Wild Ride

Wild Ride

How Outlaw Motorcycle Myth Conquered America

Tom Reynolds

NEW YORK

Library of Congress Cataloging-in-Publication Data
Reynolds, Tom, 1960–
  Wild ride : how outlaw motorcycle myth conquered
America / Tom Reynolds.
    p. cm.
  ISBN 1-57500-145-4 (hc)
    1. Motorcycling—Social aspects—United States—His-
tory. 2. Motorcycle clubs—United States—History. I. Title.
GV1059.52.R49 2000
303.48'32—dc21
                                        00-44715

The publisher has made every effort to secure permission
to reproduce copyrighted material and would like to apol-
ogize should there have been any errors or omissions.

TV Books, L.L.C.
1619 Broadway
New York, NY 10019
www.tvbooks.com

Interior design by Rachel Reiss
Manufactured in the United States of America

Dedicated to bikers everywhere.

Contents

Acknowledgments

The author would like to especially thank the following people:

- Albert DePetrillo, editor *extraordinaire,* for his keen eye and storytelling instincts, which were invaluable during the rewriting of the manuscript, making each new version better than the last.
- Peter Kaufman, Rebecca McKenna, and the entire staff of TV Books, for seeing the possibilities of publishing such a strange story.
- Dr. Martin Jack Rosenblum, for his erudition, knowledge, and sense of time and history. If I had never met Marty, I might not have written this book.
- Dave Nichols, Kit Maira, and the entire staff of *Easyriders Magazine,* for the generous use of their archives and interview materials.
- Marianne and Wayne, for the many years of friendship and support.
- L.M., for helping me keep a positive focus on things.
- Gailee, for a decade-plus of conversation.
- Willie, Peggy, Weylin, and Annarose, for the coffee, barbecues and the hauling of furniture.
- John and Christy, for their generous collection of newspaper articles, research materials, and enthusiasm.

- Jim Meredith, for his archival photographs and great stories.
- Jon S. and Dennis O., for the added support during insolvent times.
- The Boozefighters, for always knowing what being a biker is really about.
- The family of Wino Willie Forkner, for being a part of history.
- Gunnard, Jeanne, Bruce, Jane, Sam, and Rachael, for being my family.
- Denise, Erin, Kara, and William, for having me be part of their family.

January 2000

I FIRST MET TRASH ON A SUNDAY MORNING IN SACRAMENTO; HE was outside the reservation office of a Best Western on Jibboom Street trying to kick start his bike. I was supposed to meet up with him the day before, New Year's Day 2000, but his Harley blew its entire oil reserve all over the freeway during the 390-mile trip up from his home east of Los Angeles. He and his riding partners had to pull over, replace a faulty oil plug, and spend the night somewhere north of Barstow.

I'd never met Trash before but he was easy to spot. He was laconically described in his VA medical record as:

> General: Wearing biker uniform—Harley T-shirt, jeans, boots. Long gray hair and beard. Clean, clear-eyed, slightly reserved, but friendly.
>
> Skin: No suspicious lesions on head or torso; maculopapular rash, mild on rt. lateral; few excoriated lesions c/w scratching.

Other distinguishing characteristics included "chest: barreled," "neck: supple"; he is moderately obese with no "dyspnea" (labored breathing), and has a "possible hearing problem." In the flesh, Trash is 5′9″ and looks like a hung over Burl Ives. His body is filled with bone pins and he has a steel plate in his head, the result of a 1991 motorcycle crash where he collided with a truck while going 95 mph. He is a walking scrapyard at airports, setting off every metal detector he goes through. By his own admission, he hasn't held steady employment since 1974 and was two months behind in his rent. The electricity and water to his house had been shut off for non-payment and only recently turned back on. He doesn't drink or smoke but used to snort "crank"* a lot, though he claims he has not done any drugs for three years. He is fifty-four years old, has an I.Q. of 138, and can quote Robert Heinlein verbatim.

Outside the Best Western, Trash kept leaping on the starter pedal, his thirty-year-old Harley making chuffing noises like a dying locomotive. His right leg had been shattered in the 1991 accident and the hip bone and socket had cracked off from his pelvis. Nine years later, it is still utter torture for him to start his motorcycle.

"Why don't you get an electric start installed?" I asked.

"Can't afford it," he said. "Don't worry, it always does this." His bike had a cone shovelhead, a long-discontinued Harley engine whose moniker derives from the shovel-shaped covers over the cams. After his twentieth try, the engine finally kicked over. Trash looked up into the sky, raised his arms, and let out a wail like a banshee. He eased himself on to the seat and told me to hop on.

We rode over to his room where he introduced me to Brother Hank and Sheila, who were sharing the room with him and had funded his trip. The couple had ridden down from their home in Las Vegas to pick up Trash at his home in remote Kagel Canyon in California's San Fernando Valley so they could all travel together. The route had been at least three hundred miles out of their way. Brother Hank was a reformed outlaw biker, a tall thin man with a short-cropped gray beard, baseball cap, and the easy grin of a feed

---

* Slang for methamphetamine.

store owner from Decorah, Iowa. His wife Sheila had Morticia Addams jet-black hair and wore a black long-sleeved "Big Red Machine" sweatshirt, which the Hell's Angels sell commercially.

Trash, Brother Hank, and Sheila had all come to Sacramento to attend the ABATE (American Brotherhood Aimed Toward Education) Freedom 2000 Rally being held in front of the state capitol to call for the repeal of California's helmet law. Trash was also drumming up support for AB-1515, a bill authorizing a special motorcycle license plate for Vietnam veterans. AB-1515 had been authored the previous summer by Assemblyman Bob Margett (R) who represents the state's Fifty-ninth District.* Even though AB-1515 is attributed to Margett, the bill was entirely Trash's creation.

"I know shit about this governmental stuff," Trash told me as he unpacked his bag. "All I want to do is have a license plate for bikers who are Vietnam veterans." There already were California license plates available for Vietnam vets, as a bill ratifying them had been passed long ago. The problem was the earlier bill only specified "cars, trucks, and trailers" and had been signed into law as written. AB-1515 was simply a rewrite of the bill with an addendum to include motorcycles, but it had been stalled for months by State Senator Barbara Karnette (D), who chaired the Transportation Committee. Trash had a morning meeting at the capitol building with Assemblyman Margett, who was speaking at the ABATE rally, and was also planning to confront Senator Karnette in her office, though he vowed he would be "gracious about it."

The circumstances that led me to Sacramento were still on my mind. In December of 1999, shortly before Christmas, Trash phoned me, having gotten my number from Dave Nichols, the editor-in-chief of *Easyriders* magazine. Trash had seen a televi-

---

* This includes all or part of Arcadia, Bradbury, Claremont, Covina, Duarte, Glendora, La Verne, Monrovia, Pomona, San Dimas, Sierra Madre, Temple City, West Covina, and Azusa.

sion documentary I'd recently produced about outlaw motorcycle culture, and was struck by an interview we showed of an old biker named Wino. A World War II flight gunner, Wino recalled how he had been made "a nervous person" after witnessing something horrible while taking part in the U.S. invasion of Iwo Jima. After the war, Wino returned stateside and transformed himself into a pioneering icon of the outlaw biker world, a roaring, stomping semi-lunatic who spent the next five years helping to turn the image of motorcycling on its greasy head.

Wino's story inspired Trash to call and tell me he had an idea for a video program. "It's about PTSD," he said over the phone. "That's post-traumatic stress disorder. I think that's why I ride bikes, just like Wino." Trash, I learned, was a Vietnam veteran who apparently hadn't been the same after what he experienced on April 11, 1966, near the Courtenay Rubber Plantation in Vietnam's Phuoc Tuy province. He'd had severe problems for decades, exhibiting many of the psychic scars that society often associates with Vietnam veterans. There is nothing Hollywood about Trash's afflictions: he doesn't freak out every time he hears a Doors song on the radio. Rather, he has dizzy spells a few times a year, which last most of the day, and suffers from depression and panic attacks. He cannot hold a job because of problems with anger and has a history of assaulting supervisors. Trash has lived most of his adult life under the guise of the Disoriented Martyr.

We chatted on the phone for a while discussing the viability of his idea, and I informed him that I was working on a book about outlaw motorcycle culture and he sounded like someone with whom I might want to talk. I told him to keep in touch with me and hopefully we could meet in person. Over the next few weeks, Trash e-mailed me regularly. He sent me a description of the AB-1515 license plate bill and a third-person account of the

----

Courtenay Rubber Plantation battle he experienced as a nineteen-year-old member of Charlie Company. Within a few weeks, I was in Sacramento to meet Trash face-to-face.

I had to go back to the airport to pick up my rental car and Trash offered to give me a ride. Sheila volunteered her helmet and I climbed aboard Trash's bike. "I was averaging a hundred on my way up here," Trash shouted to me above the engine. "But I'll take it easy with you."

It was only while we were tearing up Interstate 5 that I remembered that Trash once hit a truck at 95 mph. The road was full of semis and even a two-wheeled buzz bomb like Trash's bike was no match for a rumbling Peterbilt being driven by a drowsy Teamster on a caffeine jag. Trash weaved in and out of traffic until we arrived at the first truck; unless we changed lanes, there was only a few seconds left before we'd go under the rear wheels. Trash pulled up a scant ten feet from the tail, then cut left in front of a Toyota and sped alongside the trailer. We were so close that I could have keyed the panels and popped out any loose rivets without stretching. When we passed by the cab, Trash shot around the left front fender, pulled in front, and raced ahead. The whole maneuver took less than five seconds and he repeated it twice more with two other semi trucks.

Later, I met up with everyone at a pre-ABATE rally party being held at Club 65, a sports bar off Highway 50 with two billiard tables and a dance floor. There was a band playing seventies rock covers off to the side and a TV set on the wall showing a rerun of *ER* with the sound off. It didn't remotely resemble the hellish image most people have of a biker hangout (some syphilitic dive built on the edge of the River Styx). A guy behind a table was selling beer from a keg at a buck a glass, but he wasn't getting many customers. Most of the bikers were at the bar ordering up expensive imports or Bloody Marys.

I got pegged as a cop inside of two minutes. It is not unusual for undercover law enforcement to hang around biker bars to monitor any outlaw action, and I'd made a point of being really obvious about taking notes, figuring it was better than being seen hunched over in a darkened corner discreetly scribbling. I had parked myself next to a pinball machine displaying my memo pad like a semaphore flag when I heard someone say cryptically, "1,001, 1,002..." I looked up and saw a well-groomed Hell's Angel in his late forties with salt-and-pepper hair grinning at me. "Make sure you get everyone's name right," he said, then turned on his heel and headed for the bar.

It was a veritable United Nations of motorcycle clubs inside the place. There were a dozen Hell's Angels plus members of the Devil's Horsemen, Resurrection El Dorado, Grand Fathers, Molochs, and Vagos, a Southern California outlaw club who lean towards anachronism (they carry themselves the way the Angels did thirty years ago, all beards and worn denim). None of the Angels showed a speck of dirt or shredded clothing and of all the outlaws at the club, they were, oddly, the most respectable looking. The one who spoke to me was wearing nicely pressed jeans, Nike sneakers, and a digital watch. If it weren't for the winged death's head on the back of his jacket, he could have been a soccer dad, for all I knew. Anyone wanting grime and decadence had to look to the Soldiers for Jesus, who are members of the Christian Motorcycle Association. There were a half dozen of them and they all sported dark wraparound sunglasses, metal studs, and pointy beards that gave them a Mephistophelean aura that belied their evangelical beliefs. Though none of them displayed the infamous "1%" patch that the Angels wear, declaring their outlaw status to the world, the Soldiers for Jesus looked like every small town's nightmare of the marauding motorcycle fiend.

By the time Trash showed up at Club 65 with Brother Hank and Sheila in tow, it was nearly seven. As Brother Hank and Sheila took over a pool table, I followed Trash as he worked the room, greeting old friends and making new ones, including several members of the Vietnam Veterans Motorcycle Club. Trash buttonholed a biker vet named Batman and showed him a color printout of his proposed license plate design. "First, there's your division insignia," he said. "Then five spaces where they'll assign you a number or you can personalize it, if you want." Trash showed how his own plate would read: C/2/16. "It stands for Charlie Company, Second Battalion, Sixteenth Infantry. That was my company." The plate design above read "VietVet," which caught Batman's eye.

"Hey, I like that one," Batman said. "Can I have it?"

"Sure, if the bill passes," Trash answered.

I'd long been aware of the high percentage of bikers who were veterans. The whole outlaw *cum* leather jacket *cum* Harley image has a long knotty history riddled with enough war angst to fill a dozen Oliver Stone movies. Almost half of the bikers inside Club 65, regardless of whether they were outlaws or not, had served in Vietnam and Trash wasn't having any problems finding someone sympathetic to his cause.

Later, while the four of us played pool, Trash casually showed me a nihilistic parlor trick using a pool cue. "Put the handle end on top of your foot," he said, demonstrating. "Then place the tip right under a guy's chin..." With that, he drop-kicked the cue with a violent upward thrust, grabbing it before it could hit the ceiling. "You can kill the guy if you do it hard enough. But if a fight ever breaks out, grab a pool ball." I took note of it, marveling at the casual nature of the demonstration. It was a bit of pub justice from an earlier era, where fights among bikers were fairly common, usually flaring up over rival colors or a disputed pool shot. Nowadays, anyone looking to witness a fight or random mischief would do better hanging out at a college bar in Fort Lauderdale during spring break.

While Trash played pool against Sheila, I went outside with Brother Hank to check out the bikes in the parking lot. Trash had told me earlier with a straight face that he would need to "keep an eye" on Brother Hank, who had a tendency to tee off on people in bars, especially drunks. "He fucking hates drunks," Trash said. "He'll haul off and smack them." I had bought Brother Hank a non-alcoholic beer but he refused to drink it after leaving the bottle unattended for a few minutes, saying, "you don't know *what* someone could slip in it."

Whatever hair-trigger tendencies Brother Hank may have possessed, I never sensed them. He was friendly, sociable, and a walking encyclopedia on Harleys and the politics of military weaponry. He had an elaborate theory regarding the creation of the M-16 automatic rifle. "It was designed for Vietnam," he said. "You never knew where the enemy was, so you just sprayed the jungle and hoped you hit somebody." Brother Hank had served in the navy from '63 to '65 and had known Trash for thirty years. He literally rebuilt the shovelhead from the cams up after Trash's 1991 accident. While Trash received barely competent care in the hospital, Brother Hank salvaged the bike and somehow put it back together, albeit replacing most of its original parts.

Trash's shovelhead was the closest thing in the Club 65 lot to resemble an outlaw "hog," the grinding skeletal bisons that sixties-era bikers rode, and that was largely because he couldn't afford to buy anything else. Even the Angels, the originators of the bike-as-Stuka-bomber thirty-five years ago, had gleaming Super Sport Glides, one of the newest Harley-Davidson models available, all with custom paint jobs and the familiar winged death's head logo emblazoned on the starter casings. Brother

Hank strolled the lot chatting to me about gear displacement, combustion, and transmissions. He openly admitted that Honda motorcycles are "incredibly well-designed," though added he would never own one. "I just like Harleys," he said.

THE NEXT MORNING, I WAS OUTSIDE BOB MARGETT'S OFFICE INSIDE the state capitol building, sitting on a stepladder that was lying sideways in the hall while waiting for Trash to show. The helmet law rally was scheduled for 11:30 A.M. on the west steps, but Trash was determined to get in as soon as possible to meet with the assemblyman and also to try to speak with Senator Karnette. He was running late so I went into the office.

Margett's staff was already familiar with Trash, as he had visited the assemblyman's office months earlier when AB-1515 was still being passed around the state legislature. "Oh, we know Trash," said Terra, an administrative assistant. "He's a great guy." It turned out Margett was flying in that morning from out of town and wasn't due in the office for another ninety minutes. The assemblyman was scheduled to speak at the ABATE rally about AB-1515 and then introduce Trash, who was speaking after him.

While I waited, a young and effusive legislative assistant named Todd greeted me. When I told him why I was there, he quickly handed me a booklet entitled *The California Public Management Casebook*. "You should read this," he said. "This explains the helmet law issue."

I knew very little about AB-7, the bill which became the California helmet law in 1991, other than the universal antipathy that bikers have towards it. One twelve-page chapter brought the whole story up-to-date.

The AB-7 helmet bill came to fruition via a distraught mother named Mary Price whose eighteen-year-old son Jimmy crashed his motorcycle in 1985 and lingered in a coma for two days before expiring. Jimmy was not wearing a helmet since the law at the time required that only riders under fifteen-and-a-half years of age were required to wear one. Jimmy had always refused to don a helmet while riding, despite his mother's pleas to the contrary.

One week after the youth's funeral, in a strange coincidence resembling a Movie-of-the-Week plot point, Mary was driving home and came upon an accident involving a motorcyclist. As they waited for the ambulance, Mary noticed that the rider was conscious, talking clearly, and wearing a helmet. She concluded that the helmet had saved the man's life and that her son would still be alive had he been wearing one. She vowed to get the state of California to pass a law requiring all motorcyclists to wear helmets.

Mary found a sympathetic ear from State Senator Richard E. Floyd, a Democrat and old-school politician who chain-smoked cigars and cursed like a marine. Floyd drafted the AB-7 bill and spent the next five and a half years trying to push various versions of it through the state legislature. It was twice vetoed by then-Governor George Deukmajian. During the legislative rigmarole, word got out about AB-7, which sent mainstream riders, outlaws, and even the American Motorcyclists Association (AMA) scrambling to Sacramento to try to head it off. Floyd regularly found his office jammed full of leather-clad bikers waiting to get a meeting with him; Mary claimed she received threatening phone calls; and Governor Deukmajian suddenly found himself aligned with the Hell's Angels, who supported the governor's veto efforts, which Senator Floyd delighted in playing up to the press. The governor, Floyd told the media, was pals with the largest criminal biker gang in the world. Finally, in 1991, California's new governor Pete Wilson, ironically a Republican, signed the Democratic senator's AB-7 bill into law. Bikers have been trying to repeal it ever since.

I was copying the *Casebook* when Trash finally walked in, having spent the last twenty minutes trying to find a place to park his bike. Todd and Terra greeted him warmly, pumping his hand like a valued constituent. Both of them were young, in their mid-twenties, probably from upper middle-class families, and had every opportunity to patronize him, but they didn't. It was he, after all, who had originated the idea behind one of the assemblyman's bills. It wasn't until I noticed Todd and Terra laughing nervously after Trash offered to "swing a sack of doorknobs" over the head of anyone who was giving Margett grief in the legislature that the differences in their backgrounds became apparent. Trash is a friendly sort who loves to kid around, but even his facetious asides seem to come from a comedic netherworld where all the joke writers once worked for Shecky the Enforcer.

Since Margett wasn't due for another hour or so, Trash suggested we wander over to Senator Karnette's office so we could talk to her about her opposition to AB-1515. He didn't have an appointment and today was the assembly's first day back in session following the holiday break. Adding to that, Trash had come dressed in all his biker finery: crusty jeans, scarred boots, a sweaty T-shirt, and his white flaring beard. I couldn't wait to see this.

We headed down one floor and walked into the senator's office. The receptionist, an older woman in her fifties with gray hair and round glasses, was shuffling together a pile of file folders when she looked up and fairly blinked at Trash's presence. "Can I help you?" she asked with a slight stammer.

"I'd like to see Senator Karnette," Trash said. "Is she in?"

"Well, she's very busy," the woman replied, not even bothering to ask if Trash had an appointment since, of course, he didn't. "May I ask what this is about?"

Needless to say, we weren't going to see the senator. Trash is not a morning person and his sleep-deprived face gave him the look of a Civil War general who just endured forty-eight hours of nonstop Yankee shelling. Everyone was extremely polite but the secretary's occasional stammer betrayed her nervousness and I could sense a subtle air of anticipation among the staff who stood off to the side eyeing us closely, as if wondering when we were going to whip out bike chains and start swinging. Finally, Trash chuckled disarmingly and confessed, "I gotta tell you, I'm totally new to this thing. I have no concept of what to do..." It was a humble request for help that seemed to relax the room and the secretary's stammering demeanor diminished. They referred us to a pair of consultants in the transportation committee who had more specific information about AB-1515, since it was coming up for a vote again in February. Trash thanked the woman and we left. "I'm glad you're here to take notes," Trash told me as we headed down the corridor. He couldn't remember where we were supposed to go and who it was we were supposed to see.

The constant walking from one office to another was beginning to take its toll on Trash's pinned-together lower body. At first, I had suggested we take the stairs so as to avoid the glacially-paced elevators but Trash replied, "Yeah, well, *you* didn't crash into a truck once." He was limping slightly and had to constantly shift his weight as we stood waiting for the elevator. After we found the transportation committee offices, we were sent to a principal consultant, who treated us with the bored diffidence of a man whose office had been invaded by two Amway salesmen. The man was gracious and let Trash have his say but clearly wondered what the hell we were doing there. When he repeated how AB-1515 would not be voted on until February, Trash innocently asked him how the vote was going to turn out. Trash pulled out his license plate design and showed it to the consultant, who gave it a cursory glance. Eventually, he walked us out to a huge copy machine the size of a Corvair and

ran off two copies of page thirty-five from the *California License
Plates and Proof of Registration* manual, showing the design for
the Purple Heart license plate, which Trash had never seen. Trash
graciously accepted them and we all shook hands. The man wandered back to his office and Trash and I hit the cafeteria.

"I'm not supposed to be here," he said, sipping a Mountain
Dew. He was still on parole after serving eighteen months in
Chino, which made his trip to Sacramento a serious breach of the
rules. "I'm required to check in with my parole officer and get permission to leave the area. I was halfway up here when I realized
I forgot to ask if I could go. It's a mandatory four months in jail
if they find out I came to Sacramento." I offered to not mention
this in print but he shrugged, chuckling. "Ah shit, go ahead and
print it. If they send me back to jail for it, I'll be a martyr."

"They were mad at me," Trash said, talking about his conviction for possession of speed in 1996. "Before I went to trial, my
lawyer found out I was a veteran and kept insisting we use it for
my defense." The result was, according to Trash, disastrous.
"Shit, the fucking prosecutor stood up in the court room and
goes, 'This is why this man should be locked up. He has a background of violence and is a menace to society.' I mean, this was
supposed to be my fucking *defense* and they used it as the reason to put me in prison." For the first time since I'd met him,
Trash became visibly upset and looked away, his normal good
humor usurped by a jaw-grinding contempt for the Man. His
eyes misted slightly and he pushed his soda away. "Let's get out
of here," he mumbled and headed for the exit.

ASSEMBLYMAN BOB MARGETT WAS A TALL OLDER MAN IN HIS SIXTIES
with silver hair and the presence of a benevolent grandfather
who enjoys fishing and reruns of *Matlock*. It was the first time
he'd ever met Trash in person. The biker gave him a warm but

throttling bear hug that made the assemblyman's eyes bug slightly, but which he reciprocated. "Now you know there are a lot of different kinds of license plates, Trash," Margett said. "Senator Karnette thinks there's too many as it is. We need to remind them that this is just an extension to include motorcycles." The plan was confirmed; the assemblyman was scheduled to speak in twenty-five minutes at the rally and he would introduce Trash. Trash thanked Margett and repeated his offer to swing a sack of doorknobs over the head of anyone the assemblyman wished. Margett laughed nervously.

When we got outside, Trash was terrified. The rally was already underway and there were around fifteen hundred bikers gathered on the west steps listening to an impassioned biker wearing a Harley jacket who kept pointing at the capitol building behind him and saying, "If they don't do what you say, throw their asses out of office!" I recognized one of the Hell's Angels standing off to the side dressed in a tailored double-breasted suit, dress shirt, and tie, flanked by two Angel prospects. He had been at Club 65 the night before, where I had seen him in the parking lot talking on a cell phone, and I put odds that he had a meeting this morning with somebody in the legislature.

"I don't know if I can do this," Trash said with a nervous flutter in his voice. "I mean, I can stand in a room of fifty people and crack jokes and shit but giving a *speech*..." He was sweating profusely and paced about like a man who had just pulled the short straw volunteering him to feed the family wolverine. I reassured him that he was among friends and that everyone was on his side. The quality of most of the speeches made me think Trash didn't exactly have his work cut out for him. One biker made rambling comparisons to show how the helmet law was a double standard. "You can't ride a bike without a helmet," he said into the microphone. "But they'll let you drive a car. I'm confused!"

The California helmet law has had a unifying effect on biker clubs, particularly those who used to be bitter rivals. In prior years, the Angels and the Molochs had little use for each other and past incidents where the two clubs crossed paths had turned ugly, but the passage of the helmet law in 1991 supplied them with a common issue; members of both clubs had gotten along famously at Club 65 the night before. Other partnerships are more surreal. At the ABATE rally, I could see Hell's Angels, AMA representatives, and state legislators all forming an anomalous assemblage around the speaker's podium. The AMA has spent decades condemning the Angels and their outlaw ilk, and no politician wants to be seen with them. Being photographed speaking at a rally while one of the Hell's Angels' Filthy Few stands a few feet behind him is hardly fortuitous for any elected official. The various assemblymen who spoke all made a point of being brief and courting the veterans in the crowd, eschewing any mention of the word "biker." "I know a lot of you out there are veterans," Margett said to the crowd. "And a lot of you were willing to give the ultimate sacrifice to defend this country and its rights and privileges."

As Margett gave his speech, Trash was standing off to the side trying to combat the flop sweat. He handed me a camera and asked if I could get pictures of him, adding, "If I pass out, just come up and drag me off." Margett was brief and he introduced Trash, who shakily walked up to the podium.

As Trash spoke, there was something vaguely Frank Capra-like about the whole scenario, with the Mr. Smith role going to a huge biker with a barrel chest, supple neck, and no dyspnea. Trash talked about the status of his license plate bill and had the presence of mind to address issues that Margett had not mentioned. He even vowed to make sure the bill did not suffer the SR-43 clause, a little-known legislative option that allows a bill to be rejected without being read. "I'm not going to quit fighting until we get it done," Trash declared. "I'm gonna go pass out now." Trash's brief speech was articulate, focused, and didn't betray any of the nervousness that had gripped him.

The rally concluded with the bombastic appearance of "New York" Mike Shelby, a San Diego-based biker who was the William Jennings Bryan of the day. He once made a run for a seat in the state assembly as a Republican in order to combat the helmet law, but lost in the 1996 primary. Now, New York Mike was gearing up to run again and began giving a frenzied speech that made Trash wistful with envy. "God, I wish I could speak like Mike does," he said.

New York Mike was a slender clean shaven man in his forties wearing a black leather jacket, whose Long Island accent confirmed his moniker. "This is about freedom!" he declared. "We can't let them forget that this is what it's about!"

"Freedom!" the crowd yelled back. "Freedom!"

"Freedom!" Trash cried out next to me.

"We're not about to roll over and let them tell us how to dress!" New York Mike continued, storming about like a biker Tony Robbins. "Because a government who tells you how to dress is a danger to its citizens. It's wrong! It's just wrong!"

New York Mike then unveiled a banner announcing his candidacy for the state assembly, which he was planning to start on (of all things) Martin Luther King's birthday. "January 17 is Martin Luther King Day," he shouted, waving his arms. "And that's the day I'm kicking off my campaign. And Martin Luther King had a dream. His dream wasn't to be rich at last. His dream was to be free at last! I have a dream! And our dream and your dream is the same dream, if you're an American! It's to be free at last!"

Seeing New York Mike do his speech showed where my Frank Capra comparison went awry. The zealousness that bikers possess

----

toward repealing the helmet law, an issue that much of the general public considers to be either good sense or a complete yawner, is probably the biggest handicap facing the anti-helmet lobby; the media regularly makes them look like loons who won't get a life.* New York Mike's Martin Luther King reference was typical of this fanaticism and especially odd, considering the Anglo heritage of the crowd he was addressing. To put no fine point on it, biker culture is a white thing. There are very few blacks or Hispanics involved in it and, while it's not overtly racist, there has long been an air of segregation hanging around the sport.

New York Mike segued over to his core platform of less government, lower taxes, and a strong national defense, all issues that no state assemblyman could really do much about. Plus, I seriously questioned the chances of anyone getting elected to the California state legislature with a name like "New York" Mike. He concluded with, "... the Statue of Liberty says 'give me your tired, your poor, your huddled masses yearning to breathe ... free!' Thank you very much."

The crowd applauded wildly and dozens of bikers went up to stuff dollar bills into New York Mike's outstretched helmet as contributions to his campaign. The rally was over and everyone slowly made their way off the west steps out to the street where the bikes were parked.

I bought Trash lunch back at the motel and we went out to the parking lot to load up his bike for the long ride back to Kagel Canyon. After tethering his bag to the long sissy bar, he gave me a rough bear hug and told me we should keep in touch. The shovelhead started up on the second kick to the starter and Trash let out a celebratory wail, climbed on and roared out of the park-

---

* This was the tone of a newspaper article about the rally that appeared the next day.

ing lot. I went back inside my room and lay down, wondering what motivated someone like Trash to wrap his mind, body, and soul around an obsolete motorcycle with an engine that barely started. I'd been around bikers for almost two years and still hadn't figured it out. The whole thing stretched back more than fifty years and was one of those weird stories that could only happen in America.

Part I

Boozefighters and Pissed-Off Bastards

CHAPTER 1

In the Beginning

WILLIAM FORKNER WAS BORN IN FRESNO, CALIFORNIA, NEAR THE heart of vineyard country in 1919, where he developed a taste for red wine when he was seven years old. He was permanently dubbed "Wino" before entering puberty. Forkner grew to be a strong muscular man with twinkly eyes, a wide mischievous grin, and a yen for alcohol that bordered on dipsomania. He bought his first motorcycle when he was sixteen, a 1929 black and chrome Indian Scout with double cams and a narrow front wheel that he paid thirty dollars for, and rode it back and forth to Roosevelt High School. Forkner had a grandmother who lived in Los Angeles, so after graduating high school he bombed his way down from Fresno on his Indian to come live with her. He caddied at the Baldwin Hills Country Club to earn money for beer and gas and fell into the local motorcycling scene, hanging around the biker bars that populated a dreary industrial area of Los Angeles known today as South Gate. It was still county territory in the 1940s, a mostly white working-class neighborhood of lumberyards, machine shops, and trucking companies. The sprawling Firestone tire plant employed much of the labor force living there.

One night in 1940, Forkner rode by the Rendezvous Bar at the corner of Florence and Central and saw a couple dozen motorcycles parked out front, their riders mingling near the front door. They were all members of the 13 Rebels, a Los Angeles motorcycle club with flashy sweaters and bikes tuned for competition racing. Intrigued, Forkner parked his 101 Scout and followed them inside the Rendezvous. Within an hour, he was on the floor as the 13 Rebels gave him a stomping. "I thought, 'Boy, this is great,'" Forkner recalled. "'I gotta join this organization.'"[1] Within weeks, Forkner was invited to join the club.

The 13 Rebels were not an outlaw club per se, as the term "motorcycle outlaw" did not exist in the public lexicon prior to World War II, a time when motorcycling had none of the stigmas it would develop later. "There have been motorcycle clubs in one form or another almost as long as there've been motorcycles," says Dave Nichols, editor of the biker magazine *Easyriders*. "But they were just groups of guys with their wives and kids. They were family affairs, people that liked to ride together, [and] the members were very nicely dressed. They had nice ties and nice caps, and they just looked spiffy. In fact, if you showed up at a meet without your tie, they'd fine you."[2]

Anyone who watches a newsreel from this time period will notice that its subjects were the last well-dressed generation, where even Detroit auto workers who rioted during the bloody 1941 General Motors strike wore vests and dress shirts. There is a series of grainy 8 mm home movies from the 1930s in the *Easyriders* archives that show motorcycle racers scrambling around a dirty field wearing white collegiate sweaters, bow ties, and riding caps. While the 13 Rebels were hardly collegiate, they also weren't the kind of club where Forkner could fit in for long.

Forkner rode with the 13 Rebels for the next two years, racing on the tracks at the Riverside, Corona, and Carrol Speedways, and going on the grueling runs up to Big Bear that were organized by the Three Points, another L.A. area club. He also married his girlfriend Marie, started a family, and worked in a machine shop. After the Japanese attack on Pearl Harbor, he joined the Army Air Corps and ended up in Hawaii, where he trained at the 124th Division's gunnery school at Hickham Field. Forkner then caught a plane to the South Pacific, an extra man on a bomber crew, and was stationed on Entiweetok Island.

Over the next thirty months, Forkner manned a .50 machine gun on a B-24 Liberator when he wasn't working on the ground as an engineer. He and his crew hit Saipan and other Japanese occupied islands for several months, and then were given a rest period. Forkner flew to Hilo, Hawaii, for R&R where he got raving drunk, trashed a bar, and ended up in jail. The next day he was thrown out of Hawaii and stripped of his corporal's stripes.

Forkner's B-24 was running raids when the American armed forces invaded Iwo Jima in 1945. The marines who hit the beach were mowed down like grass; the body count approached Shiloh-like proportions. One day, Forkner was pulled off a mission at the last minute to take the place of a gunner from another flight crew who had fallen ill. His plane then took off on a bombing run and never returned. "I saw my crew get shot down there," he recalled. "Watched them all the way to the water. Nobody got out, it blew up. Made a pretty nervous person out of me."[3] His entire crew dead, Forkner was reassigned to work as an engineer until he was transferred to a base in Hawaii, where he drank, fished, and played bridge while waiting for the bloodshed to end. Weeks before the Japanese surrender, Forkner had accumulated enough points for a discharge and was sent home in the summer of 1945.

Thirty miles south of Los Angeles, overloaded troop ships were sailing daily into the harbor at San Pedro and dropping off thousands of discharged veterans, who were each given a mustering-out check and permission to go anywhere they wanted. They were all on the 52/20 plan, meaning they got twenty dollars a week from the government for the next fifty-two weeks or until they got a job. Back then, twenty bucks bought an awful lot of beer and gas.

Forkner returned to South Gate, got his Indian Scout out of storage, and took a job driving a truck for a guy named J. D. Cameron, a local motorcycling legend who owned a freight company called the Big A off Firestone Boulevard, just around the corner from the All-American. He rejoined the 13 Rebels, most of whom had contributed to the war effort by building planes in the area's numerous aircraft manufacturing plants. Forkner was now twenty-six and totally wired, having just spent the last three years "getting shot at."

The summer of 1946 marked the end of Forkner's time with the 13 Rebels. By then, he had traded in his 101 Scout for a large hulking Indian Chief, and the 13 Rebels were sponsoring a quarter mile race at the El Cajon track down by San Diego. Forkner had no intention of attending it as his Chief had a blown second gear, but a 13 Rebel named Blackie talked him into it while they were drinking at the All-American. At closing time, Forkner and Blackie got on their bikes and shot down the freeway to San Diego, 130 miles away. The Indian Chief somehow made the trip and they arrived around dawn. The two immediately bought a bottle of liquor and rode over to the racetrack.

The El Cajon was a quarter mile dirt oval encircled by a high plywood wall, and had a sloping concrete grandstand with wooden benches. The race was the first one the 13 Rebels had sponsored since V-J Day, with Forkner's employer, J.D. Cameron, working as an official inside the track. Because of the war, many of the riders had not competed in years and the morning races got off to a slow start, the bikes making tedious laps around the dirt oval. It was dreadful and the crowd grew bored, hissing and booing. Plastered since dawn, Forkner and Blackie were up in the

grandstands wearing their wool 13 Rebels sweaters in the sti-
fling heat. At intermission time, Forkner turned to Blackie and
slurred, "Jesus Christ, man, we could put on a better show than
this son-of-a-bitch."[4] The two of them staggered out of the grandstand and headed for the parking lot, Blackie not really sure
what Forkner had in mind.

An access road off the parking lot lead to a wooden gate that
opened onto the track. The gate was closed but Forkner announced they were going to ride onto the track and put on a
show for the crowd. "We're going right through that goddamn
gate," Forkner told him. "All you got to do is just lay down on
the goddamn tank and hang on." A nervous Blackie climbed on
his Harley VL while Forkner gunned his Indian. They took off
at full tilt toward the gate hunched low over their handlebars,
but at the last second, Blackie lost his nerve and slid to a stop.
Forkner hit the barricade going sixty. The gate smashed open in
a shower of shattered wood and Forkner came bombing onto
the track, the heavy bike nearly throwing him off before he
wrestled it under control. He made a sharp turn and headed
down the straightaway.

The sight of some madman speeding around the track, leaving a trail of splintered pine in his wake, caused the crowd to
jump to its feet, roaring its approval. It was the only entertaining thing they'd seen all day. Stunned, the track officials tried to
shut the stunt down and one man ran onto the track holding a
rolled-up flag to knock Forkner off his bike. Forkner "made a
sashay" toward the infield, forcing the man to drop the flag and
flee. He tore past and made a lap.

On his second time around, the official appeared on the track
again, brandishing a chair in a white-knuckled fury. Forkner
aimed his bike and ran the man off the track again. On his fourth
lap, he lost control of his Indian and turned it over onto the dirt

track. J.D. Cameron dashed out from the infield and yanked the wires on the bike's distributor cap. It was all over. As a disoriented Forkner tried to kick start his dead Indian, track security marched out, dragged him to the back of the pits, and called the cops.

When the police arrived, they were puzzled as to what to do with Forkner. He kept insisting they couldn't arrest him for what he did because the crowd loved it and besides, the racing had been shit that day. Finally, the track official whom Forkner had twice nearly run over came up and swore out a complaint. Forkner was arrested and hauled off to the city jail where he spent the weekend, worried about his bike and annoyed with Blackie for chickening out. The following Monday, Forkner appeared in the San Diego County courthouse and pleaded guilty to trespassing and being drunk and disorderly. He paid a twenty-five dollar fine, which he borrowed from a chief petty officer who was in court that day suing somebody for hitting his car.

Forkner hitchhiked back to L.A. where he was greeted by an infuriated pack of 13 Rebels.

"Jesus, they climbed all over my ass," Forkner recalled. He quarreled with them, accusing the club of being a bunch of pansies. Whatever happened to the old 13 Rebels, the guys who once kicked the crap out of him at the Rendezvous? We don't do that kind of shit no more, they told him.[5] The 13 Rebels ordered him to turn over his colors and get out. Forkner promptly went home, retrieved his wool 13 Rebels sweater and gave it back. Upon examination, they discovered that Forkner had defecated on it.

After his ousting, an angry Forkner went over to the All-American to get loaded and sulk, ordering up Old Mission beer at a dime a bottle. As Forkner stewed, he struck up a conversation with a short, sullen biker sitting next to him at the bar. The man was barely twenty, drank even more than Forkner did, and was missing both of his legs. His name was Robert Burns but everybody called him "Dink" for his small size, as he barely topped out at 5′6″. He had grown up in the Norwalk area of Los Angeles and took up motorcycling as a teenager. Dink had started earning a reputation as a savvy racer when the war flared up. He was seventeen when he enlisted in the navy in early 1942 and shipped out on an aircraft carrier heading for the Marshall Islands. The carrier was soon attacked and sunk by Japanese forces, the very first American ship to be lost in battle since entering the war. Both of Dink's legs were blown off at the knee.

While recuperating in the hospital, he was issued a pair of wooden limbs that he had to swing forward until they locked before taking a step. Though unable to race competitively anymore, Dink continued riding, having adapted the foot pegs on his Triumph so he could attach his prosthetic legs through a small hole by the ankle joint.

At the bar with Dink that night were two other bikers whom Forkner knew casually: George Menker, a navy veteran, and a gregarious former serviceman nicknamed Fat Boy. The three men listened to his tirade about getting kicked out of the 13 Rebels. They'd all fought overseas during the war and hadn't forgotten the indelible experience of having total strangers trying to kill them. As the night went on and the beer flowed, the four bikers announced their decision to form a new motorcycle club. They just didn't know what to call it.

A regular named Walt Porter who was sitting nearby overheard Forkner and the others tossing out possible club names to no avail. "Well, what are we going to call this goddamn thing?" Forkner finally asked aloud. Porter looked up from his end of the bar and said, "Call it the Boozefighters."[6] It was an unrefined name that had little in common with other club monikers at the time, like the Jackrabbits and the Gophers. Forkner and the others laughed; they thought it was perfect.

Over the coming weeks, the Boozefighters increased their membership until they capped out at around twenty. Though Forkner had formed the club, he chose not to lead them and instead the Boozefighters elected C.B. Clauson, a former paratrooper who had hit the silk over France during D-Day, to be their president. With the exception of one, a teenager with the unlikely name of Jim Morrison, every Boozefighter was a World War II veteran.

WHILE THE MAJORITY OF THE GREATEST GENERATION RETURNED TO raise children, build Levittown, and elect Eisenhower, guys like the Boozefighters tried to exorcise their personal demons through motorcycling. They spent much of their time getting drunk, howling at the moon, drag racing in the L.A. River aqueducts, and avoiding the police. Most of them, Forkner and Fat Boy in particular, simply partied and rode hard, while a few, like double amputee Dink Burns, were bitter, full-blown alcoholics right out of *Let There Be Light,* the 1945 John Huston documentary about combat veterans suffering from battle fatigue. As Forkner recalled about Burns, "Dink just never got back to feeling the world let him live right. Just was pissed-off at everything."[7]

Other postwar clubs began springing up in the Southern California area, like the Galloping Gooses, ex-servicemen who took their moniker from a nickname they had for the middle finger gesture. There was also an active motorcycle scene around San Bernardino ("Berdoo"), a working-class city fifty miles east of L.A. that consisted mainly of Depression-era tenant farmers who had fled the Dust Bowl and settled there because they were too tired and broke to go any further. A few miles south of Berdoo in the small town of Bloomington, a particularly screwy group of veterans found civilian life to be too slow and set out to get more thrills by riding motorcycles. They were all former fly-boys: pilots, gunners, bombardiers, and navigators who called themselves the POBOBs, an acronym for Pissed-Off Bastards of Bloomington.*

The Boozefighters were a scruffy bunch, but they rarely adopted the whacked-out fighter pilot trappings that some of the other postwar clubs did, like the enigmatic POBOBS. "We didn't all wear leather jackets," says Boozefighter Jim Cameron, younger brother of J.D. and a BSA rider. "We didn't all ride Harley-Davidsons, either. Harleys are nice if you like a two-wheeled museum."[8] Anyone who rode a motorcycle in the United States during the 1940s, though, didn't have a lot to choose from, Harley-Davidson and Indian being the only two domestic bikes available back then. Both were big, heavy beasts in stock form and postwar riders soon began the practice of "bobbing" their motorcycles. Fenders were cut off, saddlebags removed, handlebars shortened; even the heavy spring-loaded seats were replaced with a tiny saddle that was bolted on the frame (which left the bikes with no rear suspension). By the time the overhaul was finished, these "bobbers" resembled nasty two-wheeled chainsaws, all engine, frame, and spokes. Originally, the whole point was to streamline the bike so it would go faster, but bobbing became more of a style than anything, since any speed improvements were minimal at best. The bobbing ritual was normally limited to the Neanderthal Harleys and Indi-

---

* Very little is known about the POBOBs. They exist in outlaw motorcycle circles almost as folk legends, the biker equivalents of Stagger Lee. They were rumored to be malcontents, a motley group of Air Corps vets straight off the pages of *Catch-22* who had no use for any of the postwar optimism that the rest of America was embracing. One member was named Otto Friedli, a short, wiry man with a pencil-thin mustache who tore around on his Harley like a man strafing an airstrip on Tarawa. The POBOBs donned their military-issue bomber jackets while riding and some painted weird decals on the gas tanks of their bikes that resembled the nose art on military planes. They ran for barely two years, then disappeared.

ans rather than the lighter British bikes like Triumph, BSA, and Ariel, which hardly needed it.

Los Angeles was largely unincorporated county territory during the 1940s and didn't have much traffic, so clubs like the Boozefighters had a lot of locations to choose from for riding and raising hell, with only two nemeses to worry about: cops and equestrians. (The latter particularly despised motorcycles because they tore up the paths and scared their mounts. One horseman even went after Jim Cameron with his riding crop, forcing the biker to douse the man with full bottle of beer.) The Boozefighters had a sixteen-foot house trailer with fourteen bunks inside that they hauled around during runs so they could pass out anywhere they wanted. Their logo was stenciled on the side and the club was occasionally misinterpreted as a temperance organization. "I'm glad to see there are some people fighting booze," one priest told them. "Alcohol is a terrible problem."[9]

It was a misconception that never lasted long. Boozefighter John Davis, for instance, owned a rare 1918 Lexington, a car made entirely of aluminum that was designed to be chauffeur-driven. It had flower pots attached to the side plus a muffler with a bypass lever that could direct the exhaust from the manifold straight into the ground. Davis tended to treat the car like an all-terrain vehicle and once drove across a field and parked it in a clearing over a clump of dried pussy willows. The Boozefighters were throwing a party when they noticed that the Lexington was on fire. The flames eventually hit the gas tank and the rare car exploded into a huge fireball, melting it into a pile of scorched parts and aluminum blobs. The bikers danced around the flames while toasting the sacrifice.

The club's loosest cannon was the misanthropic Dink Burns who regularly tore around the L.A. streets like a banshee on his Triumph while the police gave chase. During one pursuit, Burns caused a patrol car to flip over and injure two policemen while he split his head open on a curb, laying him up in the hospital for weeks. He once raced his bike up a large mound of dirt next to a gas station that was under construction and landed with a sprawl on top of the roof. As Boozefighter Gil Armis describes it, "Dink rode a motorcycle like he wanted to die."[10]

One time, Burns took the Red Car trolley down Central Avenue into the South Gate area to go to the All-American. The route ended right at Firestone Boulevard, a few blocks away from the bar, and Burns tried to pay the fare with a five-dollar bill. The ride only cost a dime and the operator had nowhere near enough change.

"What the hell am I supposed to do with this?" the car's operator demanded.

"That's all I got," Burns said. "Gimme my change."

"What are you, some kind of smartass?"

"Yeah, well, fuck you."[11]

The operator gave Burns an angry kick to his shin, only to be stunned to find his foot striking wood. Enraged, the biker promptly hauled the man off the streetcar, threw him on the ground, and stomped the man with his artificial legs. The police eventually came and broke up the assault.

Burns detested any kind of assistance from others. The federal government issued him a customized Chevrolet car equipped with a hand throttle so he could drive it. Dink promptly sold the car, bought a Norton International motorcycle, and used the money left over to ride up to San Francisco, where he drank and partied for six months.

By 1947, the L.A. Boozefighters had added two other chapters, one in nearby San Pedro, the other in San Francisco. The Frisco chapter had its share of eccentrics, including a member named Gashouse who had a strange habit of collecting other people's washing machines, using them until they broke down, then dumping them out behind his house like junked cars. The Frisco Boozefighters were led by a colorful biker named Benny "Kokomo" McKell, who liked to show up at riding events dressed in a gaudy, bright red admiral's uniform complete with braids and epaulets, looking like Horatio Hornblower. The chapter hung out at a tavern called Ratto Brothers at the corner of Eighteenth and Kapp, where Kokomo would make his entrance by riding his motorcycle through the bar's swinging doors. Though this was not an uncommon practice back then and many bar owners usually winked at it, the Ratto Brothers were not amused. Steve Ratto decided to teach Kokomo a lesson and firmly braced one of the swinging doors and waited for the biker to pull his stunt. "He comes flying through the goddamn doors," Forkner said. "Well, the one don't swing, and it knocked him on his ass. And he jumped up, and he's cussing that fucking Ratto. 'You rotten son-of-a-bitching dago, I'm going to kill you. You didn't tell me that fucking door was nailed.'"[12]

Despite all the booze-fueled escapism, the *zeitgeist* that drove the Boozefighters and other postwar clubs was racing and its sense of community. The club regularly competed in sanctioned races and they even applied for an AMA (American Motorcyclist Association) membership but were turned down by its president, E.C. Smith. "No goddamn way am I giving a name like that a charter," Smith told the club.[13] Forkner wanted the Boozefighters to sponsor races, but the rest of the members were not up for that idea. "Wino wanted to promote," recalls Jim Cameron. "But we told him, 'Hey, there's no promoting. We just want to ride. There's nobody to help you.'"[14] Forkner was persistent about getting an AMA charter and simply resubmitted the club's application under the name Yellowjackets, figuring it would be more palatable. "Me and a few guys were wrangling anyway," Forkner said, "and I told them, 'Well, I'll quit here, I'll fire up another club with a legitimate name, we'll get the goddamn sanction, and we'll put the races on.'"[15] Forkner spent the remainder of the decade riding with the Yellowjackets, whose members included most of the Boozefighters; they simply changed their colors every time they sponsored a race and the AMA was never the wiser.

The role of the American Motorcyclist Association in outlaw biker culture is somewhat ignominious. Every picaresque tale needs an authority figure to play the antagonist and the AMA has often been saddled with a monarchic image akin to the Sheriff of Nottingham (Robin Hood was, after all, the original outlaw). The AMA is a division of the Motorcycle Industry Council (formerly Motorcycle, Scooter, and Allied Trades Association), and represents riders of every type of two-wheeled motorized vehicle. It was founded in 1924, a time when motorcycle riding was more of a daring social event for the upper class. Motorcycles were fairly rare and most aspiring riders had to buy them new from a dealer. The Roaring Twenties was a good time for both Harley-Davidson and Indian. The companies made record sales, chiefly to people who already had a car and considered motorcycling as fun recreation, like polo. The AMA has traditionally looked upon their beloved sport with a great deal of reverence and dignity. They see nothing rebellious or wicked about riding a motorcycle and the stories that would come out of Hollister and Riverside were an affront to the responsible family image the AMA had always upheld. This is why the organization has been laden with a stuffy reputation by outlaw bikers who relish the fact that the AMA dislikes them so much.

It is said that the term "motorcycle outlaw" was coined shortly after the Second World War by the AMA to describe those riders who refused to participate in sanctioned racing events and simply bombed around any place they damned well pleased. By this

----

definition, many of the postwar riders like the Boozefighters were probably outlaws, what with their beer-fueled runs in dried-up aqueducts, but the entire label was a little discomfiting beyond that. It would take a single incident that would take the restless ennui of the war veteran motorcyclist and bring it to the public forum.

CHAPTER 2

"He and Friends Terrorize Town"

SINCE WORLD WAR I, THE AMA HAD ORGANIZED GYPSY TOURS, which were long-range rides to motorcycle rallies being held in selected locations. The West Coast had long been a popular region to hold these events and in the summer of 1947, a gypsy tour was scheduled to take place in the small town of Hollister, California over Fourth of July weekend. There hadn't been a gypsy tour anywhere in the state since before the war and the word spread that the rally in Hollister would be *the* biker event to attend. The three Boozefighter chapters made plans to meet at the event and the South Gate members began prepping their bikes for the long trip up the Pacific coast.

Hollister is located a few miles off Highway 101 in San Benito County, about two hours south of San Francisco. It is a prototypical American hamlet of wide streets, buildings with high facades, and gabled two-story houses shrouded by willows and ficus trees. Central downtown consists of small businesses, gift shops, and bars with burnished redwood walls covered in neon beer signs and fuzzy Polaroids of after-game parties for the tavern softball league. If you wander the empty streets on an early Sunday morning, you'd swear that time stopped somewhere between FDR's first administration and the pilot episode of *I Love Lucy*. The town, by all rights, should dwell in halcyon anonymity except for what is known as the Hollister Incident. Nobody has ever fully explained what happened in the town on Independence Day weekend in 1947 because the allure of the myth is far more tantalizing than whatever facts can be gleaned from eyewitnesses or news photographs. Descriptions run the gamut from just a wild party to a rural version of the Rape of Nanking.

Despite its quaint environment, Hollister was a big motorcycle town during the forties, with twenty-seven bars, twenty-one gas stations, and only six policemen. The city had hosted its first gypsy tour back in 1936, and motorcycle races and hill climbs were held regularly out at the nearby Bolado Racetrack. There was even a local club called the Tophatters whose members resembled bike riding chimney sweeps. The Hollister community was very familiar with bikers and that the town had been selected to host another AMA gypsy tour was of no great concern to anyone. In fact, the merchants were openly looking forward to the event as it would bring in a lot of money.

On Thursday evening, July 2, several of the L.A. Boozefighters met at the All-American in South Gate to prepare for the ride up to Hollister (only about half the chapter's members would take part; the remainder had to work). It was going to be a social weekend of relaxing and watching the races; a few like Wino were even bringing their wives and girlfriends with them. One member had a '33 Cadillac and agreed to tow the club's trailer to the rally. The Boozefighters wanted to ride at night and had some drinks for the road.

At around 7 P.M., they climbed on their motorcycles and rode up the highway and arrived in Santa Barbara sometime after eight. They stopped at a bar near the ocean, had more drinks, and continued on their way. By midnight, they pulled into the coastal town of San Luis Obispo, too wasted to go any farther. They crashed inside a bus terminal until they were rousted and thrown out by security at 3 A.M. The nine or so members bided their time on the deserted streets, letting their bodies detox in the warm night air.

An hour later, the Boozefighters headed north until they reached King City at around six in the morning, where they stopped at a liquor store to get "braced up." After a round of drinking, they headed east past the garlic fields and Diablos mountain range and rode on into Hollister.

The reported number of motorcyclists who attended the Hollister rally that weekend varies from a few thousand to more than one hundred thousand. Everyone agrees, though, that by the time the Boozefighters arrived later that morning, the streets were already swarming with bikers, most of them plastered. Seized by the spirited atmosphere, Jim Cameron promptly jumped the curb and rode his massive Indian straight into a bar called Johnny's and ordered a beer. Johnny the bartender told him to move the bike over to the wall, which Cameron did. He left it there for the duration of the weekend, never riding it.

Outside on San Benito Street, Hollister's main thoroughfare, several blocks had been barricaded off by the local police to create an area where riders could park their bikes and mingle. But as more motorcyclists converged into the town's center, the area quickly became a drag strip. Most of the riders were up for racing, and the impromptu heats went on for hours, while the sidewalks filled up with onlookers who were drinking themselves sick with bottled beer.

The Frisco Boozefighters soon arrived, led by Kokomo, who was wearing his red admiral's uniform and driving a Model-T pickup with an old wicker wheelchair rolling around in the truck bed. They checked into a hotel overlooking San Benito and started tearing around the streets. More riders—from Arizona, Oregon, Nevada, even from as far away as Pennsylvania—were coming in

by the hour. Local residents noticed that many of them were wearing fleece-lined bomber jackets "like the kind the pilots wore." By
that evening, the gypsy tour had turned into a biker's Mardi Gras.

Throughout the weekend, Bolado Racetrack was filled to capacity as the races went on as scheduled. Still, there was a major
contingent of bikers who never left town, and were staggering
around in a beer-fueled haze when they weren't tearing up and
down San Benito. Broken glass was everywhere and local service stations did a brisk business repairing flat tires. Riders by the
score were wiping out on the pavement, one man nearly sever-
ing his foot. The local hospital's emergency room was jammed
with groaning bikers suffering from fractures. The noise from the
thousands of motorcycles was deafening.

One of the more perverse acts of inebriation committed during the rally occurred on the first night. Wino, Kokomo, and a
Frisco Boozefighter named Fuzzy were throwing down drinks inside a Hollister bar when an intoxicated man staggered up to
them. "He says, 'Buy me a drink,'" Wino said, "and so Fuzzy
grabbed him and threw him in the middle, and we both got a
bottle of wine. We started pouring in the glass, said 'as long as
you keep drinking, you get more.'"[16] The drunk threw down glass
after glass of wine until he slid off the barstool and passed out.

The three carried the unconscious man outside to where they
had parked the Model-T, the old wheelchair in the truck bed.
They set him in the wheelchair, tied a rope to it, and tethered
the chair to the back of the truck. Kokomo floored the accelera-
tor and they took off, towing the drunk in the chair behind them
like a water skier. They made several loops around the outskirts
of the city as the wheelchair careened about wildly, its ancient
wheels wobbling violently. Suddenly the chair went sideways
and fell over with a tumble, ejecting the drunk man out onto the
pavement. The three men stopped the car and nervously ran

back to check on him. Figuring he was either dead or very near to being dead, they placed him on top of the car's hood and drove back toward town. They pulled into a deserted alley, laid the man down by some trash cans, covered him with newspapers, and drove back to the bar.

Residents of Hollister awoke Saturday morning to find scores of bikers passed out on their lawns. Many simply roused them from their slumber and asked if they wanted breakfast. Others, though, became concerned as the bikers started taking over San Benito for more impromptu drag racing. Some called the police, a frustrating process in Hollister as the patrolmen had no radios. Instead, a yellow light resembling a traffic signal that hung above one of the major intersections was turned on, and the first cop who happened to notice it had to call the station to find out what the problem was. For the duration of the weekend, the light stayed lit almost the entire time.

The police were beside themselves. There were only six of them and they had no idea how to handle so many people, especially when most of them were raving ex-servicemen riding hopped-up motorcycles. The drag racing continued, as bikes rocketed down the streets doing speeds in excess of 80 mph. More riders spilled onto the pavement, one man fracturing his skull. The police were making arrests by the hour. One of the first nabbed was Jim Morrison, a nineteen-year-old member of the Boozefighters (the only member who wasn't a veteran), whom the police saw urinating in public. The fact that he was pissing into a car radiator, trying to fill it up, didn't help his case any. Kokomo was arrested after trying to do a tightrope walk on a telephone cable outside his second-story hotel room window before some others dragged him back inside. Another L.A. Boozefighter named Red Dahlgren was busted for riding his motorcycle through back door of Johnny's and onto the sidewalk. The local jail was soon jammed full of intoxicated motorcyclists.

Forkner was partying inside the hotel bar with his wife, the rest of the club, and some other bikers when he got word of the arrests. Somebody suggested that they should all storm the jail and break out Red Dahlgren. Forkner put it off as just drunken talk. He soon noticed that the group was piling out of the hotel bar and into the street. He followed and saw everyone heading for the city jail.

The scene was quickly turning into something out of a John Ford western and Forkner tried to intervene. He stood between the group and the jail doors, and told everyone how Dahlgren was just drunk and needed to sleep it off, anyway. He'll be out by morning, he said. Unfortunately, the three police watching from inside the jail couldn't hear what Forkner was saying; they only saw a large biker wearing Boozefighter colors addressing a supposed vigilante mob. "Son of a bitch if they don't come out the door and grab me," Forkner said. "They threw me in jail for inciting a riot."[17] He tried to explain the situation but was quickly clapped into a cell.

Meanwhile, right outside the same bar where Jim Cameron had parked his Indian, a photographer named Barney Peterson was drawing a small crowd. Peterson worked for the *San Francisco Chronicle* and had come to Hollister to take photos of the gypsy tour weekend. He'd been in town since the rally's start, snapping pictures like crazy, clearly transfixed by the inebriated fervor going on around him and looking to capture the ultimate moment on film.

According to eyewitnesses, Peterson and another photographer positioned a motorcycle next to the curb and stacked a pile of beer bottles underneath it. Satisfied, they then saw a burly man come stumbling out of Johnny's Bar. They didn't know him, but he was drunk and wearing a motorcycle club jacket, like practically every other biker in town that weekend. Peterson stopped him and asked if they could take his picture. The man happily obliged and plopped down on the bike (a Harley bobber, one of the ugliest motorcycles ever). Peterson shoved a beer bottle in each hand; the man leered, the cameras snapped. *Click. Click.* It was the ultimate money shot, a lobotomized Viking with his booted feet resting above a pile of smashed glass. Satisfied, they thanked the man and wandered off.

Forkner appeared in court the next morning with Kokomo, Red, and a Frisco Boozefighter named Jerry Butler who'd been arrested for trying to steal light bulbs out of street lamps. Kokomo stood up before the bench wearing a pair of clown pants, huge floppy shoes, and no shirt, his entire upper torso painted red and blue. The judge, who was also the town fire chief, was wearing denim work pants and no robe. He sentenced Kokomo to another night in jail and ordered him to stay away from Bolado Track on the closing day of the races. He then asked Forkner, who had brought his wife along with him to court, if he would pay attention to her and stay out of trouble. "Hell, I've never paid attention to her before," Forkner replied. "Why should I start now?"[18] Forkner was ordered back to jail for another night. When he returned to the lockup, Forkner was stunned to see the drunk man whom he and Kokomo had towed around town in the wheelchair was locked in the cell next him. He was banging on the bars trying to get out and drink again.

It was now Sunday and the local police were fed up. The racing on San Benito had been going for three days and the maniacs were pulling hundred-yard-long wheelies. Bikers were sleeping in haystacks on the edge of town, or wherever they passed out. They were climbing on the roofs of businesses to get a better view of the drag racing. More wipeouts, more trips to the local hospital. Though the weekend was coming to an end, the Hollister police called for reinforcements.

By the time a force of forty California highway patrolmen in squad cars finally arrived, it was almost dusk. The CHP came charging in, their sirens blaring, and parked at one end of the main street. It is hard to imagine just what went through their minds when they first saw what they were up against, namely thousands of biker crazies in the center of town, most of them veterans who likely had faced down more firepower during the war than the CHP had to offer. A giggling group converged around one CHP car and began rocking it back and forth. CHP captain L.T. Torres promptly ordered his men to break out the tear gas guns and ready themselves. Moving slowly through the crowd, he and his army started herding everyone down the street toward the barricade at the other end, threatening to gas them if they didn't comply. Strangely enough, the bikers obeyed and shuffled along San Benito until they were crammed together in the block between Fifth and Sixth Streets.

Torres now faced the dilemma of what to do with them. Word had it there was a dance with live music scheduled for later that night in the American Legion Hall nearby. He and a couple of officers marched over to the hall, where they found the musicians unloading their gear from a flatbed truck.

"You guys!" Torres barked at them, pointing off at the crowd. "Go park your truck over there and start playing for those idiots!"

"But there's a dance here in the hall . . ." one of them protested.

"It's canceled! Now go play."

The small combo pulled their truck into the middle of the crowd, climbed up in the bed, and started playing swing tunes. There were a fair amount of women in the crowd, and couples paired off and began dancing, their boots crackling on the splinters of broken bottles scattered all over the pavement. The impromptu dance went on into the night, bikers and their girlfriends doing the Lindy on glass shards while three dozen cops stood around them holding loaded tear gas guns. Chief Torres went into every open bar he could find and ordered them to close at twelve, two hours early. Having already made a fortune over the weekend as it was, the tavern owners obeyed and cut off the beer flow when the clock struck midnight. The gypsy tour was over.

After Jim Cameron retrieved his Indian from the bar, he and the other Boozefighters all rolled out of Hollister, save those members who had to appear in court again the next morning. Kokomo served three more days while the incontinent Jim Morrison got slapped with ninety days for indecent exposure, the longest sentence handed out from the fifty arrests made by police that weekend.

THE NEXT MORNING, OFFICIALS DECLARED THAT THE CITY OF HOL-lister would never again host a gypsy tour or, for that matter, any type of motorcycle rally. "It's not going to happen here again," said Police Commissioner Charles Krieger. "You can quote me on that."[19] Chief of Police Fred A. Earl, who'd been with the force for forty-three years, said the rally was "the worst forty hours in the history of Hollister."[20] One could hardly blame them. It was without a doubt the biggest headache they'd ever endured as members of law enforcement. The only factor that made up for the weekend was that Hollister merchants had made a mint. The owner of the hotel and bar where the Frisco Boozefighters stayed (and which they admittedly trashed) declared that, "If I could depend on this thing happening three days a year, I could close my doors the rest of the year and just make sure things were reinforced so they won't get busted."

The rally shook up the neighboring farm towns, though. The *San Francisco Chronicle* described it vividly, reporting how the streets were "littered with the wreckage of thousands of beer bottles and other debris." Numerous incidents of bikers riding their motorcycles through bars and restaurants were cited as well as

the widespread drag racing. The *Chronicle's* account was more
or less accurate but words like "terrorism" and "pandemonium"
were used to an exaggerated extent. A bit of Hays Code-like ed-
itorializing also included observations about the many women
who were at Hollister, saying "one out of ten participants was a
girl, wearing slacks and a tight sweater and riding in tandems."
There was also a series of quotes attributed to some younger bikers that eerily presaged the kind of cauliflower-ear dialogue spo-
ken in 1950s "youth gone wild" B-movies:

> James Clearwater, twenty-three: "We like to show off. We
> make a lot of noise and everybody looks. It's just a lot
> of fun. I'm conservative, though. I haven't got a straight
> pipe." [A "straight pipe" is an unmuffled engine.]

> Jim Long, nineteen: "I like a bike with a lot of drag. Drag?
> That's pickup. See how quick you can get to 90 mph. I
> get a jolt out of that jerk takeoff. I like lots of growler
> too. Growler? Why, that's a funnel. Straight pipe. Roar."

> Jerry Witcher, twenty-one: "Autos are dead. Bikes aren't
> dangerous. They don't take much space and they go
> through traffic. I like to tear them apart and see if they
> go faster when I put them back together."[21]

Nobody outside the region got wind of what happened in Hollister at first. In terms of syndicated news, it wasn't much of a
story. During the 1940s, there were any number of violent up-
risings and labor strikes that made Hollister look like a prom
dance. The Harlem Riot of 1942 was a bloody mess where
dozens were killed. Company goons were regularly clashing with
UAW strikers outside of Detroit automobile plants, splitting
heads open. Hollister was a throwaway by comparison, and the

whole thing would have been forgotten had it not been for the emergence of Barney Peterson's photograph a few weeks later.

When the July 21, 1947, edition of *Life* magazine came out, readers thumbing through its pages were greeted with a full-page photograph of a bleary-eyed smashed buffoon draped across a Harley-Davidson motorcycle with a beer in each hand, a pile of bottles below him. It was the same staged photograph that had been taken outside of Johnny's Bar. Curiously, the *Chronicle* never ran any of the photos Peterson took at Hollister to accompany their articles about the rally. But *Life* magazine had picked up the story and chose to publish Peterson's staged picture along with their own account. It was a salacious summation of the articles that had appeared earlier in local papers:

Cyclist's Holiday
He and friends terrorize town

On the Fourth of July weekend, four thousand members of a motorcycle club roared into Hollister, California, for a three day convention. They quickly tired of ordinary motorcycle thrills and turned to more exciting stunts. Racing their vehicles down the main streets and through traffic lights, they rammed into restaurants and bars, breaking furniture and mirrors... police arrested many but could not restore order.

Again, the article was somewhat true but its tone implied the kind of mayhem normally committed by pirates on shore leave. The opening lead alone was a grabber, despite the fact that there is not a motorcycle club in the world that has four thousand members even today.* All readers could gather from the photo-

---

* The numerous HOG (Harley Owner's Group) chapters around the world are a possible exception but they operate fairly independently from each other, like franchise businesses do.

graph and the article's tone was that four thousand mobsters on motorcycles took over an innocent little town and practically leveled it. Nobody pointed out that many of the bikers who were drinking, hooting, and drag racing up and down San Benito Street actually lived there.

There were virulent reactions on both sides to the *Life* article and accompanying photo. As recently as 1999, the respected journalist Brock Yates wrote in his book *Outlaw Machine* that America was "shocked" by the drunken biker photo taken at Hollister while Paul Brokaw, editor of *Motorcyclist* magazine at the time, wrote, "You have, in presentation of this obnoxious picture, seared a pitiful brand on the character of tens of thousands of innocent, law-abiding young men and women who are the true representatives of an admirable sport."

Peterson's photo is, even by the standards of the time, fairly amusing and perfectly captures the raucous atmosphere that was the Hollister rally (it's curious that he even took the trouble to stage it; he could've swung his camera anywhere and probably gotten the same thing). The photo continues to have an ambiguous following among biker zealots who see it as both a symbol of outlaw *joie de vivre* and an example of tabloid trash. That it was staged is well-known; this was a common photojournalistic practice that dated back to the Civil War. Photographer Matthew Brady routinely rearranged the corpses of soldiers killed in battle, dragging them into the camera's frame before taking their picture.

Regardless, the notoriety of Hollister that emerged later was mostly due to the fact that, other than the *Life* article, there was very little written about it at the time. Many people's ideas about what happened in Hollister depended on who first told them about it. The most outrageous stories, the ones claiming rape, mob violence, and virtual anarchy have been kept alive

over the years by two kinds of people: those who despise outlaws and those who *are* outlaws.

The Hollister Incident has become so mythologized among
bikers that it's now widely considered the birth of American outlaw biker culture, just as the 1969 Stonewall Riot in New York's
Greenwich Village is considered to have ushered in the Gay
Rights movement. But Hollister has less in common with Stonewall, or any other riot for that matter, than it does with another
cultural touchstone, the Roswell Incident (which occurred on the
same weekend as the Hollister Incident). Even today, you can
probably find a wizened retired rancher living in Roswell who
will swear he knows someone that pulled a dying alien out of
the saucer wreckage and administered CPR. Likewise, there are
any number of outlaw bikers who will boast how their forefa-
thers locked the Hollister cops in their own jail cells and flayed
the Rotary Club.

ONE YEAR AFTER HOLLISTER, THE INFAMOUS POBOBS HAD LARGELY
disbanded themselves. A few former members were hanging out
in San Bernardino, trying to figure out what to do with themselves. One local biker who rode around with them, though he
had never been a member, was Arvid Olsen. Olsen was an ex-
fighter pilot who had been a squadron leader for Gen. Claire
Chennault's famed "Flying Tigers," the AVG (Army Volunteer
Group) that flew for China prior to Pearl Harbor. He had spent
the few years back from the war riding the barren roads of
Berdoo. One day in 1948, Olsen, Otto Friedli, and a few others
were hanging out at a fast food stand on their bikes when they
started getting hassled. "We were just sitting there having a cup
of coffee at a hot dog stand, you know," recalled Friedli. "And people were honking horns at us and young guys were going by and
making nasty signs. . . . And I said, 'We've got to form (another)

club.'"[22] Olsen apparently suggested the name of his old Flying Tigers squadron, "Hell's Angels," as the club's new moniker.*

The name "Hell's Angels" was an old Air Force moniker that dated back to World War I and supplied the title for the famous 1932 Howard Hughes air war melodrama. Besides the Flying Tigers' squadron, World War II saw no less than twelve different B-17 and B-26 bombers, plus a Marine Corps company with the same nickname. One of the most famous was the 303 Bomber Division stationed in England whose B-17F flew some forty-eight straight missions against Germany before being retired from active duty. During the late 1920s, there was an AMA-sanctioned riding club in Detroit called Hell's Angels. By the time 1948 rolled around, "Hell's Angels" was such a generic term, it might as well have been ACME. But the name stuck.

For colors, they selected an emblem that closely resembled the nose art used by another obscure flying squadron: a grinning skull wearing a pilot's helmet with wings attached to it.

Olsen never became a member.

---

* No one from any of the above mentioned squadrons or flight crews ever went on to join the Hell's Angels Motorcycle Club.

CHAPTER 3

The Celluloid Hoodlum

AROUND THE TIME THE HELL'S ANGELS WERE FORMING THEIR first chapter in Berdoo, the fallout from Hollister was slowly spreading across the West Coast motorcycle racing circuit. Boozefighter Jim Cameron, who spent much of the 1950s racing professionally, says, "I wouldn't wear the colors in competition. Of course, by then, we were getting a little bit older. I started competing in about the early fifties in events and I didn't wear my jacket because of Hollister and the word that had been spread about it. But it was all a big lie."[23]

On Labor Day Weekend in 1948, one year after Hollister, the city of Riverside had been chosen as the site of another gypsy tour rally. At the time, it was considered a pretty dull town, the kind of place where "they rolled up the sidewalks every night after nine," according to Wino. Members from all three Boozefighter chapters converged on Riverside along with a couple thousand other motorcyclists and the club camped out by a long irrigation ditch three miles outside of town, built a bonfire, and went skinny-dipping. Over the weekend, downtown Riverside turned raucous as a thousand-plus bikers recreated Hollister, drag racing on the streets, partying on the sidewalk, and tossing beer bottles everywhere. But the event took an ugly turn. One roaming pack blocking the street was honked at by an Air Force officer in his car with his wife. Instead of moving out of the way, they jumped on the car, smashed the windows, punched the driver and manhandled his terrified wife. Some revelers who were speeding through town rolled their car. One rider wiped out his bike, killing his girlfriend who was seated with him. The Riverside tour was darker than Hollister ever was.

This time, the local papers covering the rally ran a photo of Fat Boy and Jim Cameron sitting on their motorcycles with beers in their hands, looking like they couldn't wait to devour the first virgin they saw. The caption below said how the two were members of the Boozefighters, the same group who "started the Hollister Riot the previous year." None of the club's members were arrested at Riverside and they had nothing to do with the violence that occurred, but by this time, their reputation was enough. Anyone reading the papers could easily deduce that there was a nasty group of bikers called the Boozefighters who were tearing around and creating havoc in every town they entered. "Everybody jumps on the bandwagon when you're having a little party time," Wino recalled later. "And people will get unruly. You don't have to be a biker to get unruly."[24]

Yet despite all the bad press, the American public ranked outlaw bikers somewhere below locusts and bubonic plague as a threat to their well-being. There were far more insidious things to worry about, like nuclear attack and Red infiltration of the State Department. The concept of a mob of Cossacks on motorcycles invading Main Street, U.S.A., to burn the churches and rape Donna Reed was still a few years away from achieving urban myth status.

If there was a social menace that *did* concern the American public, it was juvenile delinquency. Though quaint now, the term was a 24-point headline topic during those Cold War times. The threat of teenagers suddenly turning into lawless hooligans was big news and countless numbers of books and articles were being written on the subject. It was the first time in recent history that the nation was afraid of its own. The cast of *Spanky and Our Gang* had grown up to become a real *gang* and now nobody was safe.

In 1951, amidst this national fixation, *Harper's* magazine published a short story by Frank Rooney called "Cyclist's Raid," about a motorcycle gang that rides into a tiny town somewhere on the West Coast, takes it over, and wreaks havoc. It was a *roman a clef* based on the Hollister incident, which Rooney learned about from reading exaggerated newspaper accounts. In terms of literary merit, "Cyclist's Raid" wouldn't keep John Cheever up at night, but the story was quite effective at conveying the terror felt by a quiet community that is suddenly invaded by an unexpected menace. Still, "Cyclist's Raid" would have disappeared into obscurity had it not caught the eye of filmmaker Stanley Kramer.

An ambitious producer/director, Kramer had made his first film in 1948 and by the time "Cyclist's Raid" appeared three years later, was already well into production of his ninth, *High Noon*. Kramer was one of Hollywood's first independent producers, developing his own projects and getting the studios to finance them. The old-line studio system was still running things, so Kramer was considered a bit of a maverick, with a reputation for making socially conscious movies rife with "messages." As he recalled in his autobiography, Kramer first came across "Cyclist's Raid" while leafing through a copy of *Harper's* one day while in his office:

> I was skimming through the latest *Harper's* magazine, in which I had never found any screen material. This time an article caught my eye. A gang of young, leather-jacketed, chain-bedecked motorcycle jockeys, bent on mischief and mayhem, had invaded Hollister, California, on the Fourth of July weekend in 1947 and assumed control of the town, riding up and down the streets, pushing citizens out of the way,

driving their cycles in and out of the shops, up and down the aisles, shoplifting whatever appealed to them, and intimidating everyone in sight.[25]

Time had clearly tainted Kramer's memory of Rooney's work. Not only does he refer to it as an "article" rather than a short story, there is also no mention of a town called Hollister in "Cyclist's Raid." Yet the idea of a subculture of roaming vandals cruising the highways on motorcycles proved irresistible to Kramer. Considering his interest in topical issues, it was no surprise that he was attracted to the story's premise. "It touched my sense of social responsibility," he said. "And I thought it would make a good movie."[26] The result was *The Wild One,* the film that introduced the concept of the motorcycle outlaw to the American public.

As a pop culture phenomenon, *The Wild One* is rife with contradiction. It is a classic film that is also a bad movie, the first youth-gone-wild tale in cinema history, featuring a cast of characters who are pushing thirty. In terms of portraying motorcycle culture at the time, the movie got almost everything wrong, but this didn't stop bikers who likely knew better from being influenced by it.

It is often risky to dramatize youthful rebellion since whatever themes being examined are doomed to become obsolete within a decade. Nowadays, the 1950s-era "troubled juvenile" films are as musty as unopened crypts and even a classic like *The Blackboard Jungle* is badly dated. It takes years of revisionist theories and cultural recycling to immortalize a piece of pop entertainment, and that is what happened with *The Wild One*—in spades. The movie is a rare example of how the image that surrounds a product becomes more influential than the product itself.

While doing research for *The Wild One,* Stanley Kramer learned about Hollister and tried to track down the "gang that had raided" it. "It wasn't easy," he said, "because motorcycle gangs don't hire agents, maintain offices or even fixed abodes. I eventually found several gang members in Los Angeles, and they were in touch with the others."[27] With whom Kramer talked is a mystery but whether any of them were actually in Hollister that fateful weekend was a moot point by then. Its notoriety was so widespread in the South Gate neighborhood that anybody could glom whatever stories they had heard and put their own personal spin on them. Kramer was told about the Boozefighters, but none of the members have any recollection of meeting with him. The only thing they do remember is receiving a letter. As Forkner recalled in 1987:

> The studios wrote me a letter and said they would like me to come down, or somebody from the club to come and kind of do whatever, edit, or help them program the picture, you know? But I took the letter to the club meeting on Friday night. After all that adverse publicity we had out of Hollister, nobody wanted to go. C.B. (Clauson) and the rest of the guys said, "Hey, we don't need no more shit. We already got enough that we didn't deserve, so piss on it. We ain't going to go stick our neck out for that kind of shit."

Though Forkner said the letter was from the studio, most likely it came via Kramer's office. He was producing *The Wild One* as part of a dubious contract he had with Columbia Studios, the last place that would have sent such a query as it was being run by the notorious Harry Cohn. A vile man, Cohn was widely considered to be the most loathsome studio chief in Hollywood, the epitome of the crude shrieking tyrant who bullies and terrorizes anyone under his subordination. Cohn had signed Kramer to a five-year contract with Columbia in 1951 and since then every film the producer made for the studio had been a box office flop (*High Noon* had not been released yet). Cohn was fed up with Kramer, hated his movies, and rued the day he had signed him to work for Columbia. And if there was one film project that Cohn surely despised, it was the new Kramer movie about motorcycle gangs. "When I agreed to finance your pictures, I didn't think you'd turn out to be a goddamn radical," Cohn snarled at him. "A motorcycle gang raids a town. What the hell kind of subject is that?"[28]

Undaunted, Kramer was convinced of its timeliness, confident that he was exploring a cultural movement that was only just beginning. He continued interviewing various "outlaw bikers" riding around the Los Angeles area and traveled up to Hollister to talk with the locals.

Anticipating a traumatized citizenry, Kramer was surprised to find the residents were not that upset about what had happened. Sure, the motorcyclists were disruptive, they told him, there was broken glass everywhere, but we made a lot of money on those crazy bastards. Kramer found this bit of economic irony intriguing and was eager to incorporate it into the script. Now he needed to get someone to star in his film and Kramer already knew who he wanted: a hot young actor named Marlon Brando.

Brando had made his screen debut during 1950 in the Stanley Kramer film *The Men,* playing the lead role, and was revolutionizing acting. He looked magnificent onscreen, and also loved to ride motorcycles; Brando was almost too perfect for Kramer's biker movie. The actor was currently strutting around a studio set dressed in a toga, woefully miscast as Marc Antony in the film production of *Julius Caesar.* Brando had awed critics and movie audiences alike the year prior in *A Streetcar Named Desire* playing the brutish Stanley Kowalski, but in *Julius Caesar* he looked like the bewildered member of a bowling team wrapped in a sheet. He would receive good reviews upon the film's release, but Brando was embarrassed by his performance and reluctant to grab the first role that came along. He was turning down film offers left and right when Kramer called him with his idea for a movie about motorcycle gangs.

Brando had a soft spot for the producer. They shared an interest in social issues and Brando always felt obligated to Kramer for giving him his big break. The actor accepted, though surprisingly he was not enthusiastic about the project at first. Kramer and his screenwriter John Paxton (an earlier writer had fled to Mexico to escape a subpoena by the House Un-American Activities Committee) set about crafting a script out of the research they had done. They were anxious to stay true to the real Hollister story and at the same time portray the ludicrous premise of a single motorcycle gang taking over an entire town. Kramer wanted to present the motorcycle outlaws as a new kind of disillusioned youth, rebelling against a staid Eisenhower America. This was groundbreaking stuff in 1952 and, to Kramer's credit, he was anticipating something that was only just beginning to gestate in the country. Yet he was also missing the point. It had been mostly blue-collar war veterans that cut loose in Hollister. Kramer was turning the story into a study of antihero angst and small town hypocrisy.

Kramer hired a young Hungarian director named Laslo Benedek to helm the film, a decision which he soon regretted. Benedek was a genteel man whose erudition made him more suited to direct a biopic on the life of Emile Zola than an edgy movie about marauding motorcyclists, especially one starring the most temperamental actor in Hollywood. While in pre-production, Kramer, Benedek, Paxton, and Brando all met in Hollister to discuss the film (Brando even rode his motorcycle all the way up from Los Angeles). Kramer introduced Brando to some of the bikers he had met who had been cast to play extras in the movie. Brando was reportedly enthralled by them. They were rebellious, uncivilized, and restless, all behavioral traits to which he could relate. It is also likely that they were only acting up for the benefit of these Hollywood bigwigs, anxious to make a memorable impression. "Shit, man," one of them said with exaggerated portent, "Find another little town without a main highway and get that number of bikers together and it could happen again. Yessir, we treed Hollister."[29] Kramer, Paxton, and Brando felt that they were in the presence of something new and radical. They were the products of a selfish uncaring society that had somehow let them down. The film's now-legendary line supposedly came about when Kramer asked them, "What are you rebelling against?", to which one of them replied, "Well, whatta you got?"

The script finished, it was submitted for approval to the Breen Office, which monitored every film script in development for anything that appeared immoral, blasphemous, profane, vulgar, etc. (movie ratings were years away). They, of course, had a field day with the script. "You can't show this kind of picture in public," they told Kramer. It was antisocial bordering on communistic. The town's merchants were greedy hypocrites and the hoodlums came across looking like heroes. Plus, the idea of a town being overrun by a roving biker gang was preposterous. "By God, if they tried to do that to a town where I lived," Jack Viszard, head of the Breen Office, said, "I'd shoot 'em first and ask questions later."[30]

Kramer insisted that such a thing had happened in Hollister and that they were censoring him. Unfortunately, both parties were right. The Breen Office was being censorious and the script's premise was ridiculous. Adding to Kramer's problems was Harry Cohn's disdain for the project; he was not about to go to bat for Kramer.

In the end, Kramer capitulated and agreed to change the script. The personal motivations behind the bikers' radicalism were all but excised, as was the town's collective eagerness to make a buck off them. The script, still without a working title, was now simply about some roaming thugs and their threat to American values. It told of a small innocent town disrupted by the noisy arrival of two dozen members of a motorcycle gang called the Black Rebels, led by their brooding leader Johnny (Brando). Soon, another pack of more vicious bikers, the Beetles, rides into town fronted by Johnny's nemesis, the sloppy Chino. The two gangs are very much yin and yang. Johnny and the Black Rebels are decked out in snazzy form-fitting studded leather jackets with a multitude of zippers. The Beetles dress like they just plundered an Army-Navy store, wearing pilot helmets and second-hand military gear. They all drink, fight, vandalize, and paw women until the town's elders arm themselves and do battle with the invaders. At the conclusion, the Black Rebels and the Beetles ride out of town without anyone being punished.

It was pulp melodrama and Brando hated the new script, even taking a stab at rewriting it (though he never delivered anything). The Breen Office prevailed, however, and the film went into production. Kramer had wanted to shoot on location in Hollister but Cohn nixed the idea, instead forcing Kramer to use a ranch in Burbank owned by Columbia, a cheesy backlot that had been the site of hundreds of B-westerns over the years. Cohn also insisted the film be shot in black and white in order to save money, clearly showing his contempt, since he preferred the snazzy Technicolor everyone else was using. Benedek had just twenty-four days to complete the film.

The role of Chino, Johnny's arch rival, had first been offered to the actor Keenan Wynn, son of the famed radio comedian Ed Wynn. A talented motorcyclist, Keenan badly wanted the part but was under contract to MGM Studios, who refused to loan him out for the money being offered. Crushed, Wynn volunteered to find someone to play Chino and recommended an unknown actor named Lee Marvin, whom he had been teaching how to ride motorcycles.

Marvin was the antithesis of Brando, a wild gregarious sort who loved to drink and fight (the son of alcoholic parents, Brando was at the time a teetotaler). An actor for only three years, Marvin was a decorated ex-Marine who had served during World War II, hitting the beaches of Saipan in the Japanese-held South Pacific when he was only twenty. The invasion resulted in over sixteen thousand American casualties, including Marvin, who was severely wounded. After months of recuperation (he'd been nearly paralyzed), he was discharged, after which he scraped about doing odd jobs for a few years before falling into acting.

The rest of the cast members were equally unknown. An actress named Mary Murphy, a twenty-year-old ingenue under contract to Paramount, was chosen to play Kathie, Johnny's thwarted love interest, while the Black Rebels consisted mostly of young actors schooled in the Method, a style of acting just coming into vogue. Method acting, with its emphasis on "real" emotions, was deliberately anti-technical, and old-school directors and movie stars were often irritated by it. Many a movie crew was kept waiting while some day player who had just three lines in a scene was off trying to "get into character." The Method was a useful technique in the proper hands (Brando was a master at it, as was Montgomery Clift) but too often the results were self-indulgent performances. *The Wild One* became a virtual swamp of bad Method acting.

The film's production was by all accounts grueling. They were working on a tight budget and could not afford to fall behind. Benedek was an inexperienced director and Brando made no bones about his dislike for him, feeling he didn't know what he was doing. As filming began, Kramer and his crew discovered to their chagrin that the star of the picture was not much of a

motorcycle rider. Though he'd ridden for several years, Brando
was not skilled enough for the hot-dogging stunts that the gang
members were expected to perform in the film. The studio had
supplied him with a powerful Triumph Speed Twin that he handled tentatively at best. The actor badgered the film's stunt co-
ordinator Cary Loftin to show him how to turn figure eights in
the dirt. A few days later, Brando took a friend for a ride on the
Triumph and crashed into the bumper of a parked limousine, flying off into the dirt. He ended up with a huge abscess on his hip
that had to be aspirated. Kramer summarily forbade Brando from
doing any more riding except when the cameras were rolling, a
dictate the actor ignored.

Throughout the filming, Brando made up much of his own dialogue. He didn't like the script and argued constantly with
Kramer. "We can't do it the way it's written," he said one day.
"We've got to explain that these guys are nameless, faceless fry
cooks and grease monkeys all week. They've got to belong to
something. And when the tensions build up, they do violent
things."[31] In this case, Brando was onto something insightful, but
most of the time he ad-libbed pastiches of jive-filled aphorisms
that he probably picked up in Greenwich Village. Much of the
film is filled with hipster blather, which Kramer insisted was
based on the biker lingo that he and Paxton heard. "A lot of the
dialogue is taken from our actual conversations with them,"
Kramer said. "All the talk about 'We gotta go, that's all...just
gotta move on' was something we heard over and over."[32] Yet
there is a ridiculous scene in a bar where several of the Black
Rebels play verbal dodgeball with an old man serving them
beers. "Say, Pops, gimme another one of those crazy beers, will
ya, man," yaps one, right after he finishes performing a cadenza
on a harmonica. The rest of the gang declares that the man is
"too square," that he doesn't "dig their rap." This was white bo-

hemian quasi jazz-speak and nobody ever spoke this way except in the movies, not Jack Kerouac and the Beats and certainly not the Boozefighters, nor any other riders from the South Gate area biker clubs. Adding to this corrupted milieu is the insufferably mannered acting by Brando's bad boy sidekicks whose cocky rebel shtick is so over the top it borders on parody.

When Chino and the Beetles ride into town, the film shows signs of taking off. This gang is dirtier, smellier, and less fashionably inclined than the Black Rebels but are far more interesting, particularly the leader Chino. With his chewed-up cheroot and bumblebee sweater, he is both a clown and a freak, cracking jokes while spoiling for a fight. The Beetles end up being the worse of the two clubs and they soon go on a rampage, an apparent homage to Hollister.

Later, the Beetles hunt down Kathie, Mary Murphy's character, and encircle her with their motorcycles until Johnny rides in to the rescue. The suggestion of rape is clearly evident, and it is the only truly sinister moment in the entire film. Otherwise, the scenes depicting biker mayhem range from mild to sophmoric. Even by 1950s standards, *The Wild One* is incredibly tame, and its worst act of destruction is the bizarre trashing of a beauty salon by the Beetles that climaxes with the gang members all breaking into the Charleston. For his part, the director Benedek didn't know a leather jacket from a cardigan sweater and thus had trouble staging the brawling scenes because every actor looked alike. Bikers who appeared in one angle during a fight disappeared from another.

By the third week of production, Brando, as he was apt to do, stopped caring. He felt the movie had strayed from its original intent, thought Benedek was incompetent, and just wanted to finish and go back to New York. Lee Marvin, too, cared little about getting the director's approval and started masticating the scenery every chance he could get. The scenes where Chino is drunk are particularly realistic, as Marvin was smashed at the time of filming.

Adding to the tension on the set was the undeniable fact that Brando and Marvin couldn't stand each other. "Lee was jealous of Marlon," Mary Murphy said, "and wanted to knock him off his pedestal."[33] The one-on-one fight between Johnny and Chino is especially vivid since both actors wanted to kill each other. Originally rehearsed with stunt doubles, Brando and Marvin ended up performing the fight for the cameras and stunned the crew with their ferocity, trading blows that barely missed each other and scrapping in the dirt.

Brando and Marvin managed to separate themselves from Benedek's limp direction enough to give excellent performances. Indeed, the most intriguing element of *The Wild One* is the juxtaposition of Johnny and Chino. They are essentially each other's alter ego and if melded together, the result would be the Compleat Biker.

From the opening credits, it is obvious that the movie is about Johnny. Brando's first appearance, riding grimly on his motorcycle and wearing a pair of dark sunglasses, is striking, almost to the point where you don't notice the antiquated rear projection effect behind him. With his studded leather jacket and white riding cap, Johnny is all brooding swagger and simmering sexuality. "It's like his uniform," says *New York* magazine film critic Peter Rainer. "We're seeing somebody who is being typed as a certain kind of misfit, and this was very common in fifties' movies. What Brando did was sort of break through that, so he didn't exactly play it out the way I think he was supposed to, in terms of the way the script was written."

In contrast, Chino is a big pathological nutball. Lee Marvin's presence in *The Wild One* is such that he threatens to steal the whole movie from Brando. If his is not the most positive portrayal of a biker, Marvin is enthralling to watch, and one of the biggest letdowns of *The Wild One* is that he is not onscreen more. "The one character in *The Wild One*," says Dave Nichols, editor of *Easyriders*, "that really did exemplify the American biker in that time period was the character that Lee Marvin played. He looked and dressed and acted the part of one of the real Boozefighters."

Marvin supposedly based Chino on Wino Willie Forkner, whom the actor met while riding around Los Angeles preparing for his role. This may explain why he is the only biker riding a Harley in the film (every gang member in the film is astride an English-made bike: BSA, Matchless, Arial, etc.; Forkner wouldn't be caught dead on an English bike). Though he was never the criminal Chino is, Forkner's offbeat charisma and take-no-shit disdain for authority is very much evident in Marvin's portrayal of the screwy gang leader. When Chino and his Beetles rumble into the town in their ripped denim and cast-off pilot gear, they are the lords of white trash, and far more realistic than the slang-spewing Black Rebels with their designer leather. This is probably because most of the real-life bikers that Kramer cast in the film were assigned to be members of the Beetles.

There are few riding sequences in *The Wild One*, which is also a shame. When the Black Rebels first come down the city's main street, their bikes thundering like longhorns on a cattle drive, the townspeople on the sidewalk look on with growing fear. It is only when the bikers dismount and start talking that the film goes south.

The Wild One was released in 1954 to tepid box office sales. Harry Cohn, as expected, loathed the movie and did nothing to promote it, preferring that it die a flaming death in the theaters. Critics largely panned it, deriding the film for being exploitative. "Filled with horror and sadism," decried the New York *Daily*

News, which accused Kramer of failing to place the responsibility on the shoulders of the motorcycle gangs, where it surely belonged. *Time* magazine said, "The effect of the movie is not to throw light on a public problem but to shoot adrenaline through the moviegoer's veins."

These were undoubtedly harsh words for an earnest man like Kramer who only wanted to examine an impending "social problem." (He was often admired for his didactic approach to filmmaking, but, by Kramer's own admission, it dated a lot of his work and many of his movies don't hold up well today.) Brando likewise was disappointed with the final product and publicly announced that he was going to give up acting forever, a claim he would make repeatedly throughout his career.

Naturally, motorcyclists went out of their way to see *The Wild One* upon its release. Most of the Boozefighters were displeased with it. "I thought it was terrible," says Jim Cameron. "It really degraded motorcycling a whole bunch and everybody got the wrong idea. I thought it was a big hoax, because I'd been through Hollister and they were trying to copy it and they weren't even close. Didn't even happen like that."

Wino, though, relished being the inspiration for Lee Marvin's Chino character. (Some writers have also stated, erroneously, that Brando's Johnny was based on Forkner, something the latter never objected to, either.) The film was picketed in Milwaukee, Wisconsin (the home of Harley-Davidson), banned in Memphis, and completely forbidden from being exhibited in England, a blacklisting that lasted until 1968.

By most standards, *The Wild One* was an ignoble flop but it would go to become one of the most influential films of the 1950s and the first important movie of Marlon Brando's career (not forgetting *A Streetcar Named Desire,* which preceded it).[34] While Brando may have established his acting reputation in much better films such as *Streetcar* and *On The Waterfront,* his work in *The Wild One* created an *image,* one that continues to this day. After the film's release and subsequent failure, sales of leather jackets soared. Movie posters of Brando as Johnny became ubiquitous and are still purchased even today. (Photo stills of *The Wild One* are far more arresting to look at than the movie itself.) The persona of Johnny the sulking outlaw would be revisited in movies such as *Rebel Without a Cause,* and the sneering juvenile hoodlum became a standard icon of 1950s culture. This is largely due to the influence of *The Wild One,* a movie few people saw that was based on a riot that never happened.

CHAPTER 4

American Legends

DR. MARTIN JACK ROSENBLUM IS A SHORT SLENDER MAN IN HIS early fifties who dresses entirely in black, with a Gabby Hayes beard, white flashing teeth, and round wire-rimmed glasses. When I first met him during the Harley-Davidson Ninety-fifth Anniversary Reunion in Milwaukee in 1998, he was limping around on a cane while recovering from knee surgery, damaged from years of kick starting motorcycles.

Marty is the official historian for the Harley-Davidson Motor Company and one of the preeminent chroniclers of motorcycle culture in America today. He has spent almost his entire life trying to decipher what he calls the "shaman-like experience that comes from riding a Harley-Davidson."

"Harley-Davidson is the only transportation vehicle that has associated with it a culture," Marty says. "As a matter of fact, it's the only functional object that has the kind of culture that is as powerful."[35]

Rosenblum's father was a Swedish immigrant who'd once been with the Palace Guard Corps, where he learned to dislike motorcycles. (He'd been forced to ride on the back of one being driven by ranking officer who was completely drunk. Nothing happened, but the experience was so unnerving that he vowed nobody in his family would go near one of those two-wheeled death machines.) Whether this had the reverse effect on his son Marty won't say, but by the time he was seven, the younger Rosenblum was already subscribing to Harley-Davidson's official magazine, *The Enthusiast*, having become fascinated with the company's motorcycles. What began as a childhood fancy quickly grew into a deepening obsession, and by the time he was eleven, Marty would wait at the top of a hill near his house just to see the thundering Harley and Indian riders who came tooling up the incline in packs of twenty. "They would start down at the bottom of the hill by the river," he recalls, "race up the hill, make a brief stop at the stop sign at Pacific and Leminwah and then gun it down to Wisconsin Avenue."[36]

One day, Rosenblum was watching when a motorcyclist on a huge Harley Twin hit a patch of gravel at the top of the hill and fell over. The rider wasn't hurt and asked Marty if he could use the phone to call a buddy. "I let him in the house and he was just a perfect gentleman, you know," he recalls. "He was just very kind and gracious and I went out to his motorcycle and he told me all about it, described in detail. He was dressed sort of like a cowboy, and right then and there, I started to make the connection between riding a horse and riding a Harley."[37]

The bike rider ("they were called that back then") invited the youth over to a clubhouse that was nearby and Marty got on his Schwinn bicycle, which he had decorated to resemble a Harley, and rode down the hill to visit. The riders took him under their wing and taught him to ride, showing him how to shift, work the clutch, and start the beasts up. Rosenblum bought his first motorcycle when he was still a teenager and hid it in a chicken coop belonging to his grandmother, who lived a few minutes away across a ravine. She promised she would never tell his father about it. He started collecting secondhand Harleys, Triumphs, Nortons, and the occasional junked hot rod and continued storing them on his grandmother's property. "My parents were not part of that picture," he says. "They didn't know that was going on."[38]

Even before he was hiding bikes in the chicken coop, Rosenblum had already started rolling his pants cuffs up the way the Black Rebels had in *The Wild One* and even purchased a pair of studded motorcycle boots against his parents wishes when he was in sixth grade. A few years later, Marty went to high school one day wearing sideburns, a ducktail haircut, and black leather jacket, and the principal stopped him in the hall. "He called me a 'harley,'" Marty says, laughing. "He said, 'You look like a harley.' And I got kicked out of school."[39]

Later on, Marty got swept up in the folk music craze of the early 1960s and shucked his greaser look for turtlenecks, playing guitar with a folk group and making the rounds of music festivals and coffeehouses. By 1969, he had earned a bachelor's degree in English, followed by a master's in creative writing two years later. He began teaching college English, and became more immersed in the philosophical qualities of the Harley-Davidson motorcycle. By 1980, he had his doctorate in American literature, history, and culture, and was a full-blown Harley historian.

How Harley-Davidson, a motorcycle whose popularity has largely been built on the shoulders of high school dropouts, could inspire such loyalty is all part of one of the more curious business success stories in the history of American capitalism. Harley-Davidson has survived more economic setbacks and bad press than it probably should have to become as much of an American institution as anything the nation has to offer. Whether Harley-Davidsons are the best motorcycles in the world is certainly subjective (there are plenty of riders who feel Harleys are overrated) but there is no disputing the fact that they are the most famous.

HARLEY-DAVIDSON WAS FOUNDED IN MILWAUKEE IN 1903 (THE same year the Wright Brothers made their first flight at Kitty Hawk) by William Harley and his next-door neighbors, the brothers William, Walter, and Arthur Davidson. The four men were bicycle makers who decided to take the work out of pedaling by motorizing them.* All in their early twenties, they each possessed individual skills that allowed them to collaborate with a minimum of discord. William Harley was a skilled engineer, Walter Davidson a fine machinist, and Arthur Davidson a shrewd salesman. The eldest Davidson brother, William, came on board later as a product designer.

Resourceful as they were, the men did not possess the equipment to manufacture their own parts and relied on friends and acquaintances to supply what they needed. A local maker of outboard marine engines named Ole Evinrude taught them the basics of the carburetor. They pored over blueprints of French-built motorcycles and other models. Working in a small work shed behind the Davidson household, Bill Harley and Arthur and Walter Davidson produced a motorcycle with a 3-hp single-cylinder engine, and a looping frame which Harley designed. They did not quit their day jobs, however, and the production of new bikes was slow, with just two in 1904 and eight the following year. They sold quickly and in 1907, Bill Harley and the three Davidson brothers incorporated themselves, moved out of the shed to a larger location, and produced 150 motorcycles. By 1920, Harley-Davidson was the world's largest motorcycle manufacturer.

---

* The four men were not the first to do this. Contrary to popular assumption, the motorcycle actually precedes the automobile. The German designer Gottlieb Daimler invented the internal combustion engine in 1885, which he hooked up to his son Paul's bicycle so he would not have to hear the boy complain about having to pedal up hills. Brave souls in the 1880s could even purchase steam-powered motorized bicycles (and they were as bizarre and unreliable as they sound).

Even before the Milwaukee entrepreneurs began tinkering inside their work shed, there were already a bewildering number of other manufacturers in existence, including Indian, which was founded two years before Harley-Davidson, in 1901. During the first half of the twentieth century, a total of 114 different motorcycle manufacturers would spring up in America—many with charismatic names such as Hurricane, Stormer, Scorcher, Savage, Blazer, Lightning Bolt, etc.—yet this *laissez-faire* feeding frenzy was doomed from the start. Motorcycles were in direct competition with automobiles and the introduction of Henry Ford's Model-T in 1915 dealt a serious blow to the glutted American bike market, putting most of its manufacturers out of business. America's entry into World War I two years later created material shortages that thinned the herd even more. The Depression of the 1930s combined with the import of the superior British motorcycles finally blew the rest out of the water. Harley-Davidson and Indian were the only two companies left. By all estimates, Harley-Davidson would have gone down with the rest of the Yanks but for their one saving grace, the Model 74 motorcycle.

The first Model 74s were introduced in the early 1920s and quickly carved a niche in the fading American bike industry. Their engines displaced 1,207 cubic centimeters, got forty-five miles to the gallon, and had a then-astonishing top speed of 90 mph. Over the decades, Harley-Davidson has offered a prolix number of different road models (even Harley aficionados have a hard time keeping track), as well as dirt bikes, scooters, and even snowmobiles, but the heart and soul of the company rests on its Model 74 concept: a big bike with a big engine. With the exception of Indian (which some old-timers still insist was a better motorcycle), nobody supplied a bike as powerful.

In 1953, one year before the release of *The Wild One,* Indian closed its doors and Harley-Davidson suddenly found itself the only domestic manufacturer of motorcycles left in America. For decades, Harley-Davidson and Indian had fostered a fierce competitiveness between their customers who hung loyally to the heavy touring models that both companies were offering. The Indian company produced arguably the most ostentatious motorcycles ever designed, baroque-looking monstrosities outfitted with huge hooded fenders, feathered ornamentation, and a gross of sheet metal. There was nothing subtle about Indians, and riders who were into bobbing their bikes faced a yeoman's task of trying to tear everything off. Performance-wise, both Harley and Indian bikes had their pluses and minuses, but Harley-Davidson prevailed in the end, not necessarily by having a better motorcycle but rather from Indian's own corporate mismanagement. Dealers had a difficult time keeping up with customer orders and the company made poor use of its money. Indian was almost completely bankrupt when it folded.

By the time *The Wild One* hit the theaters, Harley-Davidson's only competition came from the English imports. The timing couldn't have been more precarious, though, as a growing number of the nation's public was developing a narrow and skewed opinion of motorcyclists as beer-swilling Huns bent on spreading violence, communism, and the clap. The fifties ushered in the public's new motorcyclist-as-monster perception, which became one of the most important influences on American biker culture. A motorcycle was a mode of transportation, certainly, but with this media-led image tossed in, riders automatically inherited grit, base sexuality, and a determined badass vibe for themselves just by owning a bike, especially if it was one of those big nasty Harley-Davidsons.

The post-World War II years were the golden age of the cruisers, the big panzer bikes bought by motorcyclists who wanted to hit the highways and see America. The growth of the nation's major cities and the interstate highway system got more bike riders off the trails and onto the open road. But for many sectors of American society, more available roadways meant more opportunities for hoodlums to ride around causing trouble. Though nobody was sure where they heard them, there were stories of entire towns that had been overrun by roaming motorcycle gangs, whose members all rode "Harleys." The reports about Hollister and Riverside were not the cause of these public concerns since the average citizen couldn't recall either incident. Rather, it was from society's own confused and panicked processing of various social issues that kept popping up in the news like toadstools on a rotting oak stump. Most had little to do with one another but together they demonstrated just how much of the nation was in flux. *Brown v. Board of Education* was forcing schools to desegregate, the Soviets were detonating H-bombs, Elvis was gyrating, Lenny Bruce was swearing, James Dean was mumbling, Charlie Starkweather was killing, and now there were all these leather jacket-wearing losers on motorcycles hanging out at the malt shop.

The sight of someone wearing a leather jacket alone was enough to send people hollering for the cops. The jacket's nefarious image hit its stride during the fifties and pretty much had motorcyclists to blame for it. Bike riders had worn leather clothing for years, but only for protection in case of a spill; it had nothing to do with being rebellious. Prior to World War II, motorcycle fashion was fairly constricting, with riders wearing layers of clothing and bulky wool dusters, as the sport was messier back then. Up until the late 1930s, Harley-Davidson owners in particular had to contend with engines equipped with "total loss" oil systems; all the oil poured into the crankcase eventually leaked out. Riders squeezed a tiny hand pump to inject oil into the pistons while they rode, which was purged from the engine and came flying back on the rider. After nine hundred miles, the oil was gone. Motorcyclists were regularly seen with enormous Rorschach blots of black gunk splattered all over their legs.

The phasing out of the total loss system eliminated the need for long heavy dusters and the style gradually shifted to the pilot trappings that many of the veterans were wearing. The traditional leather bomber jackets, though, proved to be too heavy and ill-fitting for some bikers, and designers like Ross Langlitz* began making leather jackets specifically for motorcycling. The most infamous design, worn by Brando's Johnny in *The Wild One,* consisted of an angled front zipper with overlapping flaps, zippered sleeves, and a form-fitting collar and waistband to keep out the wind. Not many bike riders owned a jacket as snazzy as Johnny. Like much of pop culture, *The Wild One* image was pushed. But its outlaw symbolism was so powerful that newer riders could not help but start adopting the appropriate trappings (motorcycling is a risky sport anyway, they thought, so why not look cool while doing it?). *The Wild One's* reputation did more to sell leather jackets than any number of freewheeling ex-Air Corps veterans ever could have, even though the veterans were the ones who introduced leather jackets to motorcycling in the first place.

The irony, of course, was that the uniform of the war hero became the look of the antihero, and the whole Harley-Davidson/*Wild One* fashion ensemble was saddled with juvenile delinquent baggage. Now everyone who wore a black leather jacket *had* to be a hoodlum, convincing those hoodlums who did not wear a leather jacket to go out and steal one. There was al-

---

* Ross Langlitz is widely credited with making the first real leather motorcycle jacket. A glove cutter from Portland, Oregon, Langlitz was a motorcycle enthusiast who lost a leg in a riding accident when he was seventeen, yet went on to race competitively, winning nearly fifty races between 1937 and 1954.

ready a growing commie rep around motorcycles and the corrupting effect they clearly had on every person who dared to straddle one. If the rider was young and wore a leather jacket, he was preordained to incite mayhem and provoke a round of fisticuffs with the town constable. Just wearing one got you refused a hamburger at the Pig and Whistle.

As the outlaw myth began to take wing, more aspiring bike riders started combing the classifieds looking for used motorcycles. Some went so far as to actually buy new ones but unless they opted to go British, the only bikes available were Harley-Davidsons, which the public was associating more and more with debauchery and switchblades. It was the kind of bad press that would usually cripple a company's reputation, but the more the media spun the hoodlum image, the better off Harley-Davidson became. "Did it hurt Harley Davidson sales that the media did this?" Marty Rosenblum explains. "The answer is no."[40]

IN A DROLL VIOLATION OF EVERY RULE PERTAINING TO MARKETING and public relations, Harley-Davidson sales soared throughout the 1950s, doubling and tripling in numbers. The company name became a catchall synonym for every motorcycle on the road whether it was a Harley-Davidson or not. This boom was certainly aided by a strong economy and the company's domestic monopoly, but the real grist behind Harley-Davidson's exploding success came from a foreboding semblance that hovered over their motorcycles like a leering chain-wielding buzzard. It was all a part of the moral decline that was compromising American values, especially the noisy musical clamor that all the hoodlums were starting to listen to.

Rock 'n' roll, like X-rays and North America, was discovered accidentally. Elaborate theories have been conceived to define just where this demon music came from, but the basic explana-

tion is rather unromantic: white southern boys raised on country music heard black rhythm and blues on the radio, tried to
play it, and completely screwed it up. The result was rockabilly,
the drunken uncle of rock 'n' roll, a sub-genre of pop music that
pretty much shot its wad within three years of its birth and was
gone by the end of the fifties, yet supplied the soundtrack to the
emerging American biker scene.

The aesthetic similarities between rockabilly music and post-
Wild One outlaw motorcycle culture make them almost cosmic
twins: both were a creation of white trash sensibilities based on
a rigid attention to deconstruction. Just as outlaw bikers stripped
their bikes down to a skeletal frame and boosted the engines, so
the early rockers stripped their music down to an elementary
structure and emphasized the beat.

Rockabilly music was dumb, primitive, and fucked-up from the
get-go, largely because of a peculiar quirk possessed by many of
the musicians who helped create the music: they hated it. The
noted music producer Jim Dickinson, who worked on many fifties
rock recording sessions, says that true rockabilly was created by six
"tensions" or conflicts essential to the music. They were: (1) The
musicians' guilt about playing what they felt was "nigger" music.
(2) The musicians' anger at a society that *made* them feel guilty
about playing "nigger" music. (3) Contempt for the country music
that influenced rockabilly. (4) Contempt for rockabilly music itself
because it wasn't real country music nor jazz/R&B. (5) The public's contempt for the musicians who played rockabilly. (6) The
feeling that rockabilly music was sinful and against God's will.[41]

That most of these six conflicts contradict each other only contributed to the music's intensity. Added in was the resentment of
black performers who felt that whites were yet again ripping off
their music and getting rich from it (an understandable but specious theory as nobody ever got rich playing rockabilly). As a re-

sult, the recording sessions were often staffed with an ensemble of musicians who wanted to kill each other. In Craig Morrison's fascinating book *Go Cat Go!: Rockabilly Music and Its Makers,* Dickinson explains:

> "The guitarist is always some guy that's into playing jazz and he thinks the [rockabilly] music is shit. And the singer is a country purist who thinks it's nigger music or something.... And [there] almost has to be an insensitive producer... some jerk who's going to rattle the change in his pocket and talk about something inappropriate to get it edgy enough.... There was always some guy who thought, 'We should be playing real country music,' and there was somebody else who wanted to get a drummer, and that was the way it was. All that bitching... is part of it."[42]

Many rockabilly recordings sound like the band cannot wait to finish the song and get the hell out of there. Drummers split the skins on their trap sets, upright bass players slapped the strings, singers hiccuped the vocals, and lead guitarists played careening solos that came flying in out of nowhere. Half the players hot dogged while the other half tried to destroy the song. Much of the music's sound was serendipitous by design, the result of equipment shortcomings. The familiar "slap-back" echo heard on rockabilly records was incorporated in order to add fullness to the sparse instrumentation. Instead, with all the frenetic playing, it simply made the records sound that much more deranged. The Rock 'n' Roll Trio's 1956 recording of "Train Kept A-Rollin'" has all the classic elements of pure freaked rockabilly. The song is a remake of an R&B swinger originally recorded in 1951, but is performed so egregiously wrong that it verges on musical slander. Lead singer Johnny Burnette's voice is drenched in echo and guitarist Paul Burlison (a superb musician) rips off a distorted solo that sounds like a hundred-pound wasp. There is no drummer but nobody notices.

Like *The Wild One,* rockabilly music was not widely commercially successful, yet it was tremendously influential. It was the first music ever to sneer and this attitude was copped by more rockers than care to admit it. Though Elvis was one of the original purveyors of rockabilly, he all but abandoned it after leaving Sun Records for RCA in 1955 (his cover of Carl Perkins' "Blue Suede Shoes" was his last real attempt). The real mantle of rockabilly and biker chic has long been carried by a crippled bipolar mess of a singer named Gene Vincent. If Elvis was the King of rock 'n' roll, Vincent was its demented viscount, and the music's first outlaw. Though he lacked Elvis's swagger and booming baritone, he made up for it with a wild stage persona that verged on demonic.

In July of 1955, Eugene Vincent Craddock was twenty-year-old sailor on leave when the driver of a Chrysler ran a red light and smashed into him while he was riding his Triumph motorcycle, recently purchased with a reenlistment bonus. He was rushed to Portsmouth Naval Hospital near Norfolk, Virginia, where he drifted in and out of consciousness, his left leg crushed to a pulp. The doctors had wanted to amputate the leg, but the young seaman, not yet a legal adult, pleaded with his mother not to sign the medical consent forms. For the next six months, he lay in the hospital while his leg slowly worked itself into a twisted limb that would never completely heal.

Gene loved music and had taught himself to play the guitar, though he would never get very good at it. He was, however, blessed with a chameleon-like voice, by turns both plaintive and yowling, depending on the song and the mood he was in while singing it. Gene passed the time in his hospital bed singing Hank Williams tunes and even took a stab at songwriting. He collaborated with a Marine who was in the hospital on one composition, a loping, innocuous little ditty entitled "Be Bop A Lula."

After his release from the hospital, Gene went home to live with his parents in Norfolk and contemplate his future. He listened to the local country radio station WCMS and heard the music of the new sensation, Elvis Presley. Impressed, Gene decided to pursue music as a possible career. WCMS had started a new show called "Country Showtime" which featured local talent, and anyone could audition for a spot. Gene was one of ten finalists chosen to perform. He showed up at the Carnival Room, a local club owned by station manager Sy Blumenthal, where the show was to be broadcast live with the WCMS staff band, the Virginians, backing up all the acts. Sporting a cast on his withered leg, Gene limped onstage with greasy hair, and wailed out "Be Bop A Lula." The Virginians' leader, Willie Williams, said succinctly: " All the chicks went berserk."[43]

Over the next few months, Gene made repeat performances on "Country Showtime," electrifying audiences with his manic performances, often ending them by dropping to one knee, pounding on his guitar, and smashing the mike to pieces on the stage floor. Blumenthal and local deejay "Sheriff Tex" Davis became his managers and formed a band around Gene's freaky act. The newly formed group included a fifteen-year-old drummer and a local guitarist named Cliff Gallup who played fiery solos like a bebopper in a bad mood. Their demo of Gene's "Be Bob A Lula" was sent off to Capitol Records, which was looking for a singer to counter the exploding Elvis. Within three weeks, Gene and his group were signed to a contract and flown to Nashville to record. They played so loudly in the studio that the needles went into the red. A single was released, with "Be Bop A Lula" relegated to the B-side, as it was considered just a novelty song ("Sheriff Tex" Davis was listed as a cowriter, the unnamed Ma-

rine having sold his half of the song's rights for twenty-five dollars). Deejays ignored the A-side song "Woman Love" and instead spun "Be Bop A Lula," with its scat-like title and a beat
fairly lifted from Elvis's "Heartbreak Hotel." Within weeks, it was
number one on the singles charts and Gene Craddock, who
changed his name to Gene Vincent, and his newly-christened
Blue Caps were on their way.

With his wailing voice and Richard the III gimp, Gene Vincent,
more than Elvis, added menace to the new music that was corrupting America's youth. While Elvis swiveled his hips, Gene
staggered around on the stage and shrieked like a demon while
trying to ignore the incredible pain in his shattered leg. "Gene
Vincent's stage persona was really based on his appearance as a
bike rider," Marty Rosenblum explains. "If you see him in this
wonderful movie called *Hot Rod Gang,* you begin to get a feeling for what a bike rider really looked like."[44]

As the title implies, there are no motorcycles in *Hot Rod
Gang,** only a young Gene Vincent with his hair in a greasy coif.
He had yet to adopt a leather jacket into his stage act, but his
rayon shirt with a turned-up collar and brightly-colored panels
down the front was a favorite of motorcyclists at the time. The
film itself is entirely disposable and Vincent's acting is wooden,
but his cool and arrogant persona comes through in his few performance scenes.

But as rockabilly started to fade in the late fifties, so did Gene
Vincent's career in America. His Blue Caps had broken up, he
had no manager, and his crippled leg was getting worse. Vin-

---

* With the exception of *The Wild One,* there was a surprising paucity of motorcycle films produced during the 1950s. Still, the decade's ubiquitous youth-
gone-bad B-films regularly featured enough sneering brats in leather jackets
for the audience to assume that most of them probably had a "Harley"
stashed away somewhere.

cent's manic performances played havoc on the damaged limb, causing it to bleed and become infected. His leg became so unstable, friends noted that it bent like rubber when he walked. To dull the pain, Vincent drank heavily and was a serious alcoholic by the time he turned twenty-three. He continued to tour with pickup bands to back him up, downed martinis by the liter, and skulked around the stage like the last rock 'n' roll vampire left alive before the sun rose. Offstage, he smashed up hotel rooms, slept with countless women, and lay awake in bed sweating in agony from the excruciating pain in his leg. He woke up one morning to find that nobody was playing his records anymore.

Rock 'n' roll in America was starting to wane. Little Richard had left music to become a minister, Carl Perkins had been severely injured in a car wreck, The Rock 'n' Roll Trio had broken up, Jerry Lee Lewis's career was destroyed after he married his thirteen-year-old cousin, Elvis was singing ballads and appearing in bad movies, and Buddy Holly, Ritchie Valens, and the Big Bopper had all died in a plane crash. Gene, meanwhile, couldn't get arrested and decided to leave America after hearing that his music had developed a following in Europe and the Far East. On December 6, 1959, a disillusioned Gene Vincent limped off a plane at London's Heathrow Airport, having come to England to save his moribund career.

Prior to coming to England, Gene Vincent had done a tour of Japan where he was bewildered to find himself being mobbed by young Asian fans who could not speak a word of English. His shows at concert halls had drawn upwards of ten thousand people each night, the audiences screaming and clawing to reach him. Now he was on the tarmac at Heathrow airport where he was greeted by British music impresario Jack Good, who had invited him to headline on Good's TV music show *Boys Meet Girls,* an English version of *American Bandstand.* Good was somewhat taken aback by the young rocker's manner. Vincent was far too nice for Good, who had heard all the stories about his hotel room vandalism and crazed performances. Plus, his appearance wasn't tough-looking enough. Where was his leather jacket?

The English had always loved American pop culture and the continental drift of rock 'n' roll posing began with the Teddy boys of the mid-fifties. Teddy boys, or teds for short, resembled mutant Elvises, with piled-up pompadours, long angular sideburns, white suit jackets, and pointed shoes. They carried switchblades, drank ale by the pint, and danced the stroll. Everything about them embraced the American juvenile delinquent myth. When Gene Vincent arrived, he was still performing in his paneled shirts with the turned-up collar. Jack Good promptly outfitted Gene in black leather, greased his hair even more than usual, and told him to play up the limp. Good wanted his American import to be rock's Mephistopheles. Gene obliged, donned a leather jacket, and kept it on for the rest of his career—it became his trademark.

Within days of his arrival, Gene made his English TV debut on the *Boys Meet Girls* show dressed head to toe in black leather, and gave a frenzied performance that was everything his fans had anticipated. He embarked on a nationwide tour, playing to packed houses and nearly setting off a riot at the Paris Olympia. He released a rollicking rockabilly single called "Wild Cat" that landed in the English Top Thirty. In March 1960, his next U.K. single, "My Heart," scored even higher on the charts, peaking at Number Sixteen.

England was good to Gene Vincent. His records were getting airplay and he was a regular draw at halls and large clubs. As he had no regular backup group, Gene regularly performed with English pickup bands and even did several shows with a quartet of greasy kids in biker jackets called the Beatles.

The British enthusiasm for rockabilly persuaded other American artists to fly the pond and try their luck. The great rockabilly singer/guitarist Eddie Cochran came to England and joined Gene on a tour called the *Anglo-American Beat Show.* Gene and Eddie were great friends and frequently performed together during the tour. On April 17, 1960, Gene and Eddie Cochran finished up a show in Bristol and decided to take a taxi to London. With Eddie's girlfriend Sharon Sheeley accompanying them, the two rockers made their way through a throng of excited fans and climbed inside the cab. They took off, and within a few moments Gene dropped off to sleep.

At around 1 A.M. the cab was speeding recklessly through the small town of Chippenham, Wilshire, when it lost control going around a curve and smashed into a cement post at nearly 70 mph. Eddie Cochran and his girlfriend Sharon were both ejected from the car. The girl died instantly and Cochran was critically injured. Gene miraculously survived the crash, though he sustained a broken arm and severely re-injured his bad leg. He somehow managed to carry Eddie Cochran to the ambulance when it arrived before collapsing in a state of shock. Two days later, on Easter Sunday 1960, Eddie Cochran died of his injuries. He was only twenty-one years old.

It was an abrupt end to the dying rockabilly scene. Vincent eventually returned to America and continued to perform until the mid-sixties, when the British invasion and the San Francisco rock scene ended his career for good. He had no record contract and eked out a living playing clubs with second-rate cover bands backing him up.

Today, Vincent's influence on rock 'n' roll has been dutifully acknowledged by music critics and he has found a new generation of fans. There are several Internet sites devoted to him, and CD retrospectives of his singles as well as tribute albums have been released. Everyone from John Kay of Steppenwolf to Billy Idol to Brian Setzer has copied Vincent's onstage leather look. Meanwhile, rockabilly, the original outlaw music, has seen a huge resurgence in popularity in recent years, where it is performed in a far more worshipful manner than was ever intended.

CHAPTER 5

Cheaper, Faster...

BY THE CLOSE OF THE FIFTIES, THE AMERICAN BIKER HAD FALLEN
into two reputed categories: outlaws who rode Harleys and
hoodlums who rode English bikes. Naturally, this hinged on
whether or not the public could tell the difference between
the two, and what criteria they used in order to make their
distinction. Outlaws tended to be older, working-class, and
more racing-oriented while hoodlums were younger, teenagers even, and into zip guns and pouting. Outlaws could
tear their bikes apart, whereas hoodlums could barely change
a flat tire.

Though the word "Harley" was being thrown around more
and more, most people did not care what kind of bike was
being ridden, since just owning a motorcycle was boorish
enough. The only thing that might threaten the edgy allure to
being a biker was if motorcycles suddenly became popular.

It was in 1962, in an era where image was becoming everything, when TV audiences saw a commercial on their flicker-
ing sets that would help realize that threat. With halcyon flute
music drifting in the background, a wholesome blonde house-
wife living in San Francisco straddles a tiny scooter-like motorcycle and buzzes around happily, having lunch with friends,
running errands, and buying flowers. She flirts innocently with
the owner of a fish market and returns home to a loving fam-

ily. There is no dialogue until the very end, when a voiceover narrator tags out with, "You meet the nicest people on a Honda."

With the possible exception of cops, there are few things more aggravating to American bikers than the Japanese motorcycle. It is the devil incarnate, a soulless piece of stamped machinery that runs counter to the whole primal experience of riding. For years, one of the traditions at the Black Hill Classic Rally in Sturgis, South Dakota involves the destruction of a Japanese motorcycle. Riders pay a cash donation for the privilege of inflicting a single whack at an Asian-made bike with a sledgehammer. There is no shortage of takers. In a scene reminiscent of the Shirley Jackson short story "The Lottery," a large crowd gathers to cheer as the innocent motorcycle is slowly pounded into scrap metal. If nothing else, these "riceburners" have done more to screw with biker mystique than anything that the media could have ever done.

When Japanese motorcycles began arriving in the U.S. during the early 1960s, little did their makers realize that they were about to create a market for a product that the American public didn't even know it wanted. At the time, the domestic motorcycle industry was relatively healthy but had also hit a plateau. Bikes were thought of as a fringe mode of transportation that appealed to a select number of fools set on killing themselves. No matter how hard Harley-Davidson tried, it could not convince the mainstream public that anyone and everyone was welcome to buy their behemoth motorcycles and become a part of the family. Marketing was not one of Harley-Davidson's strong suits and their print ads (the company has never advertised on television) appeared only in motorcycle magazines, where they featured illustrations of happy smiling riders on clean motorcycles outfitted with stock accessories. It was an image the company clearly sought, but one which ran so contrary to its growing badass reputation that the ads seemed almost expedient, a politic method of throwing the hounds of moral justice off the scent. Likewise, the hard-charging English bikes that made their appearance in *The Wild One* had a nice thug-like vibe to them. All of these Anglo motorcycles were big powerful jobs that ruled the road and incited disgusted reactions from people who felt they were nuisances. But there were millions of potential customers in America who were curious, even intrigued, about possibly taking up the sport of motorcycling, but just not on one of those loud scary creatures. Enter Honda. The revolution that the company sparked soon put the entire American biker scene on its ear.

Soichiro Honda was born in 1901, the son of a Japanese blacksmith, and grew up to become a metallurgist and entrepreneur who ran a plant making piston rings for military vehicles. Japan's entry into World War II kept Honda's company bustling with orders, but the nation's eventual defeat in 1945 all but shut down his operation. With plenty of time on his hands, Honda noticed that more and more people had to walk in order to get anywhere, as there was no viable mode of transportation. The Japanese automobile industry was at a standstill and cars were scarce. Sensing an opportunity, Honda scraped up enough cash to buy 490 tiny war surplus generator engines designed to run communications equipment, then purchased a gross of cheap off-brand bicycles on which he could attach the engines. These inexpensive powerbikes were quickly snapped up and Honda set out to make more. Unable to find any more generator motors, Honda began building his own engines, then his own motorcycle frames, until finally his piston factory was converted to a complete motorcycle assembly plant.

At the time, Japanese culture was much more bike-oriented than America. Nearly 10 percent of Japan's population rode some kind of motorcycle, and within a few years following World War II, there were more than thirty-five different Japanese motorcycle manufacturers. For the next few years, Honda built small, rather primi-

tive motorcycles for the transportation-starved populace, until re-
alizing in 1953 that his machine tools had become so out of date
that his motorcycles were obsolete before they hit the market (plus
he was getting swamped by the fierce competition). Honda borrowed a million dollars to buy all-new equipment to outfit his
factory and then traveled to the Isle of Mann to study European
machinery technology. Two weeks later, he returned home in shock,
having discovered just how inferior Japanese technology was compared to the Europeans. Honda knew that in order to survive, he
would have to start over and build a better bike. He was also looking to expand his market, and he set his eyes on the United States.

The so-called "invasion" of Japanese motorcycles into America
began with a trickle. Honda field reps towing small trailers tra-
versed the nation looking for motorcycle dealers who would be willing to sell their tiny powerbikes. They approached primarily British
bike dealers, of which there were plenty, sensing they would be less
xenophobic about handling the Honda C-100 Cub, a tiny motorcycle outfitted with little ferrings* and a 50cc engine. It was easily
one-half the size of the average motorcycle being ridden at the time.

The reaction from dealers upon seeing these oriental curiosities was far from enthusiastic. Even the smallest motorcycles at
that time made the Honda Cub look like a toy. It wasn't a scooter,
but it sure as hell didn't resemble a motorcycle, either. In most
cases, dealers were loath to try to sell them and Honda reps went
so far as to leave the bikes behind on a consignment basis, with
the agreement that they would come back and pick them up later
if nobody bought them.

It was a trip none of them would ever make. Honda Cubs were
quickly snapped up by new riders and went on to sell in the mil-

---

* A ferring is a molded shell that wraps around the front of the frame. They
  are regularly found on scooters. More aerodynamic ferrings are incorporated
  on racing bikes.

lions. There was literally nothing like them. The price of a brand
new Cub was around $275, a fraction of what the average motor-
cycle cost. It weighed next to nothing, came with a push-button
electric starter, made very little noise, and anyone could learn to
ride one in the time it took to count up to twenty. At the same time,
Honda had produced two larger model bikes, the 125cc Benley and
the 250cc Dream, that were more problematic. As straightforward
street bikes, their design was awkward, either too slow or too small.
Honda corrected this problem by replacing them with the 250cc
Hawk and its awesome big brother, the Super Hawk, the latter of
which sent the Honda company on its meteoric rise to success.

The Honda Super Hawk remains one of the most stunning
lightweight motorcycles ever produced. It came equipped with a
305cc two-stroke engine, dual carburetors, and a rev of a mind-
boggling 9,000 rpm. It weighed far less than the larger English
motorcycles (say nothing of a Harley 74), handled like a dream,
and in the right hands, could hit speeds of up to 105 mph—this
in a class where 75 to 80 mph was usually the limit. The Super
Hawk was an immediate hit and went on to sell over a million
units in its first year alone.

Whether it was the fun little Cub or the swift Super Hawk,
Honda motorcycles were so sublimely designed, they were an affront to the noble heritage of rider maintenance. Bikers accused
them of being literally perfect, so perfect that they were boring.
Honda riders didn't have to carry tools with them because their
goddamn bikes never broke down.

For all their performance hubris, both Harleys and English-
made motorcycles usually required their riders to possess a certain amount of technical know-how (limey bikes in particular
broke down a lot). What sounds like an intolerable aberration,
though, was widely considered an organic aspect to being a bike
rider. If the throttle cable stuck, the transmission rattled, or the

carburetor needed adjustment, so be it. Pull over, fix it, and hit the road. Harley-Davidsons were generally more dependable but they, too, required routine engine maintenance, carburetor tuning, chain tightening, and brake adjustments. Anyone sensible enough to take their Harley or Triumph into a mechanic rather than try to fix it themselves was branded a chicken.

Japanese acumen changed all that and bikers have never forgiven them for it. Hondas were like Pringles, each one exactly the same, all flawless.* If your Honda broke down, which was rare, you either took it to a dealer and had them fix it, or you went out and got another one. There was a certain humility to Japanese bikes, too. They were tools that allowed you to experience the thrill of riding. The Honda was like a geisha, subservient, obedient, and lacking in personality, whereas a Harley-Davidson was a personal extension of the rider's self, each one a flawed, coarse, primal reflection of his inner soul. Harleys were bobbed, chopped, painted, streamlined, folded, spindled, and mutilated way beyond their original specs, all for the purpose of equivocation: it made them even more of a Harley.

Soichiro Honda knew nothing about all this primeval ceremony. He simply tossed his tiny bikes into a marketplace populated by cops and outlaws and waited to see what would happen. In yet another example of the serendipity that runs through biker culture, Honda seemed to fall into a well of consumer demand that not even he anticipated.

But much of Honda's success can be attributed to the company's heavy use of advertising. Honda (and later Yamaha) knew instinctively that their lightweight machines would never appeal to the purist set and needed to be targeted at members of the

---

* Some models could be problematic; the first Honda 750 models had so much torque that they were notorious for breaking chains like kite string, though this was an easily correctable rider problem.

"straight" public. The company's "You meet the nicest people" commercials were part of a national advertising campaign that also included full-page ads in national magazines, particularly in *Life,* with whom they had a contract for several years. Powered by an enormous budget, Honda advertisements became ubiquitous, with everyone from businessmen in suits to college students to housewives appearing in print and TV ads astride a tiny Honda power bike.

The ad campaign was an unqualified success and Honda's stock value rocketed until within a few years, they were boasting annual sales of $77 million while Harley-Davidson's, whose bikes cost far more, were less than half of that. Honda also began offering more bikes styles from which to choose. By 1965, the company also had a fairly wide line of motorcycles that ranged from 300ccs on down to 50ccs. Soon, they introduced the CB-450 with a dual overhead cam and twin carburetors which accelerated as fast as an English-made 650cc bike.

Harley-Davidson had met the British challenge back in the late 1950s when they successfully launched the Sportster, a red-hot street bike with a smaller frame than their standard cruisers but outfitted with a 883cc engine. It was a screamer of a motorcycle that sold very well for Harley-Davidson (it is still produced today) but it was never much of an outlaw rig. The Sportster was too small, not like the T-Rexes that the hardcores were riding. Though the physics behind power-to-weight ratios dictated that the heavier the bike, the slower it was going to run, there was still nothing more galling to American bikers than to have their low-slung Harley 74s getting whipped on the road by a stock Honda with a much smaller engine.

WHILE HARLEY-DAVIDSON WAS WARILY MONITORING THE HONDA presence on their home turf, a different biker scene was making ripples in England. Café racers were a velocity-minded group of customized bike riders who came into prominence in the early 1960s. Their roots go back thirty years to the "promenade percys," upper-class dandies on motorcycles who made a habit of scooting up and down the promenades at British seaside resorts for the sole purpose of showing off. World War II severely dampened the English motorcycle industry and it wasn't until the mid-1950s that it started taking off again as more and more young people started shelling out hard-earned pounds sterling to buy motorcycles. Café racer culture was born out of the explosion of roadside cafés that popped up alongside England's overloaded and winding roadways to cater to the growing needs of commuters and lorry drivers.* It became common for bike riders to meet at a roadside café, gulp down loads of coffee, and then speed off to the next café. These impromptu sprints between eateries were described as "café racing" or "burning."

"Café racer" was a term that applied to both the bikes and their riders, who were some of the most fatalistic motorcyclists ever to grace biker culture. Everything was about speed, performance, and cheating death. The ultimate rush was to "do the ton," hitting at least 100 mph, which is reckless enough on today's flawless expressways but sheer insanity while navigating a serpentine two-lane road. Al Griffin described the café racer memorably in his 1972 book *Motorcycles:*

> His motorcycle, which the manufacturer usually intended to be only a road bike, is often equipped with clip-on handle-

---

* Following World War I, the English government began developing a national highway system. Though some thoroughfares were built, they mostly just paved over the ancient twisting roads that had been around for centuries. The nation's growing number of motorists could barely average 30 mph on them and had to pull over regularly to take a break.

---

bars, dink front fender (if any), fiberglass gas tank, hump-back racing seat, and rear-set foot pegs. Everything possible is drilled full of lightening holes, as in the steering wheel of a race car—the café racer sometimes affects not only holes in the skid plate and in the mounting brackets but also the brake drums, fenders, and often in his gloves and even in his helmet. When he doesn't actually drill holes, he paints black spots that *look* like holes.

The café racer has large dents in the fenders and gas tanks, most often manually pounded in with a rock when nobody was looking. His helmet is white, to best show up the deep scratches he has gouged into it. His clothing is similarly scuffed on [the] forearms and knees, and the one-piece leather jump suit has stripes from shoulder to ankle; the boots, of course, zip up the sides. Like as not, he also sports a long whipping scarf like a World War I ace.[45]

The rise of fifties youth culture in the United States had drifted into the gritty working-class sections of south London, where it took a feverish hold and led to the rise of the "rocker," young leather jacket-wearing motorcyclists who slavishly celebrated the American biker myth. Nobody defined café racer conceit more than the rockers, who danced to fifties rockabilly and worshipped Marlon Brando in *The Wild One,* a movie that none of them had ever seen. The rockers formed a clear and exaggerated conception of what the American biker was all about and imitated it to such an extent that they soon became ultra-clichés.

Some of the finest British bikes were being produced during this period, the most well-known being the Triumph T120 Bonneville, introduced in 1960. With the best power-to-weight ratio of any day cruiser in its class (it weighed only 382 pounds) and a four-stroke 649cc engine to boot, the Bonneville could blow the wheels off most stock Harley 74s. Other demon models included the 1960 BSA Gold Star, the 1961 AJS 7R and, later, the 1968 Norton Commando, an awesome quick-handling street bike. The rockers built entire clubs around these motorcycles.

One notorious rocker club of the era was the Cheam Burners, whose half dozen members were such lunatics that they were regularly banned from riding by the police for periods of up to a year at a time. What made the Cheam Burners legendary was their skill at taking on the Deceptive Bends, hairpin curves on the English roadways. The signs that marked these turns were meant to warn drivers to slow down but the Cheam Burners saw them as a cue to drop the hammer and do the ton. The speedometer on any bike going faster than 80 mph was largely useless as the needle jumped about wildly, so Rockers who wanted to gauge their speed had to monitor the rpm counter and then calculate it from there. In a 1982 interview with *Classic Bike* magazine, Paul Morin, a former member of the Cheam Burners, calculated that at 6,000 rpm, his 750cc Norton Atlas and the Norton 650SS of his rocker pal Ted Raymond were doing 103 mph. Morin also recalled how he and Raymond would hit a set of four Deceptive Bends nicknamed "Dork Four" that made up a stretch of road outside the village of Dorking.

> We used to hold the bikes at just under 6,000 [rpm]—five to eight to be exact going through Dork Four, so we were reaching just about the ton. We had lines marked on the rev counter at 6,000 and peak revs of six-eight, and we used to glance down at the dial to see what we were doing just before going into the corner.
>
> Ted was the only one of us ever got through Dork Four at 6,000. We believed him when he told us this because our group never lied about speeds, unlike some other gangs. At

six-eight in top our Nortons were doing 117 mph, but we only saw that half a dozen times.[46]

Rocker clubs usually were associated with a particular café and often rode the same kind of English bike. The Cheam Burners were mostly Norton aficionados who hung out at the Harlequin café in the village of Cheam while making regular burns to the Tirola in Dorking, the route taking them straight through the Dork Four pass. Other rocker groups preferred Triumphs, which were cheaper than Nortons and could outrun them on a straightaway but didn't handle nearly as well. Any rocker or other café racer foolhardy enough to try and do the ton through the Deceptive Bends while on a Triumph most likely ended up wrapped around a tree. Not surprisingly, rockers had an appallingly high mortality rate. Several members of the Cheam Burners were killed in motorcycle accidents while doing a burn. Naturally, they could have done their racing on the safer confines of the track but, as Paul Morin said, "It's not the same—there's nothing coming the other way."

It was standard practice for English bike zealots to routinely swap parts and accessories from various motorcycles so that practically every café racer became a snowflake, no two exactly the same. Any available bike could be converted into a café racer but the ultimate was the Triton, a hybrid creation consisting of a Triumph 650cc engine mounted onto the featherbed frame of a Norton. Combining the speed of the former with the maneuverability of the latter, the Triton was the ultimate café racer; there was nothing in England that could catch it. Rockers on stripped-down café racers would come bombing out of the Elephant-and-Castle and Brixton districts of London to hit the beach resorts at Brighton where they could rumble with the fashionable pill-loving "mods."

The London mods were the rockers' arch-nemeses. Though of similar working-class origins, mods were far more ostentatious and neurotic than rockers. They had an obsession with designer threads and worked at menial clerical jobs so they could spend every spare shilling they earned on the sharpest clothes. They listened to the hot new London groups like the Who, the Kinks, and the Small Faces, plastered down their hair with sugar water, and wore long protective raincoats over their expensive wardrobes. Most significant were the mods' fixation with uppers and scooters; they were major amphetamine freaks who mainly rode Italian-made Vespas or Lambretta motor scooters.

The scooter never made much of an impression on bikers, negative or otherwise (they were made famous by Audrey Hepburn, who putted around on one in *Roman Holiday,* but that certainly wasn't much of an endorsement). Rockers mostly snickered at scooters, yet mods built an entire lifestyle around the little humming creations. Since they were loath to get a speck of dirt on their clothes, they liked that the scooters' cleaner burning engines didn't soil their threads. Mods customized them by attaching as many lights, decals, and rearview mirrors to them as possible. Though this fussiness runs contrary to the big bike myth, in their own nervous way the mods were just as much bikers as their leather-wearing foes the rockers were.

The mods-and-rockers scene of the mid 1960s (it was never large enough to be called a movement) was England's contribution to biker mythology,* even if much of it was just a regurgitation of something that was already becoming dated. Neither group was ever anything but a vague curiosity to American bikers of the time but their notoriety found its way into other parts

---

* Mods and rockers were celebrated in The Who's rock opera *Quadrophrenia,* a kind of *Catcher In The Rye* for motorcycle punks.

of Europe[47]. The conflict between the two groups was begrudging at best. Unlike the street gang violence that plagues much of America's cities today, mods and rockers were more likely to pour sugar into each other's gas tanks than wage war. There were no known deaths attributed to clashes between the two groups, and if any mod was ever set on exacting deadly revenge on some offending rocker, all he had to do was wait for the leather-clad fool to crash his bike while doing the ton.

Today, the mods-and-rockers/café racer scene has become a fascination for growing numbers of motorcyclists, who are mainly attracted to the customizing rituals that were part of it. It is quite easy nowadays to buy a street bike that'll do 100 mph or a scooter outfitted with a dozen rearview mirrors, but many find that to be cheating. Instead, they regularly swap old plans that show how to rebuild the transmission on a Norton Atlas or go out and buy their own mirrors. Scooter clubs in particular have grown remarkably in recent years, with their members riding Italian-made rigs only. It is all in good fun with a fair amount of *kitsch,* to be sure, an American celebration of something that pretty much started here to begin with.

CHAPTER 6

...And Out of Control

THE APPEARANCE OF THE HELL'S ANGELS (NOW HELLS ANGELS)*
on the cultural landscape during the mid-1960s is one of
those twisted American success stories that usually drives the
guardians of public morality into an apoplectic fit over the
spiritual decay of the nation. If there could ever be one group
who took the tenuous image of motorcycling and tossed it
into the sewer, it was the Hell's Angels. They remain the most
feared, reviled, and imitated outlaw sub-cultures around.

It is difficult for anyone to write objectively about the
Hell's Angels, as so much of their background and history is
riddled with contradiction. Though they don't make the news
often, to law enforcement, the Hell's Angels today are a criminal syndicate who operate a billion dollar international drug
operation. The Angels counter that they are just a club devoted to motorcycle riding and have been unfairly persecuted
by the government for decades.

It had been a dozen years since a half dozen former
POBOB members led by Otto Friedli organized the first
Hell's Angels chapter in San Bernardino. The club was fairly
obscure in 1960 and few people outside of California had

---

* For copyright purposes, the club currently lists itself as "Hells Angels."
They are referred to as "Hell's Angels" throughout this book only for
consistency.

ever heard of it. Those who did usually regarded their members as loathsome curiosities; they weren't *the* Hell's Angels, but rather a bunch of ne'er-do-wells with battered motorcycles. Their expansion had been rather disparate. In 1954, a wandering Angel from southern California named Rocky started up a second chapter in San Francisco out of a group of local bikers who facetiously called themselves the Market Street Commandos. A few years later, a chapter was founded in North Sacramento, then another in Oakland.

Curiously enough, most of the early chapters were unaware of each other's existence. For years, the club's name was up for grabs and any number of riders slapped a patch on their back and declared themselves to be Hell's Angels. Their winged skull colors, borrowed from a defunct World War II Air Corps squadron, varied in design from chapter to chapter. The older Berdoo chapter featured a crudely drawn skull wearing a leather pilot's helmet with short stubby wings, while the northern California chapters' colors were larger and sleeker-looking (the current design). The chapters all operated independently and would find out about each other only through chance meetings. Such was the case in 1957.

James "Mother" Miles and his younger brother Pat grew up in Sacramento and formed the Hell Bent for Glory motorcycle club in the mid-fifties when they were both teenagers. As siblings, the two couldn't have been more different from each other. Mother was a large muscular man with a mop of hair and thick beard known for his easygoing demeanor. "He was a big dude," says his nephew Jim Meredith, who is also Pat's son. "He was about 5′ 10″ but he weighed 240 and he was all muscle. They said he was really mellow, really nice..."[48] Mother's inherent calmness only went so far, though, and if anyone crossed him, he had a way of signaling his displeasure: he would remove the partial plate from his mouth prior to attacking. "He'd pull his two front teeth out and stick 'em in his vest jacket," Meredith says. "You knew shit was gonna happen when he took out his teeth, so people used to scatter: Mother Miles is on a rampage."[49]

Mother was widely respected for his caretaker instincts; he helped bail fellow riders out of jail, got their bikes released from police impound, and even gave indigent club members a place to crash for the night. "I think the reason he was called 'Mother,'" his widow Ruby recalls, "is because 90 percent of the time we had somebody staying with us. He always let people sleep over."[50]

Mother's younger sibling Pat was another piece of work. Dubbed "Mighty Mouse" for his small stature, Pat was a rabid loudmouth who binged on pills and regularly got into fights. Unlike the respected Mother, many disliked Mighty Mouse for his arrogance, and considered him an obnoxious shrimp. "He was barely 5´7″ and weighed only like 120 pounds," says his son Jim. "But he talked shit to everybody, he didn't care who they were."[51] Twice, Mighty Mouse's personality got him beaten so badly that he was declared clinically dead before recovering. The two rode as Hell Bent with some other bikers for a few years until a rider named Boots came to town (no one can recall from where).

Boots (aka Don Reeves) was a biker who sported Hell's Angels colors and had aspirations of being a country western singer. He met the members of Hell Bent and worked his way into the good graces of the Miles brothers, convincing them to turn Hell Bent into a Hell's Angels chapter. In order to start up a chapter in Sacramento, the three needed, bizarrely enough, the consent of the city council. The request was shot down almost as soon as it was presented. We know about the Hell's Angels, the council members told them, and we don't want Sacramento affiliated.

Just what specifically the Sacramento city council had heard about the Hell's Angels is not known. The closest existing Angel chapter was in San Francisco and they had never done much to make news other than roar around the streets, act obnoxious, and incite the occasional bar fight. The president of the Frisco Angels was the legendary Frank Sadilek, a charismatic and good-humored eccentric who oversaw the club for seven years, from 1955 to 1962, while holding down a job as a news cameraman. Sadilek dyed his beard magenta and wore earrings, but his biggest claim to fame was his purchase at an auction in Hollywood of the bumblebee-striped sweater that Lee Marvin wore in *The Wild One* (the film being a flop, nobody wanted the sweater and he bought it for peanuts). Sadilek is also reputed to have designed the larger winged skull patch that eventually usurped the older small one worn by the Berdoo Angels. To top it off, Sadilek spent his entire tenure with the Angels without ever getting arrested.

Law enforcement, though, had let it be known that the Angels were trouble, and the Sacramento city council sent Boots, Mother, and Mighty Mouse out of their chambers without official approval. Undaunted, they started up a Hell's Angels chapter any-way, and called themselves "North Sacramento," a dubious at-tempt at convincing the cops they weren't exactly *local.*

The Miles Brothers also made a pact with each other: if one of them should die while wearing an Angel patch, the surviving sibling would resign the club and turn in his colors. They shook on it and went about trying to avoid the police.

Meanwhile, a young biker living in Oakland had recently fin-ished a stretch in the military as an emancipated minor. Ralph "Sonny" Barger was born in Modesto, California in 1937 and was six months old when his mother walked out on the family, leaving him to be raised by his father. At sixteen, he dropped out of high school and enlisted in the army by lying about his age (he made it all the way overseas to Korea before his supe-riors caught on and sent him back home). Barger bought his first motorcycle as a teenager and was riding around Oakland when he met Boots, the itinerant biker who was now sporting North Sacramento colors. It was the first time Barger had ever heard of the Hell's Angels.

Barger, Boots, and several others started up the Oakland Hell's Angels in 1957, following Barger's brief tenure with the club's Nomad chapter, yet another attempt at subterfuge by the North Sac Angels to disguise where they were from. Boots become Oakland's first president, a position he held for less than a year before quitting to pursue his career as a country singer.

Stature-wise, Barger was not the yeti that many of the other Oakland Angels were. He weighed barely 150 pounds and any one of his club brothers could have overpowered him if they chose. But Barger's intelligence, shrewdness, and calm mind made him a natural leader and he quickly became the new president of the Oakland chapter. They all worked blue-collar jobs during the week and rode during their off hours:[52]:

- Sonny Barger—machine operator, president
- Swede—expert rider, vice president
- Baby Huey—building supplies, future vice president
- Cisco—former Misfits, long-standing Hell's Angel
- Skip the Scotchman—assembly line, World War II veteran
- Jerry—candy company employee, clean-cut
- Junior—three hundred pounds, lived with parents
- J.B.—truck driver, expert rider
- Waldo—shipyard painter, angry drunk
- Tommy—lather, freak
- Gypsy—hick
- Johnny Angel—welder, dangerous
- Elvis—Berdoo escapee, BSA rider
- The Brothers (Ernie, Amaro, Danny)

Barger and the other Oakland members were unaware of the Frisco Angels across the Bay Bridge at first, and only learned of the Berdoo chapter after accidentally encountering some of them during a run through the Gardena area of Los Angeles. Barger then realized that there were Hell's Angels all over the place and he felt it was important that more chapters didn't start up the way the earlier ones had. From now on, new club chapters had to get approval from Oakland first. Others soon followed in Richmond, Vallejo, and Hayward. Most of them were not very big, consisting of twenty members at the most.

The Oakland Hell's Angels established themselves within the city in a storm trooper manner that few other outlaw clubs could rival. In his 1976 book *A Wayward Angel,* former member George "Baby Huey" Wethern recalled the era:

> As long as there was gas in our tanks or a buck to divvy up, we cruised around. We'd go nonstop until thirst drove us to bars like Hazel's on Bancroft or the Hilltop Club on MacArthur Boulevard. Other patrons were expected to overlook insults or arrogance, because a critical stare, an unsolicited comment, or failure to project timidity was good for a thumping or a stomping. We cared as little about clear-cut motives as fight preliminaries.
>
> We didn't lose many fights. Since we often traveled with an assortment of goodies like chains, wrenches, razors, and knives, the advantage was ours from an equipment standpoint. And the regimen of slugfests, all-night drinking and grueling riding hardened us and gave us an experienced edge. Our psychological edge, the club patch, proved as effective as a cocked shotgun, threatening that every Angel within hailing distance would jump to the brother's assistance. Anybody who thought that he was fighting an Angel

one-to-one or that Marquis of Queensbury rules were in effect quickly discovered that "win" was the only rule. If a member was losing, we applied the latter half of the motto: "One on All, All on One."[53]

This form of mob rule strategy was *de rigeur* with the Angels and their outlaw contemporaries, the brutal means to an end. Alcohol-fueled clashes between rival clubs were the norm but sometimes the stray person would be drawn into a brawl for unwittingly "insulting the colors," the definition of which varied from member to member. The Hell's Angels dictum of "An Angel Is Always Right" was widely copied by other outlaws, and it was a sticky rule to enforce. On occasion, an outlaw group had to assist one of their more hair-trigger types to inflict a beating on some hapless soul without knowing precisely why they were stomping him.

The Angels' notoriety grew quickly. Labor Day had become the biggest weekend of the year for the club; it was when they made their annual run to the Monterey peninsula. All the various chapters around the state attended and the highways became alive with mobs of scowling bikers roaring up the coast for the three-day bash. On Labor Day in 1964, a few hundred-odd Hell's Angels rode into downtown Monterey to rendezvous at a bar called Nick's near Cannery Row. While there, two girls in the company of five teenage boys wandered inside Nick's and started hanging out with the amassed outlaws.

The next day, the headlines on the local papers ran the banner headline: HELL'S ANGELS GANG RAPE. The accompanying article told how a local sheriff's office responded to a call that two girls had been kidnapped and assaulted on some sand dunes near the Fort Ord Army training base, where the Hell's Angels were camping out. Upon arrival, the deputies came upon a huge bonfire surrounded by hundreds of bikers and were met by two hysterical girls who emerged from the darkness, one wearing only a ripped sweater, the other completely naked. The girls, just fourteen and fifteen years old, claimed that their male companions had been chased off and that they had been dragged away and sexually assaulted by up to twenty Hell's Angels.

Two days later, the story turned into a he said/she said scenario. Only four Hell's Angels were formally charged, one of them being Mother Miles, and their bail was set at a miniscule twelve hundred dollars. Mother was dismissed as a suspect almost immediately, though not before getting his name in the paper, while the remaining three, Terry the Tramp, Crazy Cross, and Mouldy Marvin made bail and loudly protested their innocence. The two girls later admitted they and the five boys left Nick's and followed the outlaws out to their campsite to drink wine and get high. What happened after that is not really known for sure. The testimonies and medical examinations were inconclusive, and the court dismissed the case three weeks later for lack of evidence.

The so-called Monterey Rape case made national news, however, and registered with the general public almost immediately: a group of dirty animals with names like Crazy and Mouldy had finally confirmed all those rumors about bikers that had been floating around for years. California State Senator Fred S. Farr contacted the state attorney general's office just days after the Monterey story hit the papers and demanded that an investigation be made into the Hell's Angels: who are they, where do they come from, how can we get rid of them? Thomas Lynch, a serious man with a Jack Webb aura of law and order around him, was new to his job as the attorney general of California. He wasted no time in starting to compile data about the Hell's Angels and contacted law enforcement agencies statewide with requests for as much information as they had on file about the club.

While Lynch began his probe, the wheels of justice began rolling right over the Hell's Angels and other outlaw clubs. The North Sac/Nomad Angels were particularly hard-hit. "It got to the point," says Jim Meredith, "to where anytime a Hell's Angel got seen in Sacramento, they got stopped. And they went to jail."[54] This draconian policy was easy for the police to justify since the Angels' own hubris made them wide open targets for busts. They were always carrying something illegal, whether it was pot, pills, or PCP. Leading the charge was County Sheriff John Miserly and a deputy named Leonard Chatoian, who both waged such an intense vendetta against the Nomad chapter that Mother appeared before the city council to protest. This was pre-Miranda, however, and the council waved aside Mother's complaints and instead gave him a choice: get out of Sacramento or keep getting arrested.

The Hell's Angels ranks dwindled to less than ninety members statewide, down from three hundred just a few years before. Besides Sacramento, other chapters like Berdoo were getting throttled by local law enforcement, and most of its members either left town or were sent to prison. It was only in Oakland and San Francisco, home of the two most notorious Angels chapter, that the police largely left the outlaws alone (though the Frisco membership was dwindling at a fast rate). More and more fleeing Hell's Angels came to Oakland to prospect for the Barger-led chapter, finally swelling its ranks so much that they went across the Bay Bridge to stomp on the Frisco Angels for allowing their membership to atrophy so badly. Frisco survived but the Hayward Angels, whose members were all absorbed from an earlier club called the Question Marks, were disbanded by Oakland through repeated assaults for not showing proper allegiance to them.

While the outlaws battled the police and each other, Attorney General Lynch finally released his report on the Hell's Angels

Motorcycle Club in early 1965. It had been assembled from information supplied by "twenty-two district attorneys, fifteen
sheriffs, and sixty-seven chiefs of police." Everyone had combed
through old files to find whatever they could, most of which were
detailed in a section entitled "Hoodlum Activities":

> Early in the morning of June 2, 1962, it was reported that
> three Hell's Angels had seized a nineteen-year-old woman
> in a small bar in the northern part of Sacramento and, while
> two of them held her down on the barroom floor, the third
> removed her outer clothing. The victim was menstruating at
> the time; her sanitary napkin was removed and the third in-
> dividual committed cunnilingus upon her....

> On April 2, 1964, a group of eight Hell's Angels invaded
> the home of an Oakland woman, forcing her male friend out
> of the house at gunpoint and raping the woman in the pres-
> ence of her three children. Later that same morning, female
> companions of the Hell's Angels threatened the victim that
> if she cooperated with the police she would be cut on the
> face with a razor....

The report also included a recounting of a Labor Day weekend
run in 1963, when three hundred members of the Hell's Angels
and other outlaw clubs allegedly took over the small town of
Porterville for several hours. Drunken displays of "obnoxious and
vulgar" behavior were reported as several outlaws stopped traffic
and tried to grope women passengers inside the cars. Their female
companions "lay in the middle of the street, where they went
through suggestive motions." A barmaid was nearly abducted and
raped and an elderly man in a tavern was "brutally beaten" by a
half dozen bikers. City officials chased the horrid flock out of town

with fire hoses and threats of arrest. The so-called Porterville raid was held up as a typical example of how the Hell's Angels could take over a town and wreak havoc. On paper, the Hell's Angels came across like leather-clad reincarnations of Hitler's Brown Shirts with their "Luftwaffe insignias and reproductions of German iron crosses." Most of the outrages portrayed had an air of nihilism to them, as if no one was safe from being randomly yanked off a barstool and ground up into bone meal.

It made for grotesque reading and created a sensation in the press, but exactly what purpose the Lynch report was supposed to serve was anybody's guess. Its tone aside, the document had a cursory feeling, reading more like an "Outlaw Bikers' Greatest Hits" than a thorough comprehensive study. It was only sixteen pages long and once you got past the knives, satyriasis, and *Wehrmacht* accoutrements, you were left with a bunch of semi-employed degenerates who rode loud motorcycles and hung out in bars. One could sense the report's writers were occasionally desperate for good copy:

> Probably the most universal common denominator in identification of Hell's Angels is their generally filthy condition. Investigating officers consistently report these people, both club members and their female associates, seem badly in need of a bath.

Another "common denominator" mentioned in the report was the "1%" patch on the Angels' jackets. It was the sort of cryptic symbol that would pique a journalist's curiosity and much speculation was made regarding what it meant. The patch was fairly new to the outlaw look in 1965, conceived just a few years earlier to inspire unity among all the outlaw clubs running at the time. As "Baby Huey" Wethern described it:

We kicked around a hostile statement from the American
Motorcycle Association, the Elks Club of biking. To draw a
distinction between its members and us renegades, the AMA
had characterized 99 percent of the country's motorcyclists
as clean-living folks enjoying pure sport. But it condemned
the other 1 percent as antisocial barbarians who'd be scum
riding horses or surfboards, too.[55]

The 1 percent* were, of course, outlaws but instead of feeling
affronted, clubs like the Hell's Angels, Coffin Cheaters, Satan's
Slaves, and others created an emblem that celebrated their one-
percenter status.

This clever bit of defiance remains an outlaw standard to this
day, although nobody at the AMA can remember any of their representatives ever making any such hostile statement (it certainly
was never issued in writing). It became the perfect maxim at
which outlaws like the Hell's Angels could thumb their fight-
scarred noses, even if they were possibly jeering at pure fiction.

In the end, the Lynch report did little but portray a small-time
group of crude bikers as a full-blown national menace, something they weren't by a long shot. The resulting publicity caused
the Hell's Angels to become fodder for TV and magazine coverage and this, in turn, transformed them into media celebrities.
Newsweek, Look, Time, and other publications wrote extended
profiles on them; they cropped up regularly on the evening
news; The *Saturday Evening Post* even featured them on the
cover. Before the Lynch report, nobody had ever given any bikers the kind of coverage and critical scrutiny that the Angels
were getting; it had been eighteen years since Hollister and that
was nothing compared to this.

---

* The ratio is more like 1/100 of 1 percent.

And it only got worse.

In June of 1965, the front pages of every major newspaper flashed on a story out of Laconia, New Hampshire. The Forty-fourth Annual New England Tour and Rally, the oldest continuous motorcycle event in the United States, had exploded into a full-scale riot that had to be quelled by the National Guard.

Laconia had hosted motorcycle rallies since World War I, but by 1965, local law enforcement had let it be known they were fed up with the rally and wanted it gone from the town, complaining of rowdy behavior and out of control crowds. Extra security was called in for the week-long event, and the National Guard was already patrolling the Weirs Beach area of the city days before the melee erupted. Besides the Guard and police patrols outfitted with riot equipment, local legislators passed an astonishing ordinance stating that two or more people gathered together on the sidewalk constituted a potential mob and was subject to arrest. The atmosphere was like East Berlin, and when fifteen thousand people streamed into the Weirs Beach area for the week-long rally, all the fuses were primed.

Lakeside Avenue was a major street that ran right through Weirs Beach and it was jammed with people attending the rally. A local resident, an older man with his son, daughter-in-law, and grandchildren accompanying him, tried to drive his car through the crowd when they found themselves penned in and trapped. A group of youths surrounded the car and began rocking it. Fearing the worst, the man and his family fled and watched as the swarm tipped the car over and set a match to the leaking gasoline. Within minutes, the National Guard charged in with bayonets and shotguns loaded with bird shot. They fired into the crowd and wounded several, including a news photographer who was shot in the face. A brief skirmish erupted as people were clubbed to the ground and sprayed with tear gas while several unsuspecting motorcyclists cruising the streets were knocked off their bikes by Guardsmen wielding their rifles like truncheons. Dozens of people were arrested and a curfew was ordered.

Unlike Hollister, the commotion in Laconia was punctuated by a decidedly unstaged photograph that appeared in newspapers and magazines showing an overturned burning car lying in the middle of the street, surrounded by drunken revelers celebrating its sacrifice. Other than the torching of the car, nothing else of note had happened during the rally, but that was a futile point in the weeks afterward. The historic Laconia rally was all but destroyed, consigned afterward to a two-day event that usually lost money.*

Life magazine later quoted local officials as saying they blamed the Hell's Angels for starting the riot, a specious accusation as there were no Hell's Angels in Laconia at the time, nor even any chapters on the East Coast. Photographs of those being arrested in the riot's aftermath revealed an alarming number of young sheepish males dressed in chinos, windbreakers, and Keds tennis shoes. None of those who were booked lived further west than Vermont and few of them even owned a motorcycle. But since the disturbance happened during a motorcycle rally, it was widely assumed that biker hooligans had caused the whole fiery mess at the behest of their idols, the Hell's Angels.

It was the kind of press that infuriated the Angels. They didn't have any problem with riots as a rule, and some of them even voiced their disappointment that they weren't in Laconia to orchestrate the madness. But the reality was they had nothing to do with the fracas; it only *sounded* like something they would do.

Almost without exception, the media's portrayal of the Hell's Angels was overwhelmingly negative, but at the same time most

---

* It was restored to a week-long event in 1992.

of the coverage had the Angels' cooperation. This peculiar dysfunction of the outlaw/media relationship was one of the first of its kind in American journalism, with both sides working together to give each other what they wanted with only one side, the press, being satisfied with the end result.

It took a certain level of fringe madness to be a Hell's Angel and those who were the best at exhibiting it were also the ones who kept getting quoted in the press. Everyone was sticking a microphone in the Hell's Angels' faces, asking leading questions, and whatever they said in response was retooled later to make them look like flesh-eating trolls. They were proud of their Rogues Of The Year status but hated how much the press kept getting the details wrong (e.g., "I said I smashed up a bar but I didn't say it was *that* bar").

Some Angels made inflammatory remarks that made the cops want to lean on them even more, and it soon got to the point where Barger forbade club members from talking to reporters without his permission. He once caught a writer taping an interview with another Angel and took the recorder away so he could edit the tape. Reporters had to talk to him only, and if one got too nosy or confrontational with his questions, Barger would order him to leave or risk getting a chain-whipping.

What the Hell's Angels had revealed about themselves in their dealings with the media was an attribute that had been around since *The Wild One* era and remains present among many bikers today. It is a Miscreant's Paradox, in which a person intentionally creates an aggressive image for himself, then vehemently denies he has such an image. With Eisenhower-era teenagers, it was dressing up like juvenile delinquents, only to become angry when their parents accused them of resembling juvenile delinquents. With bikers today, it is the adoption of skull tattoos, piercings, and scowling visages countered by feeling offended

----

when others say they're scary-looking. With the Hell's Angels of
the 1960s, it was talking and acting like maniacal razorbacks
around journalists, only to become enraged when the resulting
article or TV news segment portrayed them as such. Coupled
with this was their die-hard fanaticism about their numerous beliefs. It became pure sophistry and nobody practiced it more than
the Hell's Angels did during the media blitz.

A classic example of the Miscreant's Paradox exists in four
hours of long-forgotten film footage of the Berdoo Hell's Angels
that lie in the archives of a major TV network. The footage had
been shot for the production of a half hour-long television news
report about the club in 1965 during the height of the Angels'
notoriety. (The finished program no longer exists but the
unedited raw footage has survived.) In this footage, the Berdoo
Angels are so patently disoriented that the news producers filming inside the group's clubhouse jump through hoops trying to
get a usable sound bite. This bewildering exchange between one
interviewer and Blind Bob, a brutish Angel wearing Coke bottle
glasses, is indicative of the whole:

BOB

When people want to turn on me, they got something there
with a little bit more money into it. They tear me up, it's
fine, hey, they got that much coming. Because maybe I like
to smoke a joint every once in a while and I want to drop a
few ashes on it.

INTERVIEWER

What's a joint, Bob?

BOB

Marijuana. I'll be honest about that.

INTERVIEWER

Most of the guys smoke it?

BOB

I don't know.

INTERVIEWER

You do?

BOB

Every once in a while. Like I say, I've been riding a bike a long time. I was around weed a long time before I ever started riding a bike.

INTERVIEWER

Kind of goes together, marijuana and bikes?

BOB

In a way, in a way not.

INTERVIEWER

How does it go together?

BOB

Most people do ride bikes, smoke weed.

INTERVIEWER

Why?

BOB

I guess because the way most people in California do. I don't care if I slept with a girl or not.[56]

When they aren't being hazy, the Angels (some of those present are Satan's Slaves) sound off about the media's negative portrayal of them while excoriating the California attorney general,

whom some of the members refer to as Senator Lynch. They
deny that they rape, yet admit to sexual perversion charges. One
Angel keeps insisting how much they just want to be left alone,
yet doesn't explain why they have allowed an entire film crew to
invade their clubhouse. A female hanger-on named Donna repeatedly says that "The Angels are my whole life." The producers try to corner them with repeated questions about drugs and
underage girls. An Angel prospect named Handbone (whom the
others should not have allowed to speak on camera) waxes forth
in classic Paradox style on what defines an outlaw:

HANDBONE

It's not sanctioned by American Motorcycle Association. It's,
uh, what we'd say, they won't take confidence in us and believe in that, uh, we'll stand up to their laws. But we can't
afford to break any laws, because most of law enforcement
agencies are against us all already, so we have to believe in
our own, uh, laws. We can't break none of the laws, because,
uh, police are already keeping an eye on us and, uh, they're
on us from the beginning.[57]

Another Angel makes light of the club's reputation for taking
over small towns:

ANGEL

Well, like they say, you know, the Angels supposed to go into
towns, tear it apart, rip it up, assault a few people, I've never
been in on anything like that in the United States.

INTERVIEWER

Well, you've done it someplace else though?

ANGEL

Yeah.

INTERVIEWER

Where?

ANGEL

Mexico.[58]

However ignorant the Angels come across, there is one telling moment in the footage that likely did not end up in the finished report. The slob-like Blind Bob, who for the most part is inarticulate, shows a moment of glib insight after he says that he's not a very good "schemer":

INTERVIEWER

What would you do if you were a good schemer?

BOB

I'd have your job. [*Laugh.*]

INTERVIEWER

Think I'm a pretty good schemer?

BOB

Yeah.

INTERVIEWER

All right.

BOB

You got everything I don't have. I mean, you can talk. Like you, uh, right now, you've been leading me into questions, you know? You've been drawing me up. That's what I admire. You've got it made.

                        INTERVIEWER
    I thought you felt you had it made, too.

                            BOB
    In my own way, I do.

                        INTERVIEWER
    Do you really think you do?

                            BOB
    I figure I got as about as good as I'll ever get.[59]

If there was anything that the media ignored about the Hell's Angels, it was the utter listlessness of their day-to-day existence. Lawless behavior certainly has plenty of drama and shock value but it can be awfully banal, too. However fierce and dangerous they were, the Hell's Angels could also be tedious; adult men with no particular structure to their lives other than a rigid adherence to obtuse codes that only they cared about.

What riding footage there is consists of six Angels following a news crew who is filming them from the back of a car. They wear funny sunglasses and spin donuts in the dirt, clearly following the film crew's instructions.

Toward the end of the footage, a news correspondent is seen sitting above the back seat of a speeding convertible, addressing the camera as the Berdoo Angels follow him at the camera crew's bidding. As he records the closing to his report on the club, the Angels speed up and pass the car:

> They're on the run. Their record of rape and violence, sex offenses, and homosexuality, keeps them moving from place to place. While they talk bravely about their strength, the fact is they have trouble getting new members and they're

just beginning to feel the effect of the Attorney General's crackdown. After years of running wild in California, the Hell's Angels are hurting.[60]

The correspondent does several takes of this closing and each time, the Angels drop back behind the car and repeat the move at his behest, rushing past as he denounces them as rapists and sodomites.

Part II

The Counter
Counterculture

CHAPTER 7

Strange Bedfellows

SAN FRANCISCO'S HAIGHT-ASHBURY DISTRICT WAS UNKNOWN TO the rest of the country during the mid-1960s, a forty-square block neighborhood of crumbling Victorian houses, incense shops, and corner taverns. The diaspora of runaways into the area who would comprise the so-called Love Generation had not yet appeared, so it was a fairly cloistered community, brimming with student radicals, artists, amateur Buddhists, and a few certified maniacs. LSD was still legal and was sweeping through the district like radioactive fallout. There was a defined sense of freak power starting to settle in, with the biggest attraction being the scraggly group of mean bikers who regularly hung out there.

The Lynch report had thrust the Hell's Angels into the public spotlight and they had no idea how to manipulate all the attention to their advantage; everything they did blew up in their faces. Writers who begged the club for an interview and access to their rancid world trashed them later in print. Granted, the Angels admitted to nasty behavior, but the press kept getting everything wrong. The worst part was that while all the articles about them were selling loads of magazines, they hadn't made a dime from any of them.

While the Hell's Angels were dealing with their newfound fame, an impoverished journalist who resided in the Haight district named Hunter S. Thompson was wondering where his next paycheck was coming from. He was a failed novelist two months behind on his rent, with a wife and baby at home. The loud obscene motorcyclists he saw gunning around the streets on Harley-Davidsons had often caught his eye and he was curious about them. Thompson had never seen such bleak specimens of humanity before. They were foul-mouthed, vulgar, and wielded an awful lot of power, blocking off entire streets for hours without anybody complaining.

Such behavior appealed to Thompson. Born in Louisville, Kentucky, in 1937, he was the oldest of three sons of an insurance adjuster and raised in a household that provided him with good schooling, religious instruction, and a moral guiding hand. But Thompson was trouble almost from the start, getting suspended from school for fighting and bad behavior at a young age. When he was fourteen his father died, and Thompson's behavior worsened. He was an indifferent student but read voraciously, becoming fascinated with the books of the depressive he-man writer/journalist Ernest Hemingway. He also developed a keen interest in guns, hoodlums, and writing prose. As a high schooler, Thompson's antisocial acts widened to include vandalism, destructive pranks, and setting the occasional fire. Numerous arrests for juvenile delinquency compelled him to join the Air Force in order to escape an extended jail sentence.

After a brutal stint in basic training, Thompson was assigned to Eglin Air Force Base in Florida, where he was made the sports editor for the base's newspaper *Command Courier.* He demonstrated a knack for writing copy but got into grave trouble after printing an embarrassing article about a spurious medical discharge given to an airman to allow the man to play pro football. Thompson could have faced a court-martial, but his superiors ordered an honorable discharge just to get him out of their hair.

Thompson had always felt he was destined to become a writer; even his base commanders had complimented him on his talent just prior to shooing him out of the Air Force. He managed to get entry-level newspaper jobs but his bizarre personality invariably sabotaged them (he was fired from his copy boy position at *Time* for smashing a Coke machine that had stolen his quarter). He padded his work resume with fictional writing credits, then cheerfully admitted to it during job interviews. His employment record was brief and sporadic, to say the least, and he usually spent his jobless periods trying to write novels.

Thompson finally landed a sports writer position with a Puerto Rican sports magazine called *Sportivo,* and moved to the tiny island in 1959. The only sport of any interest in Puerto Rico at the time, though, was bowling, and Thompson's job mainly consisted of hanging out in alleys to cover the games and interview players. After a few years, he left Puerto Rico and settled in the Big Sur area of Northern California with his new wife Sandy, where he lived rent-free in a seaside house in exchange for being the property's caretaker for the absentee owner. But despite this idyllic arrangement, he and Sandy were always financially strapped. He continued trying to sell fiction, but his novels and short stories were repeatedly rejected. Money was so tight that he and Sandy often lived on abalone clams they pried off the rocks down by the beach.

While Thompson dreamed about writing the Great American Novel, people who knew him best assumed that he would be dead long before he ever succeeded at it. Despite his destitution, Hunter Thompson was a notorious hedonist. He polished off large quantities of Scotch, beer, and mixed drinks on a daily basis while indulging in whatever drugs and stimulants he could lay his hands on. He loved guns and regularly carried a .357 Magnum around with him, once using it to chase off several gay men who were relaxing in the Big Sur hot springs (he fired over their heads before setting a pack of Dobermans after them). Thompson hunted wild boar while inebriated and sent off vitriolic letters to magazine editors who rejected his work. Many of the residents of the bohemian Big Sur community were leery of him.

A sardonic article Thompson wrote about Big Sur that was published in a men's magazine called *Rogue* was the writer's undoing. The owner of the house Thompson lived in was forwarded the article, and she was outraged by his acerbic descriptions of Big Sur being a haven for "deviates" and "hopeless losers." The woman immediately evicted Thompson and his wife, threatening to call the sheriff.

Sending Sandy back east to live with relatives, Thompson secured a correspondent's position with a new daily newspaper in New York called the *National Observer,* an assignment he got by offering to travel to South America on his own meager funds and write feature articles. The editors at the *Observer* were astounded by Thompson's vivid dispatches about Colombian smugglers, vigilante soldiers, and third world political chicanery. They eagerly published them, although one editor wondered about the factuality of some of Thompson's reporting. Much of what he recounted took place in various remote villages or areas that nobody had ever heard of. Some of the events he described could be verified but many others could not.

Thompson spent a year in South America before returning to the U.S., weak from dysentery. He'd only earned two thousand dollars from his reportage and the money was soon gone. Reuniting with his wife, the couple wound up back in Northern California while Thompson continued writing for the *Observer.* His drug intake increased and it began affecting his reliability. He would sell a story idea to the paper, receive the expense money, and then blow it all on drugs, while never delivering the promised article. But the editors at the *Observer* tolerated his strangeness because when he did come through, his work was unlike anything they'd ever seen before.

That he longed to be a novelist on the par with Faulkner and Hemingway, two writers he worshipped, is telling. Thompson was obsessed with the human condition, but since he lacked the narrative skills to explore it fictionally (even his friends found his fiction weak), he let his rabid outlook on life influence his journalism. More than anything, Hunter Thompson was a reactor; he always needed something to respond to that would satisfy his need to highlight the futile absurdity of life he saw all around him. He usually arose in the late afternoon to begin drinking and drugging, working up steam until, by midnight, he was fairly incoherent. It was only then he would begin writing, banging out page after page on his typewriter in a manic fury. Often the result was just paranoid gibberish or, if he became blocked, a blank page. But he would not work any other way.

After Thompson and Sandy settled in a small apartment in Haight-Ashbury, his relationship with the *Observer* began deteriorating. Although they respected his talent, the editors of the East Coast newspaper were weary of the writer's belligerent behavior and kept finding incidents in his articles that they knew could not be true. Finally, after a dispute over a book review Thompson had written that the *Observer* refused to publish, Thompson quit in a huff and never worked for the newspaper again.

Sandy gave birth to a son in late 1964 and the unemployed writer was now faced with the ominous task of having to support two people. Freelance writing paid very little and he was always broke. The phone kept getting shut off for nonpayment and they were regularly threatened with eviction. Turned down for writing jobs at San Francisco's two newspapers, the *Chronicle* and the *Examiner,* Thompson tried anything he could to make money, even applying at grocery stores and cab companies, but was never hired. He sold the occasional article, including one to the East Coast magazine *The Nation* about the budding student political movement at Berkeley, but things were getting desperate. Sandy even shoplifted food so the family could eat. Thompson was two years away from turning thirty and felt he hadn't done anything worthwhile with his art.

Although they were all over the news and he saw them regularly around the neighborhood, Thompson knew very little about the Hell's Angels. Then, much to his surprise, he was contacted by an editor at *The Nation* named Carey McWilliams who asked him to write the "real" story behind the club. Practically every magazine in the country was covering the Angels, but McWilliams was more interested in the exploding media frenzy. The club had become the biggest circus geek act around and the public was lining up to buy tickets. Thompson, who needed the money, readily agreed to do the article. McWilliams sent him several clippings of newspaper stories and magazine articles about the Angels along with a copy of the Lynch report, a document Thompson had never seen before.

Going through the news clippings, Thompson noticed how all of them were written around Lynch's report on the Angels. But a closer reading of the document revealed that of the 104 various law enforcement offices contacted, nearly half of them had never encountered any motorcycle gangs. Most of the "hoodlum activities" described were based on hearsay and supposition; the cases were never investigated. One account told of two women being accosted in a diner by a pair of abusive men who claimed they were Hell's Angels, but were not wearing any Angels colors nor were they riding motorcycles. In others, the perpetrators were not Hell's Angels but rather identified as "Comancheros," "Outsiders," or just simply "motorcyclists." In at least two of the

detailed assaults, the victims were actually club members themselves (despite their boast of camaraderie, Hell's Angels regularly knocked the crap out of each other). Coupled with this
were several statistical errors, including the claim that "some
446 subjects have been identified . . . as members or associate
members of Hell's Angels chapters" (in reality, the actual figure
was barely 20 percent of that; "associate members" were likely
anybody standing in the same room with a Hell's Angel during
a head count).

Convinced of the report's spuriousness, Thompson set out to
learn more about the Hell's Angels. A friend introduced him to
a police reporter who worked at the *Chronicle* named Birney
Jarvis,* who was an ex-Hell's Angel from the old days. A tough-
talking man trained in boxing and karate, Jarvis was one of the
Market Street Commandos during the early 1950s when they became the Frisco Angels, and once served as the chapter's vice
president. During his time with the club, Jarvis was known for
his ability to destroy a roomful of bar patrons with his chopping
hands and for being a mean drunk; even his Angel buddies were
nervous around him. Jarvis had retired from the Angels years before Thompson came to see him, but kept in touch. He talked
openly with the writer, explaining the Angels in the same con-
tradictory manner that the club adopted with the press: they
weren't as awful as people thought, but they were pretty awful
just the same.

Thompson learned that the Frisco Angels held their club meetings in the backroom of a bar in the rundown DePau Hotel near
the waterfront. He went over one evening at the invitation of a
Hell's Angel named Frenchy, whom Thompson contacted at
Jarvis' suggestion. Thompson warily watched a few of them play

---

* Birney Jarvis is called Preetam Bobo in Thompson's *Hell's Angels* book.

pool on a drink-stained table for awhile, wondering if they were going to come over and split his head open, as others warned him might happen. Frenchy finally sat down with him for an interview. Thompson explained how he had read the Lynch report and wanted to get the Angels' side of it, an opportunity they were rarely ever given.

As the evening went on, Thompson impressed Frenchy and the other Angels with his sullen attitude and exceptional drinking ability: he put away even more than they could. Frenchy gave their version of the long-dismissed Monterey rape case, claiming at least one of the two girls was "hot to trot" with a couple of Angels; she didn't realize that meant she was fair game for all of them.

As the evening wore on and the drinks flowed, Frenchy's stories got more outlandish. He addressed the issue of their alleged bad hygiene, insisting that it wasn't them that smelled bad but rather their colors. Every Angel who was initiated into the club, Frenchy said, had urine and feces dumped all over his clothes and was forbidden to ever wash them.*

When the bar closed, five of the Hell's Angels followed Thompson back to his apartment and continued partying. They didn't leave until six-thirty in the morning, startling the neighbors as they kickstarted their bikes. It was the beginning of a relationship that would last over a year.

THE FRISCO CHAPTER INVITED THOMPSON TO ATTEND THEIR WEEKLY meetings at the DePau, where beer was passed around, grass was smoked, and club issues were addressed. At one meeting, Thompson watched as one Angel member was stripped of his

---

* This scatological ritual, one of the most notorious of Hell's Angel lore, was never witnessed by Thompson; it is quite possible that Frenchy was pulling his leg.

colors and cast out of the club. His picture had been chosen for the cover of the *Saturday Evening Post* some months earlier and he was deemed a "show-off."

After a few weeks of hard drinking and casual socializing, Thompson finished his article about the Angels for *The Nation* and sent it off. The money he received for his work, a paltry one hundred dollars, was soon spent and his phone was disconnected while he and Sandy continued to be threatened with eviction. That the Hell's Angels had been seen hanging around his place didn't help any, either; his neighbors were terrified. Thompson desperately tried to find other writing work, figuring the whole outlaw thing was behind him.

When Thompson's article appeared in *The Nation* in April 1965, it stood out from all the other coverage there had been on the outlaws. He spent much of the article tearing apart the Lynch report to point out its flaws. He also decried the current hype around the Hell's Angels, insisting that the club was just a tiny part of a much larger social problem in America, exemplified by the nation's epidemic of venereal disease. It was a slightly nutty yet incisive viewpoint of the club, where he summed up the twisted ironies of being a Hell's Angel at the end of the article with a quote from one of its members:

> Since we got famous, we got more rich fags and sex-hungry women than we've ever had before. Hell, these days we have more action than we can handle.[61]

The article drew a flurry of mail to Thompson's doorstep. Publishers across the country wanted him to write a book about the Hell's Angels, asking for outlines and proposals of how it could be done. But of all the propositions that clogged his mailbox, the only one that mentioned money up front came from Ian Ballan-

tine, founder and publisher of Ballantine Books, who offered six
thousand dollars. Naturally, Thompson was interested.

Jumping back into the Angels' social circle, Thompson resumed
hanging out with them several nights a week, sinking further into
their nefarious lifestyle. He went across the bridge to meet the
Oakland Angels' president Sonny Barger and introduce himself.
Barger was prepared to chain-whip Thompson for the crime of
being a reporter but after finally reading his *Nation* article, decided
that Thompson was on the club's side and that he could stay.

Using his book advance, Thompson bought himself a BSA
motorcycle to ride with the club, a decision that didn't endear him
to many of the Angels since it wasn't a Harley. They had several
models to sell him, but Thompson declined as they were all stolen.
The BSA purchase was seen as something of a snub, but Thompson got back in the club's good graces when he wiped out on the
bike after hitting some railroad tracks and split his head open.

For the next twelve months, the Hell's Angels regularly barged
into Thompson's apartment in the middle of the night to party
and read what he was writing about them. Thompson delighted
his companions by performing stunts, like lining up beer bottles
on his windowsill and blowing them to smithereens with a twelve-
gauge shotgun. He once tried to scare off his Asian landlord by
having one of the Angels answer the door when the man came to
demand the overdue rent. He nearly got sucked into a riot during
a run to Bass Lake when the locals threatened to attack both him
and Barger after they went into town to buy beer. No writer had
ever thrown himself into a story the way Thompson did with the
Hell's Angels, who were fast becoming the most infamous monsters in the emerging American counterculture scene. He got to
know many of the Angels well, particularly Terry the Tramp, a
large screwball of an outlaw who spent more time with Thompson than any of the other club members did. Tramp was an out-

law with a gift for extemporaneous gab and playing verbal head games on other people. Thompson found him fascinating, and featured him prominently in the book when it was published.

Thompson soon found himself being considered as a sort of ambassador for the club. He was repeatedly asked to bring various Angels along to the Berkeley student parties and political gatherings, as the campus activists had become fascinated with them. At one party, several young mothers and their children openly complained to Thompson when the Hell's Angels failed to show. Inviting the club to social functions was something that the writer was loath to do. He did not want to be responsible for how the Angels might behave in an atmosphere teeming with free beer and young, nubile college girls. Although Thompson championed the Berkeley student movement, he was mystified by their feeling that the outlaws should be a part of their various causes, since most of the Angels had as much an interest in politics as they did in making topiaries. At first, Thompson mumbled vague promises but eventually became so out of sorts that he bluntly told Beat poet-turned-activist Allen Ginsberg, who had become infatuated with the Angels, that "they are mean fuckers" who would beat them up and pry the gold out of their teeth if they ever showed up at one of their rallies.

Anyone who was paying attention could see how the Angels were misfit dinosaurs, relics left over from an earlier time when cars had fins and everybody knew how to play canasta. Even their lumbering Harley bikes were archaic, not at all like the lightweight Japanese Hondas that everyone else was riding. There was nothing revolutionary about the Hell's Angels or the philosophies they upheld; they were misanthropes, pure and simple. It wasn't by accident that one of their patches said FTW (fuck the world). But the burgeoning student movement saw the Hell's Angels as a new breed of radical insurgents, freshly emerged from huge greasy cocoons hanging in the back rooms of Harley-Davidson dealerships.

The naïve attempts of the counterculture at bringing the Hell's Angels into their fold has long drawn scornful chuckles from sixties haters, who delight in the image of wired outlaws routinely pounding the hell out of worshipful hippies who clearly deserved it. This is good nasty fun for sure, but hardly accurate. Not every Hell's Angels chapter was alike nor, of course, was every member. The San Francisco Angels, although they could be dangerous, were more accustomed to the flower power scene and some chapter members formed solid friendships with various hippies in the Haight district. Actor Peter Coyote, who was part of the sixties activist group the Diggers, was a longtime friend of several Frisco Angels, including their president, Pete Knell. In his fine memoir *Sleeping Where I Fall*, Coyote details his friendship with Knell:

> One of the reasons he liked me, I think, was because of our free-ranging discussions. While not formally educated, Pete was razor sharp, well informed, and very curious. He liked to test his ideas against mine. We had many discussions about politics and he could never understand what he perceived as the "carelessness" of the Diggers. He felt that we were reckless in assuming that our *intention* to construct a counterculture would protect us from failures of strategy in dealing with the majority culture. He discounted all leftist revolutionary rhetoric, pointing out that most people calling for the revolution failed to live alertly and cautiously as warriors and consequently were no threat to anyone. He did not understand how we could be unconcerned with organization and structure, though he had to agree that it was the Diggers' lack of structure that made infiltration by government programs like Cointelpro impossible.[62]

Many of the Hell's Angels were military veterans and had a primitive sense about rank-and-file order. The club's bylaws were strict and absolute; any wavering from them was grounds for expulsion or worse. It could be dangerous to be a Hell's Angel, especially if you were being kicked out. One Frisco prospect named Gordon Westerfelt, who had been rejected three times for membership, was shot to death one night outside his apartment door. His motorcycle and girlfriend soon started circulating around the chapter.[63]

The federal government and FBI were already accusing the Hell's Angels of interstate drug trafficking, a vice that was growing in popularity. But most of the FBI's efforts focused on monitoring fringe political groups, antiwar demonstrators, and anyone else who just plain seemed peculiar. And few were more peculiar than Ken Kesey, leader of the Merry Pranksters and one of the first members of the radical left to embrace the Hell's Angels.

Kesey was a writer who had become an overnight celebrity a few years earlier when his debut novel, *One Flew Over the Cuckoo's Nest,* was published and became a best-seller. Flush with royalties and book advance money, the young writer went out and purchased a 1939 International Harvester schoolbus which he and some fellow devotees painted with psychedelic swirls of paint. Wiring the bus with loudspeakers and sound equipment, Kesey and his group dubbed themselves the Merry Pranksters and started taking long road trips around the country. They stopped in cities along the way to dispense LSD to the curious, chant atop the bus, and blast Bob Dylan through a P.A. system. They were a traveling sideshow and, by 1965, everyone in America was hearing about them, just as they were the Hell's Angels.

While Thompson was working on his book, he met Kesey at KQED, a Bay Area public television station, where both were being interviewed on a talk show. Afterward they went to a bar

----

for a drink, where Kesey indicated to Thompson that he wanted to meet the Angels. Thompson warily complied and brought him along to the Box Shop, a transmission garage that Frenchy owned in Hunger's Point where the Frisco Angels often hung out.

There were around six Angels at the Box Shop when the two arrived and they took to Kesey almost immediately. For one thing, he'd done time in jail, which the Angels respected, and his personality was so disarmingly zonked that they could not help liking him.

After much conversation and passing of joints, Kesey began expounding on the magical possibilities of LSD, and the many "doors of perception" the drug opened in one's head. Surprisingly, none of the Hell's Angels had ever tried acid, as they were major gobblers of Benzedrine. "The Angels were never ones to lower their consciousness," Kesey says. "They'd take a lot of downers, but then they'd take a lot of speed to kind of come back from it."[64] LSD was plentiful and cheap to buy but not even the drug-frenzied Thompson had ever taken it before. A friend once advised him against it, deeming him "too violent" a person to withstand its effects.

After completing his addled lecture on LSD and raising one's consciousness, Kesey impulsively invited the Angels to a party that coming weekend at his house in La Honda, a wooded area near Palo Alto. The Angels were flattered with the offer and accepted; Thompson felt the blood drain out of his face.

After the two writers left the Box Shop, Thompson cornered Kesey and, in his usual incoherent way, yelled, "You motherfucking crazy bastard, you're going to pay for this from Maine to here!"[65] Thompson would not be held responsible for anything that might happen.

Although it meant free alcohol and grass, the Angels had only accepted invitations to Berkeley parties on occasion; showing up uninvited was more their style, and the gatherings they attended were usually a crashing bore. They always found themselves being barraged with questions about LBJ, civil rights, and whatever was the current mystical dogma. The Angels would soon become restless and leave. They wanted to get wasted and rut with "strange broads," not ramble on about stuff they didn't give a damn about. But Kesey, who lived out in the woods like Tarzan, might be different. He was offering fabulous drugs that the Angels just had to try.

On April 7, 1965, around forty Hell's Angels from the various Northern California chapters rolled into Kesey's La Honda property and found a huge banner strung across the entry road that said: THE MERRY PRANKSTERS WELCOME THE HELL'S ANGELS. As they parked their bikes and crossed a small footbridge leading to the main house, the Angels were greeted by a flock of Day-Glo painted creatures who ran up to them offering beer and acid. Everyone was there: the Merry Pranksters; Kesey; Allen Ginsberg; Neal Cassady; LSD researcher Richard Alpert (known today as Ram Dass); writer Larry McMurtry; and hundreds of paisley types and radicals. A local band called the Warlocks (later the Grateful Dead) supplied the music; Thompson took notes and prayed that the Angels wouldn't behead anybody.

The party went on nonstop for the next seventy-two hours as outlaws and Pranksters danced about under flashing strobe lights, ate fried chicken, and tripped mightily. "The common ground was the psychedelic of it," Kesey says. "I mean, it's really easy to differ from somebody. The truth is, we're born different and have to train ourselves to be the same."[66]

The local sheriff's office had found out about Kesey's celebration and was monitoring it at the perimeter of the property. Unfortunately, the Pranksters had literally bugged the forest and every word uttered by the lawmen came echoing back at them a second later from loudspeakers placed in the trees. A few of the Pranksters and outlaws openly taunted them, but, surprisingly, no arrests were made and the deputies never entered the property. When Thompson ventured out to talk with the police, he was amused to hear them ask how the Hell's Angels were behaving. Had they attacked anybody yet? What the hell was going on in there? Are there any drugs? "This was when the Angels were still outlaws," says Kesey. "Real outlaws. To be an outlaw, you have to be something of a fool and that foolish quality is still accessible to anybody who really wants to be one."[67]

The outlaws and flower children socialized together easily enough, although one partygoer almost got lynched for supposedly making a sarcastic remark about the club. Several Angels put his head inside a noose they fashioned from a rope that had been thrown over a rafter inside the main hall, stood him on a chair, and took turns kicking at it before finally letting him go.[68]

The party's nadir, though, occurred with a young woman and some twenty Angels in a backroom of a building on the property. While floating on a cloud of acid, the woman, a girlfriend of Neal Cassady, offered to have sex with two Angels, but as word spread, she soon found herself with ten times that many queuing up to take their shot. The effects of the LSD had made the outlaws impotent, however, and they spent much of the time with their pants around their ankles trying to jerk themselves to attention. Thompson watched numbly as three Hell's Angels pinned the girl down and took turns attempting to penetrate her. The girl did not protest or struggle; she was too far gone from the acid. Most of the outlaws stood by watching in a daze, playing with themselves until a few Pranksters wandered in with Cassady in tow, also loaded with LSD.

"I was astounded ... when they brought Neal into the room," Thompson recalled. "He was a friend of hers and I thought when he came in that he'd flip out. It worried me and I wanted to leave, but I was a writer and it wasn't something I could ignore.

As it was, he seemed to accept it very well. I remember her kissing him when he said, 'Kiss me,' and then *he* fucked her."[69]

Thompson became so unnerved that he left his tape recorder running in the room, went back outside and demanded some acid from Kesey; he wanted to forget what he just saw. Thompson dropped 400 micrograms and waited for some murderous psychosis to hit him. The effect was, fortunately, nonviolent and he tripped for the next forty-eight hours.

The Angels/Pranksters party finally ended after nearly three days and would be remembered as one of the watershed events of the 1960s, mostly because the Angels didn't beat anybody up. News of the event hit the circuit and for the rest of the summer, the quiet roads outside Palo Alto were taken over by outlaws coming down from the Bay Area to Kesey's acreage. Even the annual Labor Day run was made to La Honda that year. Because of the Angels' national infamy as spawned by the Monterey rape case the year before, small cities across America waited fearfully for the outlaws to *blitzkrieg* their communities. Some towns in Indiana and Arizona even called out the National Guard to defend themselves against the onslaught, and the police department of bordering Vancouver, British Columbia, set up roadblocks to prevent the Hell's Angels from invading Canada. But the club never showed up; they were all at Kesey's taking acid and dancing to the Grateful Dead.

But there was a mercenary element behind the relationship that was missed by most of the parties involved. The Hell's Angels may have liked Kesey but they had little use for his minions, who they found tiresome, and resented their intellectualism. Likewise, not everyone liked the Angels, as they could be intimidating. A few of Kesey's associates avoided La Honda whenever they knew the club was going to be there. "The Hell's Angels were hanging around too much," Prankster Lee Quarnstrom claimed.

"Many of us were not as enthralled by the Hell's Angels as others were."[70] It didn't take long for the relationship to go sour.

By fall, the Berkeley campus was becoming a maelstrom of political unrest as the antiwar movement was getting its first legs. On October 16, Ginsberg, future Yippie Jerry Rubin, and Beat poet Gary Snyder organized a Vietnam Day Committee (VDC) protest march that was to start on the University of Berkeley campus and end in downtown Oakland near the Army Terminal. The fifteen-hundred-plus demonstrators were stopped at the Oakland border by riot police who refused to allow them entrance into the city. The marchers stood their ground and did not disperse, chanting through a P.A. system wired to a truck.

Suddenly, eight Oakland Hell's Angels with Barger at point stepped past the police line and charged. A huge Angel named Tiny tore the marchers' PEACE IN VIETNAM sign out of their hands and ripped it up. The rest of the outlaws laid into the demonstrators with chains, scattering them in a blind panic. "Why don't you people go home?!!" they screamed with mad-dog fervor. "Traitors!" Tiny cut the wires to the P.A. system, silencing the chants and effectively ending the march. The Oakland riot police, barely able to contain their delight, did nothing to stop the attack; it was, after all, taking place in Berkeley, and their jurisdiction ended three feet in front of them. Police on the Berkeley side finally broke up the assaults and arrested the Angels. The monstrous Tiny broke a cop's leg after falling on him during his arrest.

The Angels later escaped prosecution for the attack, save Tiny, who received a fifty-six-dollar fine. It serves the pinko bastards right, the court figured. Several conservative newspaper columnists lionized the Hell's Angels, declaring them to be true patriots. It was the best PR move the club had ever made.

The VDC was bewildered by the attack. Many of its members, Ginsberg in particular, had looked at the Hell's Angels as allies.

They could not understand why they had broken up their march, though Kesey was not quite as surprised as the others. "I don't think you would ever want to trust an Angel not to attack you," Kesey says today. "I mean right away, when you're hanging with the Angels, you know who you're hanging with."[71]

For Thompson, who knew the outlaws better than anyone, it made perfect sense. The Angels possessed the same reactionary impulses as Ghenghis Khan. They wore *swastikas,* for God's sake, how much more of a clue does anyone need? There was no irony to their Teutonic appearance and snarling persona. He had to remind Ginsberg again: "They are *mean* fuckers."

The following month, Sonny Barger got word that the VDC was planning another protest march on the Oakland Army Terminal and let it be known they could expect a repeat of last October's attack if the Angels caught them taking a step into Oakland. Ginsberg urgently called for a meeting between the Hell's Angels and the VDC to discuss the situation and an open forum was scheduled for November 12 at San Jose State College.

The meeting resembled Fellini directing the Yalta Conference. With a roomful of reporters and local citizens looking on, Ginsberg began the proceedings by clinking finger cymbals together and chanting a mantra, to the sniggering delight of the crowd. He then read a poem where he begged the Hell's Angels not to beat them up. An Angel representative, who was flanked by members of the Gypsy Jokers and Nightriders, countered that they wouldn't think of breaking the law by assaulting the VDC, but if they had to attack in self-defense, that was a different story. The crowd, who were almost unanimously on the Angels' side, mocked Ginsberg and kept urging the outlaws to start beating on them *now,* since they were already in the room.

A few days before the November 20 march, Kesey and Ginsberg contacted Thompson for help in setting up a last-minute meeting with Sonny Barger. Thompson put it together and went to Barger's house with Ginsberg, Kesey, Cassady, and several Day-Glo painted Pranksters accompanying him. Remembering the relative harmony they had had together during the summer in La Honda, this time Ginsberg brought along some LSD. Barger was waiting with twenty scowling Hell's Angels and Kesey immediately started dosing them as Ginsberg set up his harmonium. They argued politics for a while, Kesey and Ginsberg trying to convince Barger that they were not Communists out to overthrow America.

The discussion was going nowhere and Ginsberg started playing the harmonium while reciting the Prajnaparamita Sutra, a Buddhist chant that translated into "Higher Perfect Wisdom." As the acid hit, Tiny, who had torn down the VDC sign at the last march, began chanting his own nonsensical scat, "om, om, zoom zoom zoom, om . . ." Soon, everyone in the entire room was chanting, and the atmosphere relaxed. The beatific Ginsberg, who never met an outlaw he didn't like, told the fearsome Sonny Barger that he loved him. The Oakland president was speechless. "That goddamn Ginsberg is gonna fuck us all up," Terry the Tramp said later to Thompson. "For a guy who ain't straight, he's about the straightest sonofabitch I ever saw."[72] Sonny Barger got up and went to his stereo, confessing aloud that he always liked Joan Baez and put on one of her records. The incongruous gathering of Angels and pacifists spent the entire night chanting mantras, smoking grass, and doing hits of acid.

A few days later, Barger called a press conference where he excoriated the VDC as just so much Commie scum that the Hell's Angels would rather not have to touch. Instead, he was offering the services of himself and the Hell's Angels to President Johnson to form a "crack group of trained gorillas [sic]" that would go and fight the Vietcong. The march went off without a hitch.

Meanwhile, Thompson's relationship with the Angels was getting shaky. They had accepted him because he had proven himself with his *Nation* article, but now they were questioning his motives. The Angels knew they were celebrities and quite seriously thought that they should be getting paid for all of their news appearances. They sold the occasional photograph of themselves to magazines, but that was all. After many months of Thompson drinking, drugging, and hanging around the club, the question was brought up: how much money could the Angels expect to make?

Any promises of a financial stake for the club in the book were certainly never made by Thompson (there supposedly had been a vague promise from Thompson to buy the Angels two cases of beer but he never recalled it). The advance money Thompson had received was long gone; all he could expect now were royalties if the book sold well, and Thompson was not about to share those with the club. How do you split royalties with a hundred Hell's Angels? Thompson skirted the money issue and kept writing, trying to get the book finished. The Angels' attitude toward him turned hostile.

Four days before the deadline, Thompson saw that his book was only two-thirds of the way done and he could get no peace at home. Either the baby was crying or the Angels were barging in to to see what he was writing. Exasperated, Thompson took his typewriter, some speed, and four quarts of Wild Turkey to a motel on the coast and furiously wrote for the next hundred hours, finally completing his book. ·

When the Angels found out the book's cover price would be $4.95, they demanded to know how much of it was theirs. Thompson bluntly told them that none of it was. Within minutes, he was on the ground as a hard rain of motorcycle boots came crashing down on him.

The details regarding this beating have never been fully explained. Thompson's own description of it has varied over the years, but hinges on the Angels suddenly jumping him not long after finding out he wasn't going to pay them. The intervention of Tiny saved him from getting his head caved in by another Angel wielding a large rock, and he ran to his car and drove off, bloodied and with a broken nose. The Hell's Angels insist that only one member, Junkie George, who is long deceased, beat up Thompson after the writer called him a punk. (Junkie George had slapped his girlfriend during an argument and Thompson intervened.) Sonny Barger went so far as to suspect that Thompson deliberately incited a fight just so he could have the ultimate ending for his book. "I believe he planned this whole scene in advance," Barger said.

Regardless, Thompson's book *Hell's Angels: A Strange and Terrible Saga*, sold forty thousand copies upon its release in 1966, a minor best-seller that generated positive reviews. The paperback edition would go on to sell over two million copies. The Hell's Angels never made a cent on it.

Photo Gallery

The only known extant photo of the original Boozefighters motorcycle club, circa late 1940s. *(Courtesy the Boozefighters MC)*

The legendary William Forkner, a.k.a. Wino, drinking on the street during infamous 1947 Hollister Rally. He was the basis of Lee Marvin's character Chino in the *The Wild One. (Courtesy the Boozefighters MC)*

C. B. Clauson, first president of L.A. Boozefighters, in front of club trailer, circa late 1940s. *(Courtesy the Boozefighters MC)*

Los Angeles Boozefighters members drinking on a curb during the 1947 Hollister Rally; left to right: George Menker, L.A. chapter president; C. B. Clauson; Bobby Kelton. *(Courtesy the Boozefighters MC)*

Gil Armis doing donuts on a San Benito street, Hollister, 1947. *(Courtesy the Boozefighters MC)*

Jim Cameron on his Indian Scout at the 1947 Hollister Rally. His bike was left parked inside a bar during the entire rally. He never once rode it. *(Courtesy the Boozefighters MC)*

Benny "Kokomo" McKell, president of the San Francisco Boozefighters, dressed in his red admiral's uniform. *(Courtesy the Boozefighters MC)*

Edward "Red Dog" Dahlgren, the Boozefighter member tossed in jail for riding on the sidewalk during 1947 Hollister Rally. The club made an abortive attempt to break him out. *(Courtesy the Boozefighters MC)*

The Boozefighters at the 1947 Hollister Rally. Club co-founder George Menker is at front right, making a face. *(Courtesy the Boozefighters MC)*

Left to right: Marie Forkner, Fat Boy Nelson, and Jim Cameron at the 1948 Riverside Rally. The club was once again blamed for causing the disorder that occurred during the rally.

Some of the original Boozefighter members at the fortieth anniversary party put on by *Easyriders* Magazine. *(Courtesy the Boozefighters MC)*

Rockabilly singer Gene Vincent, circa late 1950s. He would not start wearing his trademark leather jacket until he left America for England.

Hell's Angels chapter presidents, circa early 1960s: Sonny Barger, fourth from left; Otto Friedli, center; James "Mother" Miles, second from right. *(Courtesy James Meredith)*

James "Mother" Miles
and wife Ruby. *(Cour-*
tesy James Meredith)

Below: James
"Mother" Miles, presi-
dent of the North
Sacramento Hell's
Angels. *(Courtesy*
James Mered-
ith)

North Sacramento Hell's Angels (formerly Hell Bent for Glory), James "Mother" Miles on right. *(Courtesy James Meredith)*

North Sacramento Angels' choppers, circa 1960. *(Courtesy James Meredith)*

Pat "Mighty Mouse" Miles (foreground) with unidentified friend. *(Courtesy James Meredith)*

Sonny Barger's chopper. *(Courtesy James Meredith)*

The Jefferson Airplane, with lead singer Marty Balin at top left. Balin can be seen in the film *Gimme Shelter* jumping off the stage to confront several Hell's Angels.

Peter Fonda as Captain America in the 1969 film *Easy Rider*. The film almost single-handedly sparked the chopper craze of the 1970s.

Above: Ron "Trash" Haley
with family on a 1948
Harley in Ukiah, CA, circa
1963. *(Courtesy Ron Haley)*

Nineteen-year-old Ron Haley,
platoon leader, in Vietnam,
1966. *(Courtesy Ron Haley)*

Trash after discharge from service, circa 1967. *(Courtesy Ron Haley)*

Trash with his first wife, Cricket, in 1974. *(Courtesy Ron Haley)*

Trash, "New York" Mike Shelby, and Brother Hank at the ABATE Rally in Sacramento, January 2000.

ABATE Rally, Sacramento, January 2000.

Trash speaking at ABATE rally, January 2000.

ABATE Rally, Sacramento, January 2000.

Dr. Martin Jack Rosenblum, historian of the Harley-Davidson Motor Co.

CHAPTER 8

Ready for Their Close-Up

BY THE LATE SIXTIES, THE COMMERCIAL VALUE OF BEING AN OUT-law biker was at best a double-edged sword. Law enforcement was forced to look on with bewilderment as the Hell's Angels became media celebrities. It was equally unsettling for the club itself to know that most everyone in America knew about them, yet they were still scrounging around for gas money. They were finding more and more bikers who had slapped on makeshift colors and declared themselves to be Hell's Angels. Hunter Thompson's book was not going to pay off for them. The Hell's Angels were now an act without a venue, and it took the death of one of their officers to turn them into a commercial vehicle.

In January 1966, the illustrious Mother Miles, president of the Angels' Nomads, the man who moved the entire chapter out of Sacramento and over to Richmond, was critically injured in Berkeley after he crashed headlong into a truck that had pulled out of a blind alley. Mother lingered in a coma for six days before expiring at the age of twenty-nine.

Mother's funeral was immense. Over 250 Hell's Angels and outlaw bikers from other clubs gathered in Oakland and followed the hearse on the ninety-mile trip to Sacramento where he was buried. They were accompanied for part of the way by highway patrol cars who ran interference for the procession. The funeral was held inside a stuffy church where the minister spent most of the service haranguing the bikers in attendance about the godless ways of the infidel. Several of the Angels and others arose from the pews in disgust and stalked out.

At the gravesite, Mother's younger brother Pat fulfilled the promise they had made to each other years earlier. He stripped off his own colors and tossed them into the hole, effectively quitting the Angels. Nobody was sorry to seem him go. He went off to continue dealing PCP.

The funeral procession for Mother Miles was the largest in the history of Sacramento and received national news coverage, both on television and in magazines. The January issue of *Life* featured an article on the funeral and, just as a short story in *Harper's* had gotten the attention of Stanley Kramer years earlier, it caught the eye of another filmmaker named Roger Corman.

Roger Corman was an American original, a moviemaker *extraordinaire* who was to filmmaking what McDonald's was to dinner, a fast and efficient creator of cheap, lowbrow product that always found an audience. Corman was an anathema to Hollywood excess. He followed a simple formula for making movies: give the people what they want and spend as little money as possible. He worked quickly and ruthlessly, shooting scenes in one or two takes. Corman once directed an entire film in two days (*Little Shop of Horrors* with Jack Nicholson), using the set from an earlier movie he had made in five days. Corman regularly reused the same costumes, props, set designs, and even footage over and over again. (Several of his films contain shots of the same house burning down.) His actors often played multiple roles, and Teamster officials regularly hassled him for hiring nonunion crews. Critics dismissed his productions as so much asinine tripe: *Attack of the Crab Monsters, The Man with X-Ray*

Eyes, Bucket of Blood, The Cry Baby Killer, etc. Despite this, Corman was widely admired by his peers for his maverick ways and his generosity towards others. Many struggling young actors and directors who went on to become Academy Award winners got their start working for Corman.

At the time of Mother Miles' death, Corman was working as a producer/director for American International Pictures (AIP), an independent distributor of low-budget films for the drive-in and Saturday matinee crowd. He already knew about the Hell's Angels, having learned about them just like everyone else had, via the media. But the *Life* article on Miles' funeral made his head spin, as it included a photograph of the outlaws riding into the cemetery. It looked like the perfect publicity shot for a movie. "I built an entire picture around that still," Corman says.[73]

This kind of ripped-from-the-headlines concept had long been a staple of low-budget movies, dating back to the exploitation B-films of the forties and fifties. The fare was usually "based on" hot social topics: marijuana *(Reefer Madness)*, juvenile delinquency *(Teenage Doll)*, or nuclear testing *(Beast From 20,000 Fathoms)*. For every Charles Lindbergh/Glen Miller/Madame Curie movie produced by the major studios, Poverty Row independents cranked out quickies on John Dillinger, Al Capone, and Machine Gun Kelly, all cretins who were long dead by the time the films hit the screen. What Corman was contemplating doing, though, was fiendishly clever: get the cretins to play themselves.

It had been a dozen years since *The Wild One* had flamed out in movie theaters and nobody had attempted to make a biker film of any note since. Corman was not intrigued with motorcycles themselves so much as what they symbolized. "I had a theory at the time that westerns were starting to fade," says Corman, "and that the Hell's Angels and the motorcycle represented the cowboy on the horse in the west, in the open spaces, it represented freedom, nonconformity, the ability, as they said, to do your own thing."[74]

This ingenuous romanticism about outlaw bikers was not unusual for the era. It has always been a peculiar American phenomenon that the public makes pop heroes out of those whom they otherwise wouldn't want living within ten miles of their neighborhood. To the average American, an outlaw biker was like Bigfoot, an exotic beast whom they only saw grainy photos of in magazines and newspapers. Corman was planning on bringing them in living color to movie screens across America.

After putting out the word they were interested in making a film, Corman and a writer named Chuck Griffiths met the members of the Angels' Venice chapter (long defunct) at a grimy bar called the Gunk Shop on Western Avenue in Los Angeles. The two men wore their rattiest clothes to try to fit in. A dozen or so Angels showed up and Corman offered them as much beer and grass as they wanted if they would tell him stories and give their views on being an outlaw biker. Corman had seen *The Wild One,* but emphasized to the motley bunch that he was interested in showing the Angels' perspective on things. Like many, Corman incorrectly assumed that Hollister had been invaded by the Hell's Angels, and that the club basically made its living raping and pillaging small towns. The Angels undoubtedly caught on to his slanted knowledge, but did little to correct it. All they wanted to know was how much they were going to get paid.

"I negotiated with the Angels and paid them a certain amount of money for themselves," Corman says. "A certain amount of money for their choppers and a certain amount of money for their old ladies, the girlfriends. It was interesting to me that they wanted more money for the choppers than for their girlfriends."[75] Even by 1960s standards, Corman did not offer much: thirty-five dollars a day for each Angel, twenty dollars a day for their bikes, and fifteen dollars a day for their old ladies. They accepted.

After Chuck Griffiths finished the script, Corman passed it on to a struggling young film critic named Peter Bogdanovich, who was writing for *Esquire* magazine while looking to break into the film industry. Corman had hired him to be a location scout and gave him the *Wild Angels* script for reference. Bogdanovich, an ardent cinephile, called him back to say he was scouting the necessary locations and, by the way, the script was lousy. Corman asked him to give it a rewrite for no additional money or credit and Bogdanovich agreed. He and his then-wife Polly Platt rewrote 80 percent of the script and completely revised the plot.

Though the Hell's Angels would play themselves, the major roles went to actors. Corman originally cast George Chakiris, who had starred in *West Side Story,* to play the part of Angel leader Jack Black and a young Peter Fonda as The Loser, a role that required him to die thirty minutes into the film.

Peter Fonda had grown up in the public eye as part of the Fonda clan. His mother Frances committed suicide when he was just nine years old, a tragedy he was shielded from for many years. He had grown into a beanpole version of his father Henry, standing 6′ 2″ and weighing barely 137 pounds. Fonda rode his first motorcycle when he was a teenager and by the time he was twenty-one had become a full-time biker, riding around on a Triumph. Already an experienced actor, Peter Fonda was more than qualified to work in Corman's film.

Fonda took a meeting with Corman to discuss the Hell's Angels movie. It was the height of hippie thrift-store chic and Fonda walked into Corman's office wearing a pair of mirrored granny glasses that Brian Jones of the Rolling Stones had given him and an old jacket with an "Officer of Naval Intelligence" badge affixed to it. (When Corman asked him what the badge meant,

Fonda told him, "It means I get to piss on your tires, Roger.") Corman described his idea of making a film about the Hell's Angels, emphasizing that he wanted to do it "without making a statement." The actor was amused. "Now that's impossible," he says today, "because that kind of thing is a statement in itself."[76] Fonda needed the money and readily agreed to do the film for ten thousand dollars, though he wasn't thrilled with the brevity of his part as The Loser. He wanted to play the Jack Black role, which had already been given to Chakiris.

Unbeknownst to Fonda, Chakiris did not know how to ride a motorcycle. He agreed to take lessons, but after a few harrowing rides, he decided that motorcycling was not for him and requested a stunt double. Corman insisted his film was not a Hollywood western, where every actor on a horse had a stunt man covering for him. He told Chakiris that it was crucial he learn how to ride. The actor refused.

Corman panicked and phoned Fonda, who quickly guessed what the problem was just from hearing the concern in his voice. "George can't ride, right?" Fonda said. The producer admitted so and asked him to take over the Jack Black role. Fonda agreed but added that he wanted the character's name changed to Heavenly Blue.

"I told Roger," Fonda says, "that if you take 360 Heavenly Blue morning glory seeds, grind them in a fresh pepper grinder, and put an equal amount of water and then chuck it back, within forty-five minutes, you'll have an altered experience."[77] Corman had no idea what he was talking about but agreed to the change. Fonda was recast as Heavenly Blue and the then-unknown actor Bruce Dern was chosen to play The Loser.

The film's plot, what there was of it, revolved around a fictitious San Pedro Hell's Angels chapter led by Fonda's and Dern's two characters. They lead a run into a mountain to find The

Loser's stolen motorcycle, where they brawl with a Mexican gang. Two motorcycle cops arrive to break up the fight and The Loser steals one of their bikes. In the ensuing chase, one cop is killed when he goes off a cliff while The Loser is seriously injured. The Angels bust him out of the hospital and take him back to their clubhouse, where he dies. During The Loser's funeral inside a church, a riot breaks out and the chapel interior is trashed. Later, as the Angels bring The Loser's body to his hometown for burial, a brawl with some townspeople erupts and the police come charging in. The Hell's Angels flee, save for Heavenly Blue who remains to shovel dirt onto the coffin.

The defiling of the church that occurs near the end of the film was a grotesque exaggeration of a silly but true incident that had occurred near the Northern California resort town of Bass Lake in 1963. The Little Church in the Pines was disrupted by a small group of drunk Hell's Angels who entered the empty chapel and grabbed several choir robes. The police arrived to find them prancing about on foot and riding their bikes with the robes draped over them. The bikers were threatened with arrest before they returned the robes. In *The Wild Angels,* The Loser's coffin is draped with a huge Nazi flag, every pew is smashed to pieces, the minister is punched out, and The Loser's old lady (Diane Ladd) is raped by the other Angels near the altar.

When the film began production, Corman cast members from both the San Bernardino and Venice chapters of the Hell's Angels. They did not have any lines; all they had to do was show up and be themselves. Corman was then faced with the task of directing members of the scariest biker mob in the world, who took pride in not taking guff from anybody. "I figured out I shouldn't and couldn't push them around," he says. "I couldn't be a dominating director. On the other hand, if I was too weak, they would push me around."[78] Corman ended up directing *The Wild Angels* with the emotional resonance of a 411 operator. "So I tried to be as objective as I possibly could," he says. "I would say in a voice with no emotion, 'All right fellas, the bikes come in here, you drive over to there, you get off the bikes, and you run into that building there,' without trying to give any particular emotion other than the thoughts they might have in the shot."[79]

The circumstances afflicting the shoot were far more entertaining than the movie would end up being. One day, after breaking for lunch, Fonda and Dern went cruising in the desert out by Palm Springs near where they were shooting. "I had a super-fast four-on-the-floor '66 Impala 327," Fonda says. "We were doing things in the car and . . . came around and realized there's another movie going on here because we could see tanks and stuff. We came back through and mooned them, as it were. We fucked them off and, you know, showed our nasty shit and stuff out the window. Well, it was Roger's brother Gene Corman, who was shooting *Tobruk*.[80]*

A few hours later, Roger Corman was impatiently waiting for a shot to be set up when down the street came several World War II-period tanks and half-tracks. Machine guns sprayed blanks everywhere as the actors and Hell's Angels dove for cover, terrified. Corman ordered his cameraman to start filming it, saying "I'll use it somehow for *something*." A couple of soldier-actors leaped out of their tank and abducted Fonda, who was laughing hysterically. Corman later sent the Hell's Angels over to his brother's film location to retrieve him. "Those H-As were nice," Fonda says. "They said, 'Here, try our grass. It's soaked in opium.'"[81]

But such absurdities aside, as the Angels quickly learned, making the film was a boring and arduous task, even with an efficiency expert like Corman in charge. It was an extremely difficult

---

* A World War II action film starring Rock Hudson. Gene Corman also worked in the film industry as a producer/director.

shoot. The Angel's bikes never worked. Ever. As Corman recalled in his autobiography:

> They drove me crazy. We were always sitting and waiting for the damned bikes to be repaired and I said to one of the An-gels, "Look, I understand what you guys do. You come into town. You beat up the men, you rape the women, you steal from the stores, the police come charging after you, you run to your choppers, you *know* the fucking things aren't going to start. What do you do then? What is this all about?" "They start, they start," he mumbled. "Bad luck, that's all." Peter told me he never liked riding them. "You know why they call them Harleys, don't you?" he asked. "Because they Harley ever start."[82]

All during the film's production, sheriff's deputies and state law enforcement officials were shadowing Corman's locations, ready to bust the Angels. Most of them had outstanding warrants and the crew had to stall the police. They told them how acting in this movie was the first honest work most of the Angels had ever done. They were getting paid and therefore would have more money with which to pay their fines. This seemed to pacify the cops, but Corman had no idea how weird it was getting. Years later, he learned that 150 highway patrol agents had been assigned to monitor the shoot, bugging the hotel rooms of crew members, and even trying to infiltrate the cast.

Many of the Angels did not stay with the film. They collected their money and took off, irritated with the regimentation re-quired to work on a Corman production. Even Corman's normal stoicism started to break. "Roger was tired and frantic by the end," said Bogdanovich. "That's why the Angels didn't always like Roger. He was an authority figure and he was always, 'Hurry,

hurry, hurry, no time, no time, let's go, let's go!'"[83] Corman even sent Bogdanovich into one of the fight scenes because they were so short of extras. Bogdanovich simply ran into the fray, hit the ground, and curled into a ball as the Angels eagerly laid into him with their fists until Corman yelled "Cut!"

The Wild Angels was released by AIP in 1966 and received its first screening in New York City to an audience of 600 people. Most of them were exhibitors and distribution executives who were horrified by the rape and nihilism they saw onscreen. Fonda, who sat in the audience with his stepmother and his father's press agent, slunk down in his seat as the crowd catcalled at the screen. Several people walked out in disgust. Afterward, Fonda was angrily confronted outside on the sidewalk by a woman who was a fan of his. "There was a woman who had waited for me every night while I was on Broadway," he says. "She would give me presents, Christmas, my birthday, so forth, just a loyal fan. She was beating me on the head with an umbrella while I was trying to get in the limo ... going, *'How could you play this Nazi role?! How could you do this?!!'* I said, 'I'm just an actor,' you know. I got in the car and sped off."[84]

Fonda picked up his father and drove him over to a restaurant at Lincoln Center where a post-screening reception was being held. As they walked in, they were greeted by a chorus of boos and hissing from the assembled guests. Henry Fonda looked at his son in bewilderment. "We went by one table and it was all Canadians," Peter recalls. "They all stood up and applauded over the boos. 'We're going to distribute your film and we're going to make a lot of money doing it. It's fantastic. We can show this film. This will bring them in.' Started the whole thing."[85]

The Wild Angels was produced for $360,000 and went on to gross $5 million, a substantial profit at that time. People were turned away from drive-ins for lack of space. It was the biggest hit AIP ever had and the Hell's Angels, who had been paid thirty-five dollars a day to work on it, were again furious. It was Hunter Thompson all over again, and they decided to sue.

"I remember seeing it on television and the announcer started laughing when he read what it was about," Corman recalls. "They were suing me for $5 million (the entire box office gross) for defamation of character on the basis that I had portrayed them as motorcycle outlaws. Whereas, in reality, they were a social organization dedicated to the spreading of technical information about motorcycles."[86]

The lawsuit was no laughing matter to Corman, though. The Angels meant business, and he soon received a call from chapter president Otto Friedli, who told Corman, in effect, that he was going to snuff him out.

"If you kill me," Corman replied, "how are you going to collect the $5 million?"

The outlaw was silent for a moment. Corman continued. "My advice to you," he said, "is forget the momentary pleasure of killing me and go after the $5 million."[87] The man agreed and hung up. Corman eventually settled the suit for ten thousand dollars and worked with the Angels again.

Following the success of *The Wild Angels,* biker films spread across America like kudzu and became a regular presence at drive-ins everywhere. They were all built on the same rote design: amoral violence, rape, drug use, rape, bad writing, rape, long riding sequences, bad acting, rape.... Unlike the stilted social commentary of *The Wild One,* the sixties-era biker films were exercises in pure exploitation, morality tales in reverse. They served absolutely no purpose but to make all motorcyclists look like blood-crazed sociopaths.

"Biker films turned it [motorcycling] into an absolute joke," says Marty Rosenblum. "They were nothing more than Eric Von

Zipper (a buffoon-like outlaw biker character featured in the Frankie Avalon-Annette Funicello beach films.) You know, I didn't even take them seriously. I looked upon them as Three Stooges, Laurel and Hardy, Abbott and Costello. They were a joke."[88]

The films came fast and furious, with the word "angel" worked into their titles in the same associative way "Harley" was once used to describe every motorcycle on the road: *Naked Angels, Angels from Hell, Black Angels, Bury Me an Angel, Run Angel Run, Angels Die Hard,* ad nauseum. Strangely enough, hardly any of them had anything to do with the Hell's Angels (*Hell's Angels on Wheels* and *Hell's Angel '69* are the best known). The films often served as an employment refuge for many one-percenter types, Hell's Angels or otherwise. "I worked with the Oakland chapter on *Angels Die Hard,*" says veteran actor William Smith, who starred in several biker films. "They were all really nice, you know. During the day when we were working they were good. They did what the director wanted them. Even the Satan's Slaves,* which were a bad group. But you didn't want to party with them at night. They were totally uncontrollable, everything fell apart, man. They went crazy. Actors have had their arms broken."[89]

None of the hardcore biker films that followed *The Wild Angels* matched its success financially. They usually appeared as part of a triple bill at drive-in theaters, where any young teenager in his parent's car could sit for hours with his date watching pilled-out Mongols destroy everything in their path. Biker films made motorcycling look like a complete and total nightmare but again like *The Wild One,* their influence went beyond their inherent stupidity. "I'm sure they brought many people into motorcycling," Rosenblum admits. "And I'm sure those people,

---

* Founded in the late 1950s, Satan's Slaves were absorbed into the Hell's Angels in 1978 and became their San Fernando Valley chapter.

once they got into it, they realized that motorcycling isn't this grade B movie. It's a sport, it's a culture, and that these grade B movies can be made as a result of it is a testament to the culture. The movies have nothing to do with it, though."[90]

This is open to debate. Outlaw biker culture is predominately mythical in substance, and any bored yahoo who dreamt of becoming a one-percenter could live vicariously through these celluloid atrocities. One former Hell's Angel from South Carolina named Barry Mayson who left the club to become a Christian minister claimed in his 1982 autobiography *Fallen Angel* that the main reason he became an outlaw biker was from watching biker films:

> We just sat through *Born To Lose;* this one was *Hell's Angels on Wheels.* Bikers were something new to me. I had glanced once at some pictures of Hell's Angels in a doctor's office magazine, and thought they were just California hippies who rode motorcycles. Back here in '68 Georgia, long hair and earrings didn't go too well. . . .
>
> I had never ridden a motorcycle, but those long choppers dazzled and supercharged my eyes and ears with their chrome flash and thundering speed. It had to take a powerful man to maneuver one of those machines into a forty-foot "wheelie" or jump sand dunes in the desert. Just watching made me feel like that kind of man. I could do that. I *knew* I could do that.
>
> And damn, the way they lived was what I called *living*! There was a party scene on now, with bikers sitting in a circle in a room with a rainbow of lights and loud rock music pounding. They were passing around a hand-rolled smoke, must be marijuana, and guzzling beers in huge gulps. Bikers were yelling and laughing, one so hard he fell over and rolled across the room. Then some women came in and

started stripping to the music and running their hands over
their own bodies and the bikers'....[91]

Mayson was not alone in his reaction. "Guys that never rode
before," says Smith, "told me they saw the movies and started
riding, you know? [They] saw how much fun it was to ride a
chopper, you know, and just sit back and take a trip."[92]

It took a great deal of subjectivity to find anything "fun" about
motorcycling in biker films; half the characters died. If a pack
of riders were seen speeding through a golden desert at twilight, they weren't out enjoying the wind rushing in their face;
they were on their way to invade a town and rape the home-
coming queen.

What aspiring outlaws saw on the screen was pure exploitation and bent fantasy. They didn't see what the film's directors
saw, namely outlaw day players spending thirty minutes of valuable production time trying to get their choppers to start. They
didn't see the bikers camping out in the woods because the producers could not afford to put them up in a motel or trailer. They
didn't hear Sonny Barger, who acted in several biker movies, say
to William Smith, "These movies are just a bunch of junk. They
have nothing to do with us."[93]

Following the success of *Wild Angels,* Peter Fonda was offered
a three-picture deal with AIP and had just completed his next
picture for them, a psychedelic piece of malarkey entitled *The
Trip,* written by a then-unknown Jack Nicholson. In late 1967,
he was in Toronto for a film exhibitors convention to promote
The Trip, where he was scheduled to speak. It was the height of
the biker film phenomenon and Fonda was seen as the genre's
poster boy. The convention's host, Jack Valenti, president of the
Motion Picture Academy Association (MPAA) took the podium
and spoke first. He fixed Fonda with a stern glare and said, "My

friends, we have to stop making movies about motorcycles, sex and drugs, and make more movies like *Doctor Dolittle,** which cost $27 million."[94] Not to be outdone, Fonda took the mike and retorted that movies should earn $27 million, not cost that much. His remark got him a standing ovation from the exhibitors; Old Hollywood and New Hollywood were struggling for control of the moviegoer's wallet.

Fonda's assessment may have gone over well with the crowd, but just how it could be made a reality was another matter. He was simply an actor who had starred in a film fluke that catered to the unwashed pot-smoking crowd, an audience with the attention span of a fly. No studio film had ever made a $27 million profit, let alone AIP with its cheap, exploitative fare. It seemed like a fantasy to think any movie could bring in the kind of grosses that Fonda had mentioned in his speech.

---

* *Doctor Dolittle* was a huge flop, costing its studio millions of dollars.

CHAPTER 9

The High-Water Mark

As THE SIXTIES CAME TO A CLOSE, THE PUBLIC IMAGE OF MOTOR-cyclists was at its all-time worst. Every drive-in theater was featuring a triple bill of biker films and people who never saw them suspected they were all documentaries. It was getting more difficult for average mainstream motorcyclists to separate themselves from the one-percenters, even if they vastly outnumbered them. Motorcycling was a sport, not a means to create chaos, and it wasn't fair that these movies were making them all look like felons.

Still, none of this affected the marketplace. Motorcycle sales kept increasing while racing and hill climbs grew in popularity; they sometimes even showed up on television and in feature films. The 1966 documentary *On Any Sunday* memorably featured an open desert motorcycle race, easily one of the most apocalyptic competitions in sports. Desert racing was so environmentally destructive that it bordered on vandalism. "I don't think they do it at all anymore," says former desert racer Bill Hayward, who competed in the film. "I think ecologically, it was completely unsound but the word 'ecological' hadn't entered the vocabulary at that time."[95] Up to a thousand riders on dirt bikes would make huge grinding loops around miles of unspoiled desert terrain, tearing up cactus and sage brush, terrifying wildlife, and sending up a tidal wave of dust in their wake.

Before becoming a racer, Bill Hayward grew up in Beverly Hills as the youngest of three children whose parents were archetypes of seemingly blessed Hollywood royalty. His father was the famously flamboyant agent Leland Hayward, who oversaw the careers of Jimmy Stewart, Henry Fonda, Humphrey Bogart, Judy Garland, Greta Garbo, Montgomery Clift, and Fred Astaire, among others. His mother was the beautiful and gifted actress Margaret Sullavan, a Broadway luminary and the star of *The Shop Around the Corner* with Jimmy Stewart. Bill was raised in the lap of luxury with servants, beautiful homes, and vacations to Europe. His two older sisters, Brooke and Bridget, doted on him and his closest friends were the Fonda children, Peter and Jane.

But by the time he crashed his bike in the desert, Bill was emerging from a highly traumatic childhood. His parents had divorced when he was young, with Leland marrying a total of five times, Margaret four. He eventually moved to Connecticut to live with his mother and attend various private schools. It was an era of knee-jerk Freudian theorizing, and Hayward's "rebellious" behavior at school (i.e., watching TV under his bedcovers) got him committed for two years to Menninger's, a psychiatric hospital in Topeka, Kansas, when he was sixteen. He ran away four times, only to be caught and returned each time. Both his mother Margaret and sister Bridget spent time in the Austin Riggs mental hospital in Stockbridge, Massachusetts, for manic depression, and both women committed suicide eight months apart of each other when Bill was eighteen. He finally escaped by enlisting in the army in the 82nd Airborne Division. After finishing his hitch, he drifted back to California and settled there. He had taken up motorcycling as a teenager and went through a Triumph 500cc, a Bonneville, a BMW, a Norton Atlas, and a Bultaco dirt bike.

In 1966, Hayward was a twenty-five-year-old competing in an open desert race in Nevada that looked like something out of

Dante's *Inferno*. Smoke bombs marked the course, and the one thousand racers who had lined up side by side were forced to ride into a torturous narrow pass filled with gullies, rocks, and prickly pear cactuses. Between the smoke and billowing sand, visibility was nil and bikes wiped out by the dozen. "I got through the pass," Hayward says, "not from any skill but strictly out of luck, and then had some kind of disaster not long after and I hurt myself pretty good."[96] He hit a deep rainwash that sent him flying, tearing up his leg and trashing his Matchless 500. "I kind of ended my racing career right there."

Hayward also worked in the film industry doing production, but that didn't last long. After a falling-out with some executives while working on *Camelot,* he "got all bent out of shape" and walked away from the movies to become a still photographer.

Around this time, Hayward's sister Brooke was an actress living in Los Angeles and enduring a tumultuous marriage to Dennis Hopper, with whom she had a daughter. A dynamic actor, Hopper was also a very talented photographer, and a serious collector of modern art. But despite his gifts, he was, to put no small point on it, unemployable. He possessed a belligerent personality and a proclivity for bizarre behavior which had made him a pariah in Hollywood. A successful actor in his youth, his last major film was in 1959 where he had clashed so violently with the director Henry Hathaway that he was effectively blackballed by the studios. Once a costar in films like *Giant* and *Rebel Without A Cause* (both with his close friend James Dean), Hopper had been reduced to taking parts in Z-grade cheapies like *Queen Of Blood*. His last acting job had been on a *Wild Angels* rip-off called *The Glorystompers* and he spent the rest of his time peddling film scripts that nobody wanted to buy. More than anything, he wanted to direct.

Hopper and Peter Fonda had known each other for years and

formed an unusual friendship around their individual quirks. Both were antiestablishment types with long hair who liked to get high, and both chafed under the calcifying studio system. Equally headstrong, the two often fought but were always trying to develop film projects together. This was seen as a dubious pairing, though, by many who knew them. Despite his family pedigree, the film industry regarded Fonda as something of a black sheep while Hopper was just plain crazy.

After Fonda's speech to the exhibitors in Toronto while promoting *The Trip,* he returned to his room at the Lakeshore Motel, a suite with black and red walls that resembled a gothic bordello. He downed a couple of beers, smoked a joint, and began to autograph promotional photo stills of his AIP films for the exhibitors. While scribbling his name on the glossies, he came across a large 8x10 color photo from *The Wild Angels* showing him and costar Bruce Dern standing in silhouette next to their motorcycles. The combination of the beer, grass, and the room's hooker ambience made him give pause to the picture. "I said, 'That's it, that's the next movie,'" he recalls. "No more motorcycles, sex, and drugs, huh? We're not going to be a hundred Hell's Angels on the way to a Hell's Angels funeral. It's going to be two of us riding across the country, my journey to the East."[97] He came up with the basic premise for another biker movie, envisioning a motorcycling version of *The Searchers,* featuring two men on choppers heading across America. At the end, some rednecks driving a pickup filled with ducks blew the bikers away with shotguns.

It was a radical idea and Fonda couldn't think of anyone better to do it with than Dennis Hopper. He immediately phoned him with his inchoate idea. "You'll direct, I'll produce, we'll both ride and act," Fonda told him. "It will save some money."[98] Hopper was thrilled and they immediately went to work on their film, which they entitled *The Loners.*

Both were aware they didn't know a hell of a lot about the technical aspects of filmmaking and started drumming up help from friends. Hopper called his brother-in-law Bill Hayward. "He said, 'Look, we've got this little movie we're going to put together,'" Hayward says. "'We want you to kind of produce the thing and we don't have any money but it won't last very long.' Dennis was my brother-in-law* and Peter I'd known forever so I said, 'Sure.' I became a kind of line producer, and I had never done anything remotely like that before."[99]

Though they had taken stabs at screenwriting before, Fonda and Hopper agreed to find someone who could generate a script for them based on their story idea. While acting in a garish costume drama film in France, Fonda met a bearish Texan who was considered *the* hottest writer working in the film industry, Terry Southern.

Almost forgotten today, Southern was one of the most controversial and revolutionary scribes of American letters. His screenwriting credits included *Dr. Strangelove, The Cincinnati Kid,* and *Barbarella.* Southern also authored or coauthored several cult novels, including *The Magic Christian, Filigree, Flash,* and the best-selling *Candy.* He was so hip that the Beatles included his picture in the montage of famous faces that adorned the cover of their *Sgt. Pepper's Lonely Hearts Club Band* album. Fonda admired Southern and told him the basic premise for his motorcycle movie. To Fonda's surprise, Southern liked it and asked to help work on the script. "It's the most commercial idea I've ever heard," Southern told him. Unfortunately, Southern was a gifted writer but a horrible businessman. Nothing regarding his contributions to the project was ever put into writing.

---

* Hopper and Brooke Hayward divorced not long after this.

With Southern on board, Fonda and Hopper took the project to AIP to get financing, with Roger Corman acting as a liaison. They had no script or even a story outline, just the promise of a film with a couple of motorcycles and a bloody ending. They pitched themselves as costars, with Hopper directing. AIP smelled a hit and agreed to put up the money.

However, it was not to be. After a few days of pre-production filming, AIP suddenly hit Hopper and Fonda with a stipulation that ended up screwing the entire deal. "One of the executives of AIP," Corman recalls, "said that they wanted to have the right to fire Dennis as director if he fell more than a day behind schedule, not an unreasonable request if you knew Dennis's background. But not phrased as well as it might be."[100]

This was unacceptable. It was the first film Hopper would be directing and the chances were they would get off schedule to some degree. Much to Corman's regret, Fonda and Hopper stormed out of the meeting and took their project with them.

Unfortunately, AIP had been their only source of financing. The major studios were not about to finance a lowly *biker* film, especially with Fonda and Hopper, the Hekyll and Jekyll of Hollywood, at the helm. Discouraged, the two actors felt their biker project was stillborn and tossed it aside. They went about pitching another film idea of theirs entitled *The Queen,* a twisted political allegory about the JFK assassination performed in drag; they wanted sixty thousand dollars to shoot it in four days.

Through connections with Jack Nicholson's agency, they got a meeting at BBS with Bert Schneider and Bob Rafelson, two maverick producers who had gotten rich by creating the Monkees and were racked with guilt for doing so. The two men saw themselves as Hollywood insurgents (a somewhat self-aggrandizing perspective considering Bert Schneider's father Abe was the chairman of Columbia Pictures) and both were extremely shrewd. They were ripe for a schizoid duo like Hopper and Fonda to wander into their offices.

The two actors met with Rafelson first, who rolled his eyes at their *Queen* project and instead inquired about their biker film, having gotten wind of it. As they bemoaned their problems with AIP, Schneider walked into the meeting and overheard them talking about *The Loners*. Intrigued, he asked, "How much do you want for that one?" Fonda grabbed at a Corman figure off the top of his head and said, "$360,000." Schneider, who was the money man, asked Fonda to come to his house later that night to tell him the story.

Weeks earlier, Fonda and Hopper had sat down with Terry Southern, plied themselves with grass and cognac, and rambled off *The Loners* story line into a tape recorder. Fonda claims that Hopper was going to start first, but he froze up, so Fonda took the mike from him and narrated the plot on to the spinning tape recorder for forty minutes: two drug dealers named Billy the Kid (Hopper) and Wyatt, aka Captain America (Fonda), ride from California eastward across the country on Harley-Davidson choppers. They have a batch of cocaine hidden in their gas tanks that they plan to sell in New Orleans and they plan to retire in Florida for life on the proceeds. During their trip, they encounter hippie communes, get harassed by small town bigots, get jailed for "parading without a permit," meet an alcoholic ACLU lawyer named Hansen, ride some more, party with hookers, before finally unloading their coke stash. Billy is ecstatic, Captain America is disillusioned. Around a campfire, Captain America quietly says, "We blew it," and rolls over to go to sleep. The next morning, two rednecks in a pickup truck blow them away with a shotgun.

When Fonda met with Schneider at his home, he pitched the script, mentioned that Terry Southern was involved, and gave him a copy of the tape, which later disappeared. After a few days of consulting with other people, Schneider agreed to put up $360,000 of his own money to help finance the film.

Though in hindsight it was a brilliant investment, at the time Schneider's decision sounded reckless. They had no studio lined up to distribute the film, there was no screenplay yet, and the director had never directed before. Just to be certain, Schneider only gave forty thousand dollars up front to Hopper and Fonda to get them started. That would be enough for them to shoot something to see whether or not Hopper knew what he was doing.

Somewhere during the recounting of the movie's plot line in the BBS offices, Mardi Gras was mentioned. Hopper and Fonda decided to use the forty thousand dollars to travel to New Orleans and shoot some of the film's scenes there. Two immediate problems presented themselves. First, since there was no script, they didn't have the slightest idea what it was they were going to shoot. Second, they completely miscalculated when Mardi Gras was going to happen.

"There was no time to prepare for the shoot," recalls Hayward, "because it was supposed to be in Mardi Gras and Mardi Gras that year came unusually early in the calendar. A film crew was quickly thrown together by Hopper, several members of who had little or no experience at their assigned positions, and they all headed for New Orleans with only ten days to film.

The shoot was, by all accounts, a veritable comedy of errors. Hopper reportedly became so paranoid the crew was going to take over the film that he would begin each morning with a shrieking tirade directed at everyone, declaring "This is *my* fucking movie!" over and over again. Crew members started quitting left and right. Even Fonda, who knew Hopper better than anyone, was stunned. Hopper got into a ferocious fight with the cinematographer Barry Feinstein over control of the exposed footage and broke a guitar over his head. He was guzzling wine and speed on an hourly basis, exacerbating his already manic state of mind. Fonda would end the shooting day by dosing Hopper with Placidyl, a depressant, to get him to calm down.

They wandered all over the French Quarter during Mardi Gras and filmed whatever they could think of. Hopper, Fonda, and actresses Karen Black and Toni Basil (who were cast as hookers), filmed a nightmarish scene in a graveyard where their characters trip on acid, made more realistic by the fact they *were* tripping on acid. Basil even got naked and crawled into an open crypt. In the midst of everything, Hopper somehow persuaded Fonda to declare his anger at his mother for committing suicide. Fonda, as his character Captain America, stood atop a grave monument and tearfully expressed his long pent-up feelings while Hopper filmed it. Both Fonda and Bill Hayward would later admit that Hopper's idea worked. However, every morning Fonda was secretly taping Hopper's paranoiac invectives at the cast and crew; he was getting set to have Hopper fired from the picture.

After returning to Los Angeles following the New Orleans pilgrimage, Fonda and Hayward secretly went to see Schneider and played him the tapes of Hopper's tirades. "Dennis is insane," Fonda told him. "He cannot stand the fact that I'm the producer and that I hired him to direct the film."[101] Fonda offered to give BBS back their forty thousand dollars, although he was hoping that Schneider would just fire Hopper and get another director. Instead, Schneider offered to step in for Fonda as producer to oversee the film. Maybe he could keep Hopper in line. (Hopper later claimed Schneider was irritated by Fonda and Hayward's covert effort to kick their friend/in-law off the film, and warned him about it.)

Schneider's decision to keep Hopper on as director was a tremendous show of faith, as the dailies from the New Orleans shoot were dreadful. They resembled a Ken Kesey home movie, dark, murky, and out of focus. The lab had to "push" the film's exposure during the developing process just to get a visible image, a procedure that added graininess. Every frame looked like it had been printed on toast.

They still did not have a script. Southern had gotten fed up with the anarchy in New Orleans and eventually drifted away from the project, but not before witnessing Hopper get into a ridiculous knife fight with Southern's good friend, actor Rip Torn, who was originally cast to play the alcoholic ACLU lawyer Hansen. During a dinner at a New York City restaurant, Hopper supposedly made a critical remark about Texans at which Torn, a proud native of the Lone Star State, took offense. Torn claims he offered a handshake in friendship but Hopper opted instead to grab a steak knife off the table, brandishing it. Torn, who was once a military policeman, easily disarmed Hopper and both men challenged each other to a fight outside. Torn exited the restaurant and waited for Hopper, who never showed.

Rip Torn soon left the film, much to Hopper's regret. He wanted a southerner to play the Hansen role. Jack Nicholson, whom Fonda and Hopper knew from his work on *The Trip,* offered to play Hansen (his acting career up to that point had been so inglorious that he reportedly begged for the role). Fonda was open to it but Hopper was skeptical; Nicholson was from New Jersey. Schneider urged them to hire him, as he wanted Nicholson to act as a wedge between Hopper and Fonda to keep them from killing each other. Finally, Hopper relented and agreed to cast him.

After months of blowing cannabis and all-night babbling, a screenplay was finally created; this is where the *Easy Rider* saga becomes serpentine. According to Terry Southern (now deceased), he took the tripped-out ideas supplied by Fonda and Hopper, added his own, and wrote the entire script. "They couldn't even write a fucking letter," he groused to other people.[102] Southern also claimed he changed the film's title to *Easy*

Rider (both Hopper and Fonda acknowledge this is true). Fonda, on the other hand, insists that all three of them collaborated on the screenplay and Hopper dictated the scenes into a tape recorder for Southern's secretary to type up later. According to Hopper, Fonda and Southern were originally responsible for generating a script but kept failing to complete it. Frustrated, Dennis went off for two weeks and wrote the entire script by himself. "Terry never wrote one fucking word," Hopper has repeatedly insisted, "not one line of dialogue."[103] The only thing that is known for certain is that Southern departed after a script was created.*

Through Bert Schneider's family connections, a distribution deal was set up at Columbia, the same staid studio that buried *The Wild One* years earlier. Fonda, Hopper, and Hayward resumed production with their script in hand. "All the descriptives of it, what the scenes were supposed to be were scripted out," says Fonda. "The scene of Jack's speech [around the campfire] about the Venutians was scripted out. Most of the rest of it was just the way we did it. Not necessarily even improvised."[104]

Hayward, who had never cared for Harley-Davidsons, supplied the two Bultaco motorcycles Billy and Captain America use to meet with a buyer, played by a mute Phil Spector, near the beginning of the film. Flush with money, the two characters ditch their proletarian bikes and acquire a pair of gleaming chopped Harley-Davidsons, with Captain America's sporting a set of extended front forks, and painted up like the Star-Spangled Banner. The metaphor was as obvious as a rhino in a ballet class.

---

* When the film was released, Southern, Fonda, and Hopper were all listed as cowriters, but years later rumors persisted that Southern was the lone writer of *Easy Rider*. Unfortunately, Southern also agreed to work for a flat five-thousand-dollar fee, while Fonda and Hopper each shared 50 percent of the film's profits, making them millionaires. When Terry Southern died in 1995, he was virtually penniless.

"That was the first time I had ever ridden a Harley Davidson," says Hayward about the Captain America chopper. "I'd never had any interest in them because they were kind of slow and poky. And I rode the one that Peter rode, that big stretched-out job and it was a nightmare. It was just insane. Peter deserves a medal for riding it as much as he did in the movie. It had no front brake. And you couldn't conceivably do a U-turn."[105]

Hayward was not the only one who felt that way. Though both he and Fonda were avid motorcyclists, Hopper disliked bikes and was fearful of the chopper he rode. He had once crashed a motorcycle on the Sunset Strip years earlier and wound up in the hospital for ten days. As soon as any scenes involving Billy on his chopper were completed, Hopper rolled the bike right back on the truck.

Throughout the remainder of *Easy Rider's* filming, the tension remained high on the set, especially between Hopper and Fonda. The director was aware that his partner had tried to fire him and was not about to let him forget it. Fonda kept a bike chain wrapped around his waist as a belt lest he had to fend off a surprise assault from Hopper.

They shot guerrilla-style all across the Southwest, often stopping in small towns to film without permits. Hopper used curious locals as extras, sticking them into scenes for atmosphere. It was all very impromptu and lent a documentary feel to the proceedings. "We did almost a week and a half of shooting in town without riding," Fonda says. "Doing the stuff that was never shown at the beginning of the picture, including the hippie compound. And then comes the big time to start the rides. All of us met in Needles and we started very early in the morning and rode from Needles to Cayman, which is fifty-five miles. But, of course, we crossed the Colorado River at least a dozen times."[106]

During the road trip part of the filming, Fonda experienced a strange affliction after riding for hours on the Captain America bike, his arms stiffly locked on the handlebars while wearing a pair of purple pants. They had gone hundreds of miles before winding up in Kingman, Arizona, where they checked into a motel. Fonda wanted to go for a swim, but after peeling off the sweat-saturated pants, he discovered the perspiration had caused the dye to leech out of the fabric and stain his legs purple. Embarrassed, he pulled on a pair of jeans and headed for the hotel bar instead. He ordered up a frosty mug of beer, but then discovered he was unable to bend his arm all the way up to his face; the long ride had locked his elbow joints. Fonda sheepishly asked for a straw. As for dinner: "I had to be fed that night by the script clerk."[107]

They finally wrapped the production and returned to Los Angeles, exhausted. A week later, all the bikes used in the movie were stolen from a storage garage in Simi Valley. As the film had yet to come out and there was no advance publicity about it, the thieves had no idea what they had taken and undoubtedly chopped them up for spare parts. Fonda and Hopper also discovered that they had forgotten to shoot the final climactic campfire scene in the script, with its famous "we blew it" coda. They hastily gathered together a crew and went up to the Santa Monica Mountains to film it.

"When we finally shot the ending," Fonda says, "I simply said, 'We blew it,' much to Dennis's consternation." Hopper became angry, insisting that he could not be that cryptic. "He wanted me to do a whole explanation of *why* we blew it," Fonda continues. "And I wanted to stay enigmatic." Fonda told Hopper that he wanted to do the scene "like Warren Beatty. Warren cuts all his lines in half and mumbles the ones he *does* speak." They shouted at each other for fifteen minutes before agreeing to shoot it both ways. Fonda uttered his terse line and rolled over. "It worked just perfectly, just great," he says.[108] The director agreed and kept the take.

Hopper, his mind swirling with chemicals and an *auteur's* hubris, went to work editing the film. He locked himself away for months, watching the footage spool out before him and falling in love with most everything he shot. He envisioned an epic motion picture that would travel the country like an art exhibit; there would be reserve seating and an intermission. After twenty-two weeks, Hopper emerged from the editing room with a four-and-a-half-hour cut of *Easy Rider* that he deemed perfect.

Fonda, Hayward and the representatives from Columbia were horrified. Very little of it made any sense and they pleaded with him to cut it down. Hopper instead assembled various versions of the film, none of them running less than three hours long.

"We screened it for anybody that asked to see it," says Hayward. "We had the highest projection room bill that Columbia had ever had at that time."[109] The rough cuts of *Easy Rider* soon gained notoriety around Hollywood as being something of a freak attraction, a celluloid Elephant Man. The Columbia screening room became *the* place to go, get doped up and watch a hypnotic biker flick that never ended.

This went on for almost a year, adding an additional $141,000 to the budget until everyone threw their hands up and asked Bert Schneider to do something. Nobody wanted to fire Hopper because they were terrified of him, so Schneider bought him two first-class tickets to Taos, New Mexico, and asked him to "take a break." Hopper went on vacation with a girlfriend and Schneider hired an editor named Don Cambren to cut the film down. They wisely chose to keep the temporary soundtrack that Hopper and Fonda had thrown on, a collection of then-current rock songs, most of which would become classics.* By the time Hopper re-

---

* Fonda originally hired Crosby, Stills, and Nash to score the entire film but Hopper quashed it.

turned from Taos almost two months later, he discovered that his film had been trimmed down to a neat ninety-five minutes. He was outraged but was too tired to fight anymore and yielded.

The film was finally screened for Columbia executives, men who had come up through the ranks during the Harry Cohn era. They detested it and most walked out before it was finished. Biker films and motorcycle outlaws were for Corman and his drive-in dullards. There was nothing noble about this *Easy Rider* crap, they thought. Bring us *Doctor Dolittle*.

But the word on the street was different. The drugged-out Columbia screenings had created a buzz around the town. *Easy Rider* was literally the first major film to gain publicity by word of mouth. There was no ham-fisted promotional campaign for it. "Bert Schneider was the genius behind the distribution part of it," says Fonda. "Instead of having any TV, radio, or print ads, he did all these screenings in little fifty-seat theaters in New York, Denver, Chicago, San Francisco, Seattle. Everyone was buzzing about this film."[110]

A week before it opened, people around the nation opened up their newspapers to see a full-page ad for a movie. It showed a picture of Fonda looking off into the distance with an American flag on his back. The ad's tagline was: *A man went looking for America and couldn't find it anywhere,* a disillusioned aphorism that came not from Fonda or Hopper but rather the Columbia Studios sales department. It was the perfect marketing phrase.

On July 14, 1969, *Easy Rider* was released to an astonishing response. Theater showings sold out in minutes; lines went around the block. Even with the editing overruns, the film cost only around $501,000 to produce. It went on to earn $19 million in its first year of release, one of the most profitable movies of all time. "It cost so little that I always assumed that it would make money," says Hayward. "But I never in my wildest imagination believed that it would become the kind of picture that it did. Dennis always did, to his credit."[111]

Easy Rider was the toast of the Cannes Film Festival and won Hopper the award for best director. It also made a star out of Jack Nicholson, who, like Lee Marvin in *The Wild One,* almost steals the movie from its leads. His performance as the drunk attorney Hansen is both hilarious and tragic. The soundtrack was also a revelation, the first film to be completely accompanied by popular songs (nowadays, a cliché) rather than with an original score.

The film has fared better over the years than *The Wild One* or any of the infamous outlaw biker films, though it remains more of an icon of its era rather than a timeless classic. Indeed, it only occasionally shows up on the late show nowadays and even its thirtieth anniversary re-release in 1999 went by with little fanfare. The dialogue in the film makes it practically scream of the sixties. Even Fonda regularly jokes about the omnipresent use of the word "man" in the film. The let's-kill-the-hippies portent that runs through it is slightly fatuous today and the acid trip in the New Orleans cemetery plays for laughs; the famous campfire scene with Nicholson talking about Venutians is especially silly. But if one can deal with the archaic nuttiness that runs through much of it, *Easy Rider* is a fascinating film. "You get a contact high just watching the thing," says *New York* magazine film critic Peter Rainer. "I think it tells you a lot about the sacrificial nature, the sentimentalism of the hippie movement and how they felt that the whole world was against them."[112] Indeed, behind *Easy Rider's* revolutionary pulse was a sense of "it's all over now." There's a huge smear of cynical capitalism that runs through the film; Billy and Captain American are dealing cocaine, that decadent elitist drug that only the rich could inhale. The hippies mostly look pathetic, like war refugees waiting for someone to come and wash their burlap for them. Meanwhile, every southern male over eighteen is a drawling vigilante with barber shears in one hand and a gun in the other. Whatever its celebratory themes, much of *Easy Rider* is a downer.

Bikers today remain on the fence as to what the film is "about." During its heyday, Hopper would expound for hours on what messages could be gotten from it, though more recently he has qualified it as just "a biker film that we did to make money." For his part, Fonda says, "I don't really think of *Easy Rider* as being a biker film. There are just bikes in it. It's a western. I wore spurs."[113]

Easy Rider's real legacy remains the enormous amounts of money it earned, and this may be why the film was ruled as groundbreaking cinema rather than a B-movie with great scenery and no real plot. The film practically demolished the aging studio system and terrified the wizened executives who just did not get it. There was an entire generation of moviegoers out there that had no interest in the frothy musicals and bloated costume epics that Hollywood had been offering. They wanted to revolt, ride, and party.

Like *The Wild One, Easy Rider* succeeds best when nobody is saying anything. There are numerous riding montages in the film that serve almost as a television commercial for Harley-Davidson. Motorcycling never looked more spiritual, more free, more soul-inspiring, and America never looked more wide open. The motorcycle was elevated to a level of cultural chic that it had never attained before.

Easy Rider served as both the zenith and swan song of biker films. They would fizzle out after just a few short years and were gone by the early 1970s. Today, they are rarely revived at theaters as most of them have simply disappeared. Biker films served their purpose, though, earning money for their producers while taking outlaw mystique to a new level. The timing of *Easy Rider's* release could not have been more perfect. They had begun production in 1967, at a time when the counterculture was in the throes of stoned idealism. It was pure serendipity that Hopper was such an obsessive madman that he unintentionally delayed the film's release until the twilight of the so-called Revolution. Two years earlier, paisley types were less likely to accept the notion that Bubba Roy and his hick cousin were going to blow holes through them with an Ithaca 12-gauge and get away with it. By 1969, this seemed almost prophetic.

CHAPTER 10

It's All Over Now

THE ALTAMONT SPEEDWAY IS ABOUT FIFTY MILES EAST OF SAN Francisco, buried off of Highway 580 among tracts of rolling farmland near the town of Livermore. You cannot see the track from the highway and if it were not for the billboard marker, you would miss it altogether. The speedway is surprisingly small, a quarter-mile asphalt oval with a modest grandstand. Anyone can rent Altamont by the hour or for an entire day and tear around the track in the vehicle of their choice. The area behind it was filled in years ago to create a sloping knoll that accommodates a ramped access road leading down to the track. For decades, horses and other livestock have grazed in pastures a few hundred yards beyond the barrier wall, oblivious to the grinding din of high performance engines emanating from the track during the summer racing season. Like Hollister, Altamont should otherwise be unknown to the nation except for the many cultural historians who consider it as the place where the 1960s died.

The JFK assassination aside, the major social milestones that defined the sixties mostly occurred within the decade's final twenty-four months, as if some harried program director felt compelled to cram everything in at the last minute. The Summer of Love of 1967 has traditionally been a part of the milestone list, but in reality, the summer was already

three years old and on the way to implosion by the time everyone in the nation began hearing about it. Likewise, Altamont is
seen as the denouement where all the hopes and dreams of a
restless generation came crashing down to a tragic end rather
than just a hastily planned rock concert where, unfortunately,
one man was killed.

The story as it has been repeated over the years follows the
same plot line: the Rolling Stones host a free concert at the Altamont Speedway that is attended by well over three hundred
thousand people. The Hell's Angels are hired to do security and
guard the stage throughout the day. Throughout the day, the outlaws brutally attack the teeming crowd with pool cues. Finally,
during the Stones' performance, a member of the Hell's Angels
stabs a concertgoer to death, an act that is caught on film by documentary cameras. The event is never forgotten and dubbed forever as the Death of the Sixties.

Yet if you ask Dick Carter, the manager of Altamont who
helped orchestrate the entire event, he'll tell you a slightly different version: "The Hell's Angels weren't hired for security.
That's a bunch of bullshit."[114]

DURING THE FALL OF 1969, THE ROLLING STONES WERE IN THE
midst of their first U.S. tour in several years, promoting *Let It
Bleed*. They had replaced the erratic Brian Jones (who died soon
afterwards) with guitarist Mick Taylor, a shy musician who could
play circles around Jones, and the group never sounded better.
With the Beatles on the verge of disintegrating, the Rolling
Stones were set to become the biggest and richest rock band in
the world and therefore, since it was the sixties, had every reason to feel guilty.

The group had played a free show in London's Hyde Park over
the summer in honor of the deceased Brian Jones and it seemed

only logical that they should stage one for their American fans. Before they left England to start their U.S. tour, the Stones had met with Rock Scully, who was then the Grateful Dead's manager. Scully had gotten word that the Stones were coming to America and flew to England to discuss the possibility of them putting on a free show in the States. "The discussion about the Rolling Stones having a free concert in America had started in London," Scully said, "mainly because I brought with me all this bad press about their ticket prices. I said, 'Look, you're getting lambasted now. It's going to get worse when you get there.' They were generally interested in doing it. After Hyde Park, they were up for it."[115]

The Stones' tour had begun in New York City and was making its way to the West Coast, where they knew of the wonderful spirit of community that existed there, especially in the San Francisco area. Their intention was to put on a kind of West Coast Woodstock, as the original mud-soaked festival had taken place a few months earlier. The buzz about Woodstock's good vibes was the talk of the nation, mostly of how everyone got in for free (although they were not supposed to; the crowd had simply busted down the fences and walked in.) Though Woodstock's organizers lost their shirts on the event, it was deemed a success and suddenly everyone was expecting free entertainment.

Anyone living in Haight-Ashbury during the closing months of the 1960s could see how much the neighborhood had changed over the past four years. Whatever halcyon vibe it once had was being replaced by the consumptive pall of tourism, homelessness, and ugly crime. It was always raining in the Bay area and the streets turned wet and cold. Many of the hippies crashing there were simply runaways who were sleeping on the pavement. Rapes, assaults, and overdoses had skyrocketed. More of the flower children were getting into hard narcotics like speed and heroin, and the whole paisley dream was succumbing to the delirium tremens. Haight-Ashbury was falling apart.

Sam Cutler, a vexatious Englishman with the emotional amplitude of a vampire on morphine, was overseeing the Stones' American tour. It was up to him to finesse the band's free gala rock festival and he pretty much knew nothing about the West Coast. While talking with Scully, Cutler suggested hiring the Hell's Angels for security, as he had used the club's London chapter for the Hyde Park Concert. Scully, who was friends with some of the Frisco Angels, told him he was nuts. The London Hell's Angels were a low-key strain of outlaw, bikers with a stiff upper lip. *"No, no, no, no. No way!"* Scully exclaimed. "This isn't the same."[116]

Everybody was up for having the Stones do a free concert in the Bay area and began planning it long in advance. Scully and others in the Dead's camp set their sights on Golden Gate Park and began meeting secretly with San Francisco city officials to obtain permission. In mid-November, Cutler flew out to the Bay area where the Dead's organization introduced him to the radical Diggers, who had ideas on how the Rolling Stones should stage the concert. Two Digger members, Peter Coyote and Peter Berg, suggested a day-long series of events and exhibits, with the park surrounded by multiple bonfires that people could gather around while the bands played on a stage off to one side, thereby establishing an instant community for the audience and performers. The idea of a dozen bonfires and tribal huddling sounded too much like *Lord of the Flies* to Cutler, and he was not about to stick the biggest band in the world on a side stage as if they were playing a wedding reception. He ignored the Diggers and instead approached the Hell's Angels.

The Hell's Angels had always been a regular presence at outdoor rock shows in the Bay area. It was easy to deal drugs and they could hobnob with the performers. The Frisco Angels especially counted a number of local rock bands like the Grateful Dead among their friends. One Angel even managed the group Blue Cheer, a power trio known for their execrable cover of Eddie Cochran's "Summertime Blues" and for having a drummer who claimed he filed down his drum sticks to get a "blunter" sound.

Some rock luminaries of the era like Grace Slick have claimed the Hell's Angels had done security at their concerts before. In fact, many concertgoers assumed the club worked security jobs regularly since they were a common sight at the shows on the West Coast; there exists a little-seen concert film of the Doors where several Hell's Angels can be seen hanging around the stage. The more likely reason they were there, though, was because they had just barged in backstage to hang out and watch the concerts up close. No one dared stop them or ask them to pay. But because they were always seen displaying their colors, hobnobbing with the bands, and looking mean, people concluded they were working security far more often than they really did. In reality, the Angels simply liked crashing rock shows.

This proved to be the case when Pete Knell, the president of the Frisco chapter, took a meeting with Cutler to discuss the Stones' free concert. Cutler envisioned a more traditional venue, a big platform stage at one end of Golden Gate Park. Could the Angels help in any way? According to ex-Digger/actor Peter Coyote, who was close to Knell, the conversation went rather smoothly:

> [Knell said] "Tell 'em to come. We'll pick 'em up at the airport, bring 'em to the Panhandle, and let 'em do a free concert." Pete went on to guarantee that the equipment would be set up and ready for them and that all they had to bring was their guitars. The Hell's Angels knew what "free" meant, too.
>
> Sam asked Pete how much the club would want to serve as "security" at the event, and Pete told him, "We don't po-

lice things. We're not a security force. We go to concerts to enjoy ourselves and have fun."

"Well, what about helping people out—you know, giving directions and things?" Cutler queried, angling to have the Angels attached to the event in some official capacity. When Pete agreed that they could do that, Cutler returned to the question of price, and Pete said, "We like beer."

"How does a hundred cases sound?" Cutler responded, and the deal was struck. The Angels intended to give the beer away and felt that this would be good for the club's image.[117]

This account was related to Coyote by another Angel, a former Digger associate-turned-outlaw named Bill "Sweet William" Fritsch, who was in the room at the time. It was the closest thing to an offer ever made to the club to be involved with the Stones' free concert.

Meanwhile Dick Carter, who managed the dilapidated Altamont Speedway on a shoestring budget, was caught in a Catch-22 with the state of California. Carter had applied for a permit to erect some billboards on the highway to help draw more people to the track. The state refused his request, the reason being that his racetrack did not draw enough people to warrant putting up the billboards. Carter ran the obscure speedway almost as a one-man operation and on a good night maybe five hundred people came out to watch the races. He had been a professional racecar driver for most of his adult life and worked diligently to promote a venue that most people had either never heard of or did not know how to find.

On Thursday, December 4, Carter was at his desk putting together crew passes for the upcoming race weekend when the phone rang. "I got a call from Stanford University," Carter recalls, "and they said, 'I hear the Rolling Stones are going to be in San Francisco Saturday.'"[118] The caller told him the group was trying to find a location to put on a free show over the coming weekend. This was news to him as he had never heard of the Rolling Stones, and had no idea that anyone would care that they were giving a free concert.

Unbeknownst to Carter, the Rolling Stones had held a press conference two weeks earlier in New York City where Mick Jagger announced they were staging a free outdoor concert in San Francisco's Golden Gate Park. Unfortunately, Jagger did not know that the terms of the arrangement to use the park included one big requirement: everyone had to keep their mouth shut about it until twenty-four hours in advance of the concert. The city did not want a million people descending on them. The majority of San Francisco residents were pretty much sick of the Haight community and the impromptu rock concerts in city parks, with their bad P.A. systems and interminable drum solos. Furious over the press conference, city officials rescinded their offer and announced that Golden Gate Park would not be available.

The Rolling Stones' camp quickly approached the Filmways Company who owned the Sears Point Raceway in the North Bay. They had lots of room, easy highway access, water and toilet facilities, everything they needed. The concert site was moved there and work crews started working around the clock, building a stage platform and erecting the scaffolding for the lights and sound system. Then, two days before the scheduled show, the Rolling Stones fell into a bitter quarrel with Filmways over money and ended up canceling the Sears Point location.

Everyone began to panic. It was already Thursday and they still had no location to stage their Woodstock of the West concert. Everyone knew there was a free show going on and the Bay area was getting flooded with fans wondering where it was going to be held.

By the time Dick Carter finally learned about all this, he had a brainstorm. He would offer the Altamont Speedway as a location for the concert. The publicity would be great and if he could at least draw a few thousand people, he'd get his billboards. Carter got on the phone and started calling around, trying to track down the Stones' representatives. He phoned a number in Sausalito and got ahold of some of the tour staff. "I said, 'This is Dick Carter of Altamont and I've got a better place to hold your concert. And I'll give it to you for free.' So he said, 'All right, we'll see you in the morning' and I said, 'No you won't, because if we're going to do this thing we've got to do it now.'"[119] Carter told them to meet him at an inn in nearby Hayward at midnight to discuss the offer.

Carter walked into the Doric Inn, where he was greeted by two hippie types wearing earrings and faded Levis who were in charge of the lights and sound for the concert. One of the two was the semi-legendary Chip Monck, who designed most of the light shows at Bill Graham's Fillmore West and had overseen the construction of the stage and scaffolding at Sears Point. Carter thought they were the Rolling Stones.

Carter talked up his track to the two men until they asked to see it. The three drove back out to the speedway in the middle of the night and Carter showed them the area around the track. Monck and his partner saw possibilities and said they'd do it in two weeks. Stunned, Carter told them there were going to be fifty thousand people pouring into the city tomorrow and that they'd better do it *now*. Skeptical, Monck declined until Carter promised them that as long as they got the sound and lights up and running, he would take care of everything else. All he asked for was that they pay for it. When asked how much, Carter estimated thirty thousand dollars and asked for three hundred thousand. No problem, they replied, and he watched in astonishment as the two men pulled out a thick wad of hundred-dollar bills and peeled them off.

The next morning, Carter was asked to come to the San Francisco office of famed attorney Marvin Belli to finalize the deal. He stepped into a feeding frenzy of swarming cameras. "All the news media was there," Carter remembers. "All the TV stations and magazines, newspapers, and everybody was there. The place exploded like a bomb with the flashbulbs. And so we started talking about it and I told them what I would need. We needed all kinds of trucks. We needed helicopters. We needed blankets. We needed food. We needed water, hospital, tents, all these things."[120] As the negotiations proceeded, two brothers named Albert and David Maysles were filming off to one side.

The Maysles Brothers were documentary makers hired to shoot the Stones' U.S. tour for a concert film. "We wanted to make a film," Albert Maysles says, "so it would be a concert film-plus. Just what the plus would be we didn't know, but I guess we just felt with the Stones anything could happen."[121] They had recently recorded the Madison Square Garden concert in New York City where the Stones played in front of twenty thousand people. Now the venue was going to be a free concert at an outdoor speedway and who knew how many were going to show up for that.

The deal finalized, Carter drove back out to Altamont only to find a battalion of equipment trucks parked at the track gate that stretched a mile back. In addition, the word had gotten out about the new location and the roads were starting to jam with concert fans trying to find the speedway. Carter called a racing friend of his named Roy Miller in desperation, pleading for help. Like Carter, Miller had never heard of the Rolling Stones and knew nothing about rock concerts. He laughed when Carter told him that fifty thousand people were coming to the track, and said they'd be lucky if five hundred showed up.

Carter called the phone company and told the customer service rep about the concert and that he needed twelve phone lines installed immediately. When told it would take at least two weeks, Carter informed the man that without the lines he'd have to cancel the concert and then tell fifty thousand Rolling Stones fans the name of the customer service rep who had not cooperated. The phone company immediately disconnected service from twelve private residences in the area and rerouted their lines to the track.

Next, Carter and Miller set about chartering helicopters at twice their normal hourly rate to haul equipment, scaffolding, and over a thousand outhouses from Sears Point over to the track. They corralled hundreds of high school kids to set up concession stands and hired extra crew people to help Chip Monck build a stage platform. Meanwhile, a hundred thousand people were amassing near the gates while another hundred thousand were clogging the roads trying to find it. "My son took a call," says Carter. "A Greyhound bus driver was in Tracy and he was lost and wanted to get here. And my son asked, 'How many of you are there?' They were coming from New York and the guy said 'There's thirty-five.' My son said 'Thirty-five people?' And the guy said 'No, thirty-five buses.'"[122]

Carter called up another friend who was in the grape surplus business and bought ten thousand grape stakes to erect around the perimeter of the track. He had them strung together with kite string to form a makeshift barrier to control the flow of people. "By then, we had the sound system up," Carter says. "So we announced to the crowd that if they'd stay outside of the gates, the concert would be free. If they came through, there would be no concert."[123] Surprisingly, the crowd complied—for the time being.

There were around 350 Hell's Angels from all the various California chapters, and most of them were in Oakland for some sort of makeshift convention. Oakland was just across the Bay from San Francisco so everyone in the area knew what was going on fifty miles east of there. Even though it was free, not many of the Angels were interested in attending the Rolling Stones concert. They had gotten word that Highway 580 was a thirty-mile long parking lot; it sounded like a hassle. The only members who were geared up for the concert were the Frisco chapter, who had already taken off once the site had been confirmed. A few of the Oakland Angels were planning on going later. They had heard they could all hang out with the Rolling Stones, drink some beer, and watch the concert.

Besides the Rolling Stones, the other artists on the bill included the Flying Burrito Brothers; The Ike and Tina Turner Revue; Santana; Jefferson Airplane; Crosby, Stills, and Nash; and the Grateful Dead. The weather was perfect, with a warm sun beaming down on the grassy acreage. There was no chance of this event turning into a monsoon as had Woodstock.

Altamont was a sea of humanity. Everyone was surprised by how many people had been able to find the racetrack. "When we got there very early in the morning," recalls Albert Maysles, "somebody was tearing down a fence so we could pass over and get closer to the site. They heard Keith [Richards] saying 'First act of violence...' and thinking back on it, he had some kind of a premonition, I guess."[124]

A massive stage platform that was barely four feet high had been hurriedly thrown together in a bowl-shaped area behind the speedway. There were cows mooing out in a field nearby and the smell of manure drifted over the grounds. The Frisco Angels arrived and wormed their massive Harleys through the crowd to the front of the stage, where a six-foot high cyclone fence had been erected to keep the crowd away from the proscenium edge. The Angels parked their bikes in the area in between, climbed up around the perimeter of the stage and kicked back to watch the show. Cutler had even supplied chairs for them.

The Flying Burrito Brothers took the stage first and started playing their country-laced brand of hippie rock to the newly gathered crowd. Parked off to one side of the stage was a truck full of beer; it was, according to Carter, available to anyone. This seems to mesh somewhat with Sweet William's account of the Angels' meeting with Cutler, who knew he was going to supply beer for the bands anyway and may have dangled the lure of a free truckload of it to the Angels. Several of them climbed on top of the truck to get a better view, making them clearly visible to the three hundred thousand people sitting in the grass.

Carter claims that there was never any intention, at least on his part, to use the Hell's Angels for security. Three hundred New York City police officers that had worked the Woodstock festival had been flown in, plus personnel from Fox Security Patrol and several other firms were there to help oversee everything. Carter insisted that none of them carry weapons or wear uniforms so they could blend in the crowd. "So the only badges our security people had," he says, "were Oakland A's baseball caps turned backwards."[125]

Cutler had never met Carter and didn't care who was patrolling the crowd. All he was concerned with was protecting the stage and his band, so it is likely he simply hoped that having the Hell's Angels show up and be seen would be enough to keep order. Nobody liked cops because they could bust people, and having a bunch of long haired outlaws instead would go over better.

As the Burrito Brothers continued their set, the chain link fence in front of the stage toppled as the crowd surged forward. Within no time at all, people were right up at the edge of the stage. Sweet William Fritsch looked down and saw someone sitting on his bike. He yelled at him to get off, but the man either could not hear or chose to ignore him. Fritsch leaped off the stage and attacked, laying into the man with a chain. When his bike fell over, Fritsch went ballistic and brutally stomped the man into the steaming turf. "I didn't even want his ghost around," he said.[126] The members of the Burrito Brothers pleaded for calm. The concert continued as more people piled into the area.

Albert and his brother David were already filming the concert with a small army of cameramen assisting them. Stunned by the ferocity of the assault, Albert gingerly worked his way through the crowd with his camera. "One of the oddities of the whole thing," Maysles says, "is that there was, whether I liked it or not, a Hell's Angel helping me, carrying my stuff and being as sweet a guy as you can imagine."[127]

When the Oakland Hell's Angels showed up, all bets were off. They were much more intolerant and spiteful of the Haight community and had brought pool cues with them. As the crowd begrudgingly parted, they rumbled slowly to the stage, chugging wine and showing off their old ladies. They parked their bikes wherever they could find a spot and joined the Frisco chapter up on the stage. There were anywhere from seventeen to twenty-four of them sprawled around the platform, in plain sight of the crowd. Whether or not people thought they were doing security was irrelevant; the Angels had taken cuts and now had better seats than everybody else plus their own personal supply of beer. Several in the crowd began booing them.

When Sonny Barger came up on the platform, he was livid. "We're keeping the stage!" he screamed at Fritsch. "Do you realize that if all these people had their minds together they could crush this whole thing?"[128]

Throughout the morning, a few of the other acts played to the festive crowd while the Angels glared about, looking for anyone who'd dare touch their motorcycles. As the day progressed, though, more drugs were consumed by everyone. Many in the

Altamont crowd did not want the Hell's Angels there and hurled insults at them. A few members tried to appease the crowd by tossing unopened bottles of beer to them. Unfortunately, most people were too stoned to notice and several were conked on the head. The Maysles' cameras caught an obese man staggering about stark naked chugging from a jug of wine. His nude corpulence so offended the Angels that they dragged him off behind the stage and beat him bloody.

Jefferson Airplane, a last minute booking, took the stage in the afternoon. They had known the Angels from past gigs and did not think anything of seeing them sprawled around them. The band had flown to the track, arriving just moments before they had to take the stage. They knew nothing about all the folderol that was going on.

"I remember just getting off the helicopter and going right to the stage and starting to perform," recalls lead singer Marty Balin. "I was starting to sing the first song and I heard some noise and I opened my eyes and there were these six guys with pool cues beating up this guy right in the front of the stage."[129] Another motorcycle had been knocked over and various Angels had gone into the crowd, flailing away madly with their pool cues. Balin threw a tambourine into the melee and dove off the stage. "I just thought, man, this guy needs some help, you know," he says. "Nobody was paying attention to me anyway."[130] Balin jumped into the middle of the assault and started pushing the Angels away. One of them looked at him incredulously and asked him what the hell was he doing. "You're gonna get killed down here, Marty," he told him. "You should be onstage singing." Balin replied that he was *trying* to sing but they were acting nuts.

The assault subsided and the bruised victim scurried off. Balin returned to the stage and the band resumed playing. Within minutes, though, the singer heard a ruckus behind him and turned to see the same man getting beat up again by a lone Angel wearing a wolf's head. Balin, who had had a few drinks, became perturbed from being upstaged yet again and stormed off to the rear of the stage. As the rest of the band watched incredulously, he stepped up to the Angel and punched him so hard he cracked his wrist. The man being assaulted joined forces with Balin and the two of them continued pummeling the outlaw. Unfortunately, the Angels' "all on one" rule interceded and Balin found himself under attack by several Angels. He was kicked to the ground and knocked unconscious. When he came to, he found boot marks all over his body, like obscene tattoos. "They kicked the shit out of me," he says.

Guitarist Paul Kantner chastised the Hell's Angels over the P.A. system for beating up their lead singer, causing Barger to march onstage, grab a spare mike, and start yelling back. While they argued, yet another beating broke out as more Angels attacked someone near the stage. People tried to intervene, pleading for calm. The Angels would not hear of it.

Jefferson Airplane had been onstage for only a few minutes and it was already the end of their set. They quickly packed up and left in disgust. Outside in the racetrack's parking lot, members of the Grateful Dead stepped off a helicopter to discover that their pals, the Hell's Angels, were running amok. "They're beating up *musicians*?" bassist Phil Lesh exclaimed, bewildered. The band declined to play and departed.

With no acts left save the Rolling Stones, both the crowd and the Hell's Angels had nothing to do but sit, wait, and continue loading up on drugs. The Stones were in no hurry to play, though, and hours went by. By nightfall, the atmosphere at Altamont turned chaotic. Masses of human bodies pressed toward the stage, trying to climb up while the Angels shoved them off. More bikes were knocked over, more pool cues whistled through the night air, leaving dozens of people bleeding. Carter and Roy Miller became so unnerved that each of them shoved a ball-peen hammer into the waistline of his pants; the protruding steel head underneath their shirts resembled the outline of a handgun. People who brushed up against them quickly backed off.

Finally, a frantic Sweet William Fritsch barged in on the Stones in their trailer and ordered them to go on. The crowd was getting out of control, he said. When they replied they were not ready yet, Fritsch declared, "People are gonna die out there. Get out there! You've been told."[131]

The Rolling Stones finally ambled out onto the stage hours late. Until the wild-eyed Fritsch had charged in on them, they hadn't been aware of what had gone on throughout the day. Jagger calmly told everyone to take it easy and the band went into their first song. Like the crowd, most of the Angels had been gobbling acid and pills all day and they were feeling the effects. One, whom Maysles filmed for several minutes, went into a hallucinatory trance at the side of the stage before another Angel noticed him and threw him off. The Stones stopped playing several times to break up the beatings going on in front of them. Keith Richards was especially irate and berated several of the Angels to cease their pool cue assaults.

According to Dick Carter, what happened next began as a lover's quarrel. "There was this black fella, Meredith Hunter," he says. "He had a blonde girlfriend, and she mentioned that she loved Mick Jagger."[132] Despite the immensity of the crowd, several of the Angels were already familiar with Hunter. He was one of a tiny handful of African-Americans in a sea of white people and, at 6'2" and wearing a lime green suit, he was easy to spot. Fritsch had thrown him off the stage six times throughout the day. The fact that Hunter had a white girlfriend did not endear him to the swastika-wearing outlaws.

Hunter allegedly took his date's admiration of Jagger completely wrong. "This guy was a little high, I think," continues Carter. "He went out to his car, got this long barrel six-shot revolver and came down through the crowd saying, 'I'm going to kill Mick Jagger.' He actually pointed the gun at him and took a shot."[133]

It is highly unlikely that Meredith Hunter left the grounds in the darkness to retrieve a gun from his car amidst a crowd in excess of a quarter million people. There remains no question, however, that he did have a firearm on him, as dozens of people saw him fire a shot at the stage. The bullet whizzed past Jagger's head, though he never felt it. "My brother was up in the scaffolding with another cameraman and they saw the scuffle," recalls Albert Maysles. "They didn't know exactly what had happened...."[134] They swung their cameras around and began filming.

What the Maysles got was footage of several people swarming all over a staggering Meredith Hunter who has a pistol in one hand. A short Hell's Angel from Frisco named Allen Passaro* charges in with a large knife and stabs him as other Angels come rushing in to assist. Mick Jagger stops the band and announces that they're "splitting." An Angel informs him that "there's a guy with a gun out there."

The concert was over but most everyone in the huge crowd didn't know what happened until they saw the lifeless figure of Meredith Hunter being taken to the side of the stage. He'd been stabbed at least five times and severely beaten. "We got him into a bread truck we had," says Carter, "and brought him up to my office and we took all the security people to guard the office."[135] The

---

* Passaro had only recently been made a member of the Frisco Angels. He didn't own a motorcycle and, after being voted in, acquired a Harley by calling on a man who was selling one in the paper. He beat him unconscious and stole the bike.

police arrived later, arrested Passaro and took statements. They demanded to see the gun that Hunter had fired but it was gone.

The killing at Altamont made national news, with the press describing it as a murder; some reports even claimed Passaro had the gun and shot Hunter. Because the Hell's Angels were involved, the authorities handed down sweeping indictments on everyone who had been part of the concert. Attorney Melvin Belli contacted Carter and told him that unless he wanted to get charged as an accessory to murder, someone had to track down the gun. Carter located Sonny Barger at his Oakland house and went over to talk to him, somehow getting past two Dobermans that Barger owned to guard the place. He told Barger that Belli needed the gun for the good of everybody. Did he know where it was? Barger speculated that one or two of the Angels probably had it and that he'd try to track it down for him.

The next day, Barger phoned to say that he found the gun. Belli instructed him to wipe off all the fingerprints, put it in a cardboard box and mail it to his office. The recovery of the gun along with the Maysles' film footage of the killing was later introduced in court. Passaro was found not guilty and released. Several years later, his body was discovered floating in a ravine.

For years, the Hell's Angels have blamed the Rolling Stones for the Altamont debacle, claiming they were duped by the band to run interference for them and then were left to take the fall for Meredith Hunter's death. When the Maysles released their Rolling Stones concert film *Gimme Shelter*, the club tried to sue them for $1 million, claiming they were actors in the movie and, thus, should be paid as such. The brothers met with some of the Angels to settle the issue and barely escaped a beating.

More than three decades later, Altamont has hung on in memory as Dante's *Inferno*, where all the indulgences and transgressions of the sixties era were swiftly punished; the dark underside of Woodstock. This is odd considering that more people actually died at Woodstock. "The film *Woodstock* was somewhat deceptive," says Maysles, who attended that festival, too. "There were four people that died. There wasn't all the flower generation happiness that was reported in the film."[136]

Altamont is thought to have resulted in four violent deaths but Carter insists it is not true. "Two days after the concert," he says, "there was a kid that was walking along the canal down there, and a cop went after him. The kid jumped into the canal and he couldn't swim and . . . drowns. So that was a death. Then a couple days after that there were two fellas that had hitchhiked out here from Illinois. They were miles from the track and they were sleeping in their sleeping bags and some guy went off the road and ran over them. And so that's two more deaths. So they said we had four deaths at Altamont. We had one."[137]

If Hunter had survived his wounds or at least had not been filmed being stabbed, the concert would be little remembered today. But the image of a knife-wielding outlaw killing a gun-wielding hippie on film was seen as the perfect tragic ending to a long strange trip. But Altamont was only guilty of bad timing. The concert took place in the final month of 1969, making it a convenient door hook on which everyone could hang their disillusionment with the sixties. Less than ten years later, eleven concertgoers were trampled to death at a Who concert in Cincinnati, a tragedy that barely registers as a footnote.

The sixties did not die at Altamont. The big rock festivals continued, drugs were still bought and sold, and the Vietnam War dragged on. But everything was changing, as it had been for quite some time. If anything had ended, it was the counterculture's romance with motorcycle outlaws, and Altamont was the nail in the coffin of a relationship that had been deteriorating for quite some time. The Hell's Angels had been bullying their way into rock concerts for years, getting the flower children hooked on nasty drugs like speed, and raping errant runaway girls who were naïve enough to hook up with them. They were seen as mean fascists who had come into the garden and pissed all over the blossoms. For outlaw bikers, though, what happened at Altamont shouldn't have been a surprise to anyone. As one ex-Oakland Hell's Angel put it:

> The wishful thinkers assigned us as protectors of the flower people. We were supposed to be the counter-society's police force, a benevolent Gestapo which would, by our heavy presence, discourage alley-seasoned thugs from preying on the gentle people.... Those people had no idea what we were about.[138]

CHAPTER 11

Things Get Bloody

AS ANY FIRST-YEAR ECONOMICS STUDENT KNOWS, THE BEST WAY to take over a public company is to buy up as much of its stock as possible until you are a majority shareholder, then vote yourself in charge. Though popular opinion associates corporate raiding primarily with the 1980s and after, there was a wild frenzy of company mergers that occurred during the *laissez faire* sixties, expanding the profit base of business entities like TRW and Litton.

By late 1968, Harley-Davidson had been a public company for almost four years, after issuing 1.3 million shares of stock in order to raise operating capital. Their once powerful hold on the American motorcycle market had long been usurped by the Japanese and they were down to just 16 percent of domestic bike sales. Adding to Harley-Davidson's troubles was the fact that the English were starting to run more of their bikes off the racetracks.

For years, English motorcycle companies and their racing teams had accused the AMA of creating track rules that favored Harley-Davidson, who had always been a major contributor to the AMA. The controversy lay in the elemental differences between American and English engine design, specifically their compression ratios. Basically, an English vertical twin engine ran at higher compression (9.5:1) than an equivalent-sized Harley flathead engine (7.5:1). These differences were inherent to their design. Since the 1950s, the AMA had set limits on engine compression in racing competition and many English bikes were disqualified.

When more American racers started switching to Triumph, Matchless, and BSA, they were able to force an easing of the rules regarding compression, and the more maneuverable British bikes started mopping up the racing fields. The English hemorrhaged a lot of money in the following years on developing customized racing bikes that would beat Harley-Davidson racers, as if they were out to avenge their loss of the Colonies. Winning races always helps to sell motorcycles, but the heavy investment would cost the English dearly within the next ten years.

Meanwhile, Harley-Davidson's struggles had not gone unnoticed in the business world. The company received many offers from other corporations to buy it outright, including Chrysler and International Harvester. Though less profitable than it had been earlier, Harley-Davidson was soundly managed and had a fiercely loyal base of customers, several of whom either had a criminal record or looked like Sasquatch. The second generation Davidsons, who were running the company, declined the bids to sell.

But being a public company that was somewhat cash-poor, Harley-Davidson became vulnerable to a hostile takeover bid from anyone who wanted it badly enough. Bangor Punta, an East Coast-based firm with heavy investments in the railroad industry was one of the companies whose purchase offer had been rebuffed. They had recently bought the Waukesha Engine Company, who were right down the street from Harley-Davidson, and decided to set their sights on nabbing the intrepid motorcycle company.

Bangor Punta also had a notorious buy-and-chop policy that would've make Ivan Boesky proud; the firm was surely going to dismantle Harley-Davidson if they took control of it. Harley-

Davidson President William H. Davidson, son of company co-founder William A., and his board of directors watched in alarm as Bangor Punta started buying up Harley stock. They had to act quickly, and Davidson resumed talks with American Machinery and Foundry (AMF), who had also once made a purchase offer.

AMF was a conglomerate mostly invested in the industrial sector but whose name was more associated with sporting goods than anything else. Motorcycling, too, was a sport, so it didn't seem *that* awkward for Harley-Davidson to partner up with them. A deal with AMF would keep the company intact and supply a generous boost in the value of the stock. Davidson urged shareholders to vote for the merger and sell any outstanding stock to AMF. On January 7, 1969, Harley-Davidson was saved by officially merging with AMF.

The AMF/Harley-Davidson merger was a wise and prudent business decision but to the outlaw faithful, it was nothing short of heresy, like Bob Dylan going electric. "People today often talk about the AMF years," says Dave Nichols of *Easyriders* magazine. "This is when a company that makes sporting equipment, most notably bowling balls, was the primary owner of Harley-Davidson. It's sort of a dark area in the history of Harley."[139]

Yet despite that pessimism, sales soared: for the next ten years under the AMF banner, Harley-Davidson sold more motorcycles than they ever had before, even more than during the halcyon fifties following the demise of Indian. The company more than tripled their annual sales throughout the 1970s, a jump largely due to the parent AMF committing the ultimate blasphemy: running Harley-Davidson like Honda. The company known for its big, seventy-four-inch cruisers and dressers also started cranking out 350cc, 250cc, 175cc, 125cc, and 90cc model motorcycles by the thousands. They wanted to be both Asian *and* English at the same time. In 1977, AMF/Harley-Davidson even began producing the XLCR Café Racer with a 1000cc V-twin engine, a blatant attempt to mimic a limey crotch rocket. Though the XLCR was a powerful bike, it disappeared two years later. "The Code of the Customer philosophy started to deteriorate somewhat," Rosenblum admits diplomatically. "Quality started to go somewhat. There's no question about that."[140] It didn't take long for Harley loyalists to loudly declare AMF/Harley bikes to be junk.*

Though AMF/Harley-Davidson was selling more motorcycles, the profit margin was not up to the parent company's standards. They were also making a lot of models nobody wanted and the company's leadership was continually in flux. Six different men, two of them from the Davidson family, came and went as president of AMF/Harley-Davidson within a span of ten years. The 1974 oil crisis raised the cost of hauling drive trains and engines from Milwaukee to the assembly plant in York, Pennsylvania, adding to the already increased operating expenditures. By then, certain statements by AMF officers that showed up in annual corporate reports made it clear to everyone that AMF, disappointed by the profits being yielded, would eventually be selling off Harley-Davidson to someone else.

One must ask why none of the English motorcycle companies ever made an attempt to buy their biggest competitor. Though such a move would have increased their foothold in the United States, by this time it was fruitless. If Japanese ingenuity had caused Harley-Davidson to stumble, it wreaked havoc on the grand institution that once was the British motorcycle; by 1978, every manufacturer of them was out of business.

THE DECLINE AND FALL OF THE BRITISH MOTORCYCLE INDUSTRY REmains one of the more humiliating events in the history of trans-

---

* In retrospect, this viewpoint is seen as somewhat exaggerated.

portation. Since the turn of the century, the British had led much of the way in advancing motorcycle technology and design. Following World War II, there were nearly eighty different English manufacturers of motorcycles, with one of their supreme achievements being the Vincent Black Shadow, the fastest stock motorcycle in the world at the time. It was a 1,000cc bike that had the unusual distinction of having no frame; everything was bolted together and connected to the engine. Any nervy Brit could stroll into a Vincent dealership, randomly pick a model off the floor, and within minutes go screaming through the countryside at 120 mph, scaring the sheep. The early-to-mid 1960s was the zenith of the British bike, with Triumph, Norton, BSA, Matchless, Ariel, Royal Enfield, Sunbeam, and others resonating through the culture as symbols of English pride and resourcefulness.

They are all gone now, remembered mostly as fossilized curios with dripping crankcases. Harley at least could rely on the xenophobic loyalty of the American biker to see them through, but the riders of English bikes were more apt to ditch their leaky models and go buy a Honda or Kawasaki that they wouldn't have to screw around with.

The English companies had dumped so much money into trying to wax the competition on the racetrack that they didn't see how the Japanese were completely overwhelming them on the commercial front until it was too late. Suddenly Asian companies were producing bikes that were as fast or faster than the English machines, cost half as much, and always worked. When Triumph introduced their three cylinder 750cc Trident, Honda beat it to the punch with a 754cc bike that ran like a rocket and could be started with a push-button. The company even introduced disc brakes.

"The Japanese motorcycle industry did a superb job of cloning the best of the British look and feel," says Marty Rosenblum. "The

British motorcycle industry was getting erased right there in front of me during the sixties. By the mid-seventies, you couldn't find anybody to work on them, you couldn't find a good dealer, you couldn't do anything with the British bike anymore. I couldn't get my Norton to go around the block more than once."[141]

With the English gone, the domestic bike market was narrowed down to a tug-of-war between Harley-Davidson and Honda. When one considers that Honda produced an average of over three million units per year compared to AMF/Harley-Davidson's peak of seventy thousand, it looked like a one-sided competition. What's more, biker purists were refusing to buy the AMF/Harleys while the other customers who did were destined to ditch them later and go Asian. Who knew how long Harley-Davidson could hold out before they followed the English to the Museum of Obsolescence.

The Harley mystique, though, was being kept alive by something that the Japanese could never poach upon: the chopper. They weren't anything new; riders had been customizing their bikes for years since after-market parts virtually didn't exist. But after the popular success of *Easy Rider,* the elongated custom bikes became one of the hottest modes of transportation around. Literally everyone who owned a Harley had seen the film and left the theater mesmerized by Captain America's bike. The 1970s became the decade of the chopper, as thousands of bikers set about converting their banged-up piece of crap into one hip-looking motorcycle.

Choppers were all about excess. It took no small amount of arrogance to ride one, which was entirely the point. Early choppers were Frankenstein-like creations known as much for what they *didn't* have as for what they did, i.e., no front brake or rear suspension. The choice to "ride rigid," with nothing to cushion a rider from bumps on the road became a point of honor with many bikers (though some destroyed their spines after years of riding this way). Because of their futuristic appearance, many people erroneously assumed that choppers were performance machines, though bikers knew better. "There is no way in heck you can tell me that a chopper goes faster with an extended front fork," says Marty Rosenblum. "If you try and turn a corner you're going to end up on your head. Choppers are visual."[142]

While the outlaw faithful had always been able to weld some mutant creation together in a cousin's workshed, more and more bikers were looking for someone else to upgrade their machines. Two seventies-era pioneers who made their name customizing motorcycles were Ron Simms and Arlen Ness. "There's only a handful of people that really originated chopping motorcycles," says Dave Nichols. "In the early days, we had Ron Simms [and] Arlen Ness who chopped these bikes and they were just fabulous-looking. They started out as these young guys that were just tearing into these bikes and doing things no one had ever done with metal and fabricating."[143]

Though both men are still legends in the craft of custom-building choppers, the two could not have been less alike. Simms was a stoic sort who wore sunglasses indoors while Ness was more outgoing with silvery hair and a goatee. Simms' bikes appealed primarily to hardcore types who favored long gleaming outlaw rigs with Hieronymous Bosch depictions of beasts, devils, and grinning skulls on the gas tanks. Ness built wildly baroque creations that ran the design gamut from Bauhaus to the *Alien* movies. Later, he started making custom-designed cruisers whose parts and accessories were individually selected from his catalogs by the customer. Ness still steadfastly refuses any requests from clients to paint skulls on his bikes and usually refers them to Simms.

"Whoever the first guy was actually to come out with the extended front ends, I'm not sure of," says Simms. "You know, most of the stuff that happened with the custom bikes actually started around the San Francisco Bay area."[144]

The long-forked chopper craze lasted throughout most of the seventies before subsiding later, to be replaced by more subtle and sensible forms of customizing. What forced their decline was the limitations to being excessive. "Everybody kind of did what their friend did," says Ness. "They wanted to be so different but everybody's bike ended up looking pretty much alike."[145]

AS MOTORCYCLES BECAME MORE OSTENTATIOUS, OUTLAW BIKER CULture started to fracture. The fallout from Altamont and their declining reputation in the Bay area served to prove a point about the Hell's Angels that Hunter Thompson had stated years earlier: "They are *mean* fuckers." Their one-percenter novelty had worn off, and more and more motorcyclists just wished they'd go away. Outlaws were giving their sport a black eye and kept showing up at venues where they were not welcome, occasionally bringing their beefs with them. Such was the case in Cleveland on May 6, 1971.

The Fourth Annual Motorcycle Custom and Trade Show was being held for the third year in a row at the Polish Women's Hall, sponsored by the AMA-chartered Cleveland Competition Club. The event had taken place without incident in the preceding years but this time the atmosphere was different. Three months earlier, an outlaw biker had marched into a seedy Cleveland tavern, stepped behind the bar and spray-painted on the wall, in letters two-feet high: BREED—H.A. STOMPERS. The stompers in question were an upstart outlaw club from the eastern seaboard called the Breed, with a total membership of around two hundred. They had recently expanded into parts of the Midwest, including Cleveland, and were bent on squashing the city's local Hell's Angels chapter.

Shortly after the tagging, a dozen Breed members had entered another bar called the Golden Nugget where an equal number of Hell's Angels were hanging out. Within seconds, a full-scale brawl erupted and the Breed out-slugged the Angels, leaving them in a groaning mess on the floor. Puffed with pride, the Breed decided they were ready to vanquish their rivals. Unfortunately, none of the Breed members could keep their mouths shut about their *coup d'etat* plans for the Angels and everybody from the mayor's office on down got wind of an impending war between the two clubs.

At the Polish Women's Hall, a battalion of law enforcement was guarding the entrances. Every Hell's Angel member who tried to enter the hall was immediately made to surrender anything that resembled a weapon to security. An arsenal of chains, walking sticks, and hunting knives was confiscated. The Angels, though, were not searched for concealed weapons. At around 10 P.M., an army of an estimated 150 Breeds rolled up in front of the hall, riding in pickup trucks, overstuffed jalopies, and, fittingly, a hearse. They piled out and headed for the door. Security made them check their bike chains and walking sticks although, like the Angels, none of them were searched for concealed weapons.

The Breeds marched two abreast in a long column into the large hall and started lining up against one wall. Around two dozen Hell's Angels were congregating in front of a stage where a cover band called the Innovators was playing Stax songs. The Angels silently watched the Breed congregate around the room. Other show attendees paid little attention to what was happening and continued walking the floor. The Breed encircled the smaller pack, preparing to waylay them; the Angels were outnumbered six to one. Word had gotten out over the wire and 150 policemen converged on the hall.

In a matter of minutes it was over. Someone was heard yelling, "It's on!" and a battle erupted. The Angels blunted the impending attack by striking first, charging in with knives and slashing away like mad reapers. Many of the Breeds were expecting a fistfight and had no weapons on them. Panic ensued and bystanders fled the hall in terror. The police who were outside heard the melee and charged in to break it up. Cops and outlaws slipped on the pools of blood that gathered on the floor. Shrieks of pain filled the room as knife blades cut holes in limbs and thoraxes. A blinding cloud of teargas filled the room as mass arrests were made.

Five bikers died in the brawl, including four Breed members, and more than twenty were injured. It was, to date, the worst biker gang fight in history.

Outlaw mystique was gradually being eclipsed by the grim realities that can overwhelm the life of a one-percenter. In October 1972, the day before Halloween, around three dozen sheriff's deputies and other law enforcement officials served an arrest warrant on an outlaw biker named George Wethern who resided in Ukiah, California. A former Hell's Angel, Wethern lived in a secluded redwood house on several acres of hilly ranch land with his wife Helen and two children. After arresting the couple, the authorities made a thorough search of his home and uncovered narcotics and several weapons.

During their interrogation, investigators confronted Wethern with the accusation that there was likely more than just contraband hidden away on his ranch property. After hours of repeated denials, Wethern finally sighed, "I'll show you the wells."

"Baby Huey" Wethern was a 280-pound behemoth who had helped form the Hell's Angels' Oakland chapter in 1957 and became their vice president before quitting four years later. When the Angels became big news following the Lynch report, Wethern rejoined the club in 1966 and began orchestrating LSD sales in Haight-Ashbury with the help of three reticent hippies named Chuck, Chuckie, and Steve. The airy trio had floated in from across the Bay into Oakland one day looking to buy LSD. Wethern scored them eight thousand tabs of Owsley acid for eight thousand dollars and, a week later, they returned for more. For the remainder of the 1960s, Wethern ran a psychedelic industry, raking in over $150,000 a year while piecing off the action to other Angels. Competitors were dealt with promptly. He would go to their residences with a couple of Angels in tow, kick in the door, and tell the rival dealers they either work for him or he would blow their brains out. He punctuated his threat by shooting a .45 an inch away from their ears. Drugs were not a part of some cosmic ritual; they were a business.

By 1969, Wethern was a very wealthy outlaw and a jittery mess, dealing more and more in methamphetamine and PCP. He was taking both drugs by the handful and his personality became more erratic and paranoid. One night at his Ukiah home, he went into a rage with one of his partners, an Angel named Zorro, over a financial dispute and blew seven holes into Zorro's chest and abdomen with his .45. Zorro somehow remained alive and Wethern was lucid enough to rush the man to the hospital for treatment. While waiting in the lobby, Wethern saw police officers slowly surrounding him and he attacked. The cops maced the outlaw and took him to jail, where he was charged with, among other things, attempted murder. Police waited for word from the hospital to see when they could upgrade the charge to homicide. Miraculously, Zorro survived his wounds, emerging from the hospital half-crippled and with a limp arm. Wethern plead down to misdemeanor assault and received a 180-day suspended sentence.

The shooting of Zorro might have gotten Wethern killed by the Angels but instead he was allowed to resign for a second time; too many members were making their living working for him. He continued dealing drugs and stayed in contact with the club. Then one day in 1970, a chapter president came to Wethern's front door with a grim request: he needed to use the ranch property to dispose of a body. A twenty-six-year-old woman named Patricia McKnight who had been hanging around the Angels for months had committed suicide at one of their parties. She had just endured a gang rape while tripping on drugs but Terry the Tramp pushed her over the edge with one of his sadistic mind games and she shot herself in the head. Wethern reluctantly complied with the request and the girl's body was buried in an empty well hole.

One year later, the limping Zorro arrived on Wethern's doorstep with more news. Two outlaw bikers from Georgia named Tom Schull and Charlie Baker, itching to become Angel prospects, had gone to a party being held by the Richmond chapter. Hours later, they were both dead, one from a forced overdose, the other via strangulation. Wethern again volunteered another well hole to dispose of the bodies, though it made him more paranoid than ever.

The senseless murders of the two Georgia bikers split the Richmond chapter in half. Some members were sickened by the killings and panicked. One Richmond Angel named "Whispering Bill" Pifer suspected he was about to be eliminated for witnessing the murders and turned himself into the authorities, requesting protection in exchange for his testimony. The information supplied by Pifer brought the law to Wethern's doorstep.

Wethern numbly took the authorities back out to his ranch and pointed at a couple clumps of grass. A backhoe excavated the remains of three decomposed bodies. Later, as he sat in an interrogation room back at the station, Wethern requested a notebook tablet and a couple of pencils so he could write out his confession. After receiving the materials, Wethern suddenly rammed the sharpened pencil tips straight into both eye sockets, in a grisly attempt to pierce his brain and commit suicide. He was rushed to the hospital where he ended up strapped to a bed, preventing him from removing his bandage dressings. His eyeballs somehow healed enough to where Wethern regained his sight. He eventually testified against the club and entered the Witness Protection Program.

As THE YOUNGER OUTLAWS FELL DEEPER INTO CRIME AND NARCOTICS, their elders had either retired or were dying off. Nineteen seventy-one saw the passing of two originals: Boozefighter co-founder Robert "Dink" Burns and rock 'n' roll rebel Gene Vincent, both profoundly unhappy men who never stopped battling the demons that tormented them.

Gene was living in a cheap apartment in West Los Angeles, bloated and ashen. He had not eaten in three days and had spent his last seventy-two hours drinking. His bad leg bled all the time and kept developing infections; alcohol only numbed the pain. The last few years of Gene's life had been one long downhill slide. Both bad management and three failed marriages left him totally broke, and his house had been seized by the government for unpaid back taxes. His music was no longer being played anywhere and he could not even get gigs on "oldies" shows. The rock 'n' roll maverick, whose whole act had been ripped off by countless performers, was dismissed as a one-hit wonder whose time in the sun had passed a decade earlier.

Gene collapsed, vomiting blood, as he began hemorrhaging internally. He did not try to fight; more than anything, he just wanted to die. His wife and mother found him later. He expired with a slight smile on his lips. Gene Vincent was only thirty-six years old.

Across town, in Norwalk, Dink Burns had spent most of his years after the war driving a truck and riding when he could. But he was unable to stop drinking, fighting, or being angry. He never recovered from the loss of his legs while still a teenager and his bitterness stayed with him ever since. As Forkner said, "The guy was always pissed at the world."[146]

One morning, Dink's wife awoke to find him outside in their driveway, slumped over in the front seat of his car. He had gone out drinking the night before and somehow made it home before passing out behind the wheel. The years of drinking had caused his insides to collapse. Dink Burns was dead at the age of forty-seven.

Part III

Trash:
An Outlaw's Tale

Chapter 12

The Young Soldier

Gulf of Tonkin resolution—(1964) A Congressional resolution authorizing military action in Southeast Asia.

RON HALEY WAS IN THIRD GRADE IN THE EARLY 1950S WHEN HIS family moved to Ukiah, a town of three thousand people two hours north of San Francisco. He was the middle of nine children born to an abusive man, "a nasty sonofabitch," who his mother kicked out so they could all get some peace. The family was on welfare, but once the father was gone, they managed to organize their finances enough to get a phone and a black and white television.

Ron grew to be a muscular youth with dark straight hair and white corn-fed teeth, excelling in sports but never trying out for any of the school teams. At age sixteen he was working after school at the Erickson-Ford Box Company, making redwood planters, and saved up enough money to buy a used 1947 Harley with a sixty-one cubic-inch knuckle-head engine. He knew little about the bike until a year later, when the Hell's Angels rode through Ukiah during a run, shortly after the 1964 Monterey rape case. Ron rode into the middle of the pack and followed it for miles until a couple of Angels pulled over to the side of the road. Ron parked alongside and proudly showed them how he had a bike just like theirs. The Angels asked him why he kept "all that garbage" on it, indicating the saddlebags and fenders. Within minutes, the outlaws broke out tools and stripped everything off the bike that didn't make it run, dumping it in a pile on the side of the road. "Then I had a chopper," Ron says.

A loner by nature, Ron rode his Harley to high school every day. After graduating in 1964, he took a hard look at what his options were. He had his menial job at the box company, and the bike had a blown oil ring. Ron decided on his best course of action: he would move to Hawaii and become a gigolo. "I wanted to go there and live off of women," he says.

Ron flew from San Francisco to Oahu with $250 in savings, checked into a YMCA, and started hitting the tourist bars and nightclubs on Ala Moana Drive in Honolulu to meet rich older women. (Though he was only seventeen years old, Ron passed for much older so nobody ever carded him.) But Ala Moana Drive was an expensive commercial strip for the tourist trade and the bars had high-priced drink minimums. Within two weeks of his arrival, Ron was broke.

Unable to afford his room at the Y, Ron moved out and began living on the beach. "I was eating coconuts off of trees," he recalls. "Tried to find some odd jobs but no one would hire me." He was contemplating turning to crime when a man from the YMCA tracked him down at his beach squat and offered to buy him a plane ticket back to the mainland. Ron readily agreed and asked for the money but the man refused. He took him to the airport, bought the ticket there, and watched Ron get on the plane.

Ron flew back to California and returned to Ukiah, where he hung out around the house unwilling to go back to his job at the box company. After a few weeks, his mother told him she couldn't afford to feed him and suggested he go find something to do with himself. He decided to enlist in the army.

In July 1964, after signing up as "RA-Unassigned" (which meant he didn't care where he went or what he did), Ron was sent to Fort Ord to complete his basic training. His test scores indicated an aptitude for clerical work, and he was assigned to a Los Angeles recruiting station for seven months as an administration specialist. While on the phone with his mother one day, Ron learned someone was offering $150 to buy his crippled knucklehead. "I told her, 'Sell the damned thing. That's good money.'" The bike was sold.

Ron was transferred to a base in Germany in April 1965, as the war in Vietnam began heating up. Germany was just as slow as Los Angeles, so Ron requested a transfer to Saigon where all the action was. He was quickly reassigned to Army Headquarters, First Infantry Division, under the command of Major General William DePuy, a short, reckless cowboy who was under the delusion that the war in Asia would be over in a few months. Ron went through six different jobs in three weeks at the base, all of them involving typing. While working as a company clerk for the motor pool, he marched into his C.O.'s office and rashly told him he was tired of typing statistics. "I wanna *make* statistics," he said. Ron requested a transfer to field duty and produced a report on a company that had suffered heavy casualties and needed men.

The C.O. glanced at the report and shook his head. It was Charlie Company, part of the Second Battalion, Sixteenth Infantry Regiment. "They're a Ranger outfit," he told Ron, "and you're not qualified." Ron kept persisting, until the officer gave in and agreed to his request. "You aren't gonna live through it," the C.O warned him as he signed the transfer papers.

Charlie Company was not technically a Ranger outfit, though most of its members wore Ranger patches, making them the most aggressively trained infantrymen in the U.S. Armed Forces. To be an Army Ranger, one had to have a fatalistic view of life and war. They were like coal mine canaries, sent in to sweep hostile territory first, engage the enemy, and knock out defensive positions. Rangers were chosen from the Army's infantry and airborne divisions and the competition to qualify for a patch was fierce; men died during training.

Ron had done little but type for the past fourteen months and had not handled a weapon since basic training. But he was sent off to join Charlie Company who was out patrolling the jungle-infested area near Xa Binh Gia east of Saigon. "They asked me what kind of weapon I wanted," Ron says. "I told them, 'Give me the biggest weapon you got.'" He was issued a forbidding M-60, an air-cooled .50 machine gun that weighed nearly eighty pounds, and made a platoon leader in a company of 150 combat veterans. He was nineteen years old.

In the spring of 1966, Charlie Company was moving through the jungle and engaging in firefights with stray Vietcong (VCA) patrols. The company was carrying out Operation Abilene, its primary mission being to track down D-800, a massive VCA battalion thought to be hiding somewhere in the heavy thicket. The operation consisted of little more than marching around and strafing the vegetation, hoping to hit something.

On Easter Sunday, Charlie Company stood in a clearing near the village of Xa Cam My as a visiting Protestant chaplain held Easter services for the men. "Think of your loved ones back home," the chaplain told them. "They will be going to church on Easter and praying for you." The chaplain's benediction was interrupted by the sight of three VCA scouts in black pajamas crossing the other side of the clearing four hundred yards away, near the Courtenay rubber plantation. Charlie Company unloaded on them and hit two; the third scout disappeared into the jungle. A first lieutenant got a dying confession out of one of the wounded scouts by twisting his testicles: D-800 was nearby.

The information was relayed back to First Division headquarters and within hours, a Huey helicopter flew into the field just before dusk, dropping off Major General DePuy. Now was the time, he told Charlie Company. They were going into the jungle tomorrow morning to draw out D-800. "What they wanted everybody to do," Ron says, "was to make as much noise as they could. We were told [D-800] was not going to engage a smaller unit. They'd only engage battalion size or bigger." Once D-800 was lured into the open, reinforcements were standing by and they would be slammed.

The next morning, Charlie Company set out to draw D-800 into an attack, and tromped through the jungle like drunk Shriners. They stepped on fallen branches, rustled palm leaves, and talked loudly. Ron marched with First Platoon all morning, the M-60 balanced on his shoulder like a battleaxe. They moved through the plantation, and then, around noon, Fourth Platoon was fired upon. Charlie Company dug in and fired back into the jungle. They could see that several of the enemy were dressed in the khaki uniforms of the North Vietnamese Army (NVA). D-800 was much larger than anticipated.

D-800 had been listening to Charlie Company crashing through the bush for hours, and encircled them like a noose. They opened up with withering fire. Third Platoon called in an artillery strike and a barrage of 105mm shells came screaming in but fell short. Ron was knocked over by an artillery blast that nearly shattered his eardrums. Several members of Charlie Company were blown to bits by friendly fire. Enemy mortars thumped all around them. Nobody knew who was firing at whom.

Charlie Company was trapped in a bowl-shaped area surrounded by thick overhanging tree foliage. There was no way helicopters could come in with supplies. Several soldiers frantically tried to chainsaw through the thick jungle cover for helicopters to come through. D-800 came out of the jungle and launched another attack. Vietnamese officers with bullhorns were barking out orders to VCA snipers up in the trees. They fired down on the disoriented Charlie Company, cutting down men left and right. Ron dug into an artillery hole and raked the VCA firing line with his M-60, his ears numb from the shell blast.

By nightfall, D-800 pulled back into the bush, as scores of wounded men lay in the field, screaming in agony. Medics, having long run out of morphine, bandages, and medical supplies, could do nothing to help them. Scavenging patrols of Vietcong women and children crept out of the jungle with lit candles to pilfer guns and ammunition from the dead; wounded GIs who tried feigning death were executed with their own weapons. The patrols stole what they could and vanished back into the thicket. Ron lay off in the bush, listening to the anguished cries all around him and waited for another assault wave to come. Then something happened to him:

> Late in the night, when the fighting had been over for a while, I suddenly found myself pulled into a sphere of warm, bright light. I was in a place where I felt at peace. Totally at peace. There wasn't anyone else in that light that I could see, no relatives, no winged beings. There were many other points of light in the distance, sort of like at the end of a tunnel. There were no feelings of this being a religious moment, but of a step toward a new level of existence, a new beginning. A warm, welcome exciting new place that we were all meant to go to. Also, I had another strong feeling. I felt that everyone who dies goes to where I was going, except suicides. I had the strong feeling, a mental image, that suicide would prevent me from going with the light.

> I don't know how long this trip lasted, but I suddenly
> found myself back where I was, laying in the dark and quiet
> of a bloody battlefield....

The promised reinforcements never came. Second Battalion's Bravo Company was too far from the firefight and could not get to the combat perimeter in time. As the sun rose on the morning of April 12, Bravo Company came upon the battle area to find over one hundred dead and wounded members of Charlie Company sprawled everywhere. Huge black flies swarmed around the corpses bloating in the morning heat while most of the survivors lay on the ground crying uncontrollably. More helicopters finally arrived, hovering overhead but unable to land. Medics and para-rescue men lowered themselves to the ground from dangling cables to attend to the wounded.

Television news crews got wind of the battle and swarmed into the plantation with cameras rolling. Several soldiers screamed at them to stop filming their dead comrades. Major General DePuy arrived and was berated by an outraged lieutenant who accused him of using them for bait. DePuy, who saw the carnage around him, did not reprimand the officer for insubordination.

Charlie Company suffered an appalling 80 percent casualty rate during the Courtenay Plantation battle. Ron was one of just twenty-eight men who had survived the battle. The next day, he and the others stood in a daze as General Westmoreland personally congratulated them for their valor and issued field citations. The company was quickly re-supplied with members from other units and returned to their routine, slogging through the jungle looking for the VCA and engaging in brief skirmishes.

Ron spent five more months in the field until his year of combat duty ended in November 1966. He was rotated out and sent to Fort Carson, Colorado, to serve out his last seven months of service. Fort Carson was an enormous base that mainly served as a way station for Army personnel awaiting discharge; there were thousands of men stationed there with nothing to do. To keep them busy, base commanders ordered Ron and everybody else below the rank of sergeant to stand shoulder to shoulder and walk the entire sixteen-mile length of the base, picking up trash and cigarette butts.

Fort Carson was an intolerable bore. Ron got caught with a forged pass and busted down to E-2, his rank during basic training. He also missed a bed check and later went AWOL for three days. His surly attitude around the base had been duly noted and the Army saw an opportunity to get one more man out of the overflowing base. An Army psychiatrist ruled that Ron had "showed a lack of responsibility resulting in poor conduct and efficiency. He has failed to meet the required standards of the Army, as evidenced by his past record of conduct in this unit." Because of his combat service, Ron was given a General Discharge Under Honorable Conditions. "It's the same thing they give if you get your leg blown off," he says. "Except mine was a medical discharge for character and behavior disorders."

RON HAD TEN CENTS IN HIS POCKET WHEN HE WAS DISCHARGED IN June 1967. He hitchhiked to Ukiah and got back his old job at Erickson-Ford making redwood planter boxes. He started to drink heavily, and stayed drunk much of the time, even coming to work inebriated. Then one morning Ron came to work completely sober. His behavior was so different than usual that the foreman accused him of being drunk and fired him.

Ron decided Ukiah left nothing for him and hitchhiked east. He moved around until settling in Biloxi, Mississippi, where he landed a job putting up Super Slides, the giant slides found at water parks. After a few months, he was able to put a roll of cash together, and bought himself another motorcycle. It was a '56 Harley Panhead that cost him three hundred dollars. Not long afterward, he was riding on a street in Gretna, Louisiana, near New Orleans, where he was doing a Super Slide job when a car ran a red light and clipped the Harley's back wheel. Ron flew through the air and crashed into a fire hydrant, ending up in the hospital with a badly injured foot.

By coincidence, Ron's brother Utah came to Gretna two days later on a visit, and found him lying in the hospital with a huge cast the size of a football on his right ankle. While Ron recuperated, Utah fixed the panhead and got it running again. After his release from the hospital, Ron went on unemployment and met a girl named Cricket, who was dancing topless in a strip club in the French Quarter of New Orleans, and they hooked up. Cricket soon moved in with the two brothers. When he was able to get around without the need of crutches, Ron noticed how expensive New Orleans could be and suggested they all return to Biloxi and party with the seven hundred dollars Ron got as a settlement from the accident.

In 1968, Biloxi was a fledgling resort town mostly known for shrimp, Civil War memorabilia, and being the birthplace of Elvis. Ron, Utah, and Cricket settled in an apartment that was just down the road from Keesler Air Force Base. Cricket continued dancing in strip clubs while Ron and Utah picked up the occasional odd job. They worked on shrimp boats and did security at bars, all the while collecting $123 a week in unemployment. Since Ron was still hobbling around on a walking cast, he carried around a .22 High Standard automatic for protection.

The two brothers decided to start raising hell and felt they needed nicknames. There weren't many motorcycles in Biloxi and the panhead had already established them as bikers. "My older brother always used to call me Trash when I was a little

kid," Ron recalls. "So I decided that Trash was my name."
Utah's new moniker would be equally inglorious. Lacking a
toothbrush, he realized that he had not brushed his teeth for
three weeks, and felt like he had trench mouth. The alliteration
was too much for the brothers to ignore and Utah was quickly
dubbed "Trench."

Keesler was full of bored airmen who were always looking for
parties where they could drink and cut loose. Trash had gotten
to know several of them and one day, an airman asked him if
he knew where there were any parties going on. Trash facetiously told him "Oh, down by the beach. Nine o'clock." Later
that evening, Trash and Trench were riding the Harley along
East Beach Boulevard when they came upon a huge party going
on by the water's edge. The brothers stood dumbfounded as various airmen staggered up with beers in their hands, thanking
them for arranging the party. "They came down there and
started the party," Trash says. "And they all thought we did it."
The two brothers ate and drank for free all night while getting
most of the credit.

The impromptu beach parties grew in popularity and became
so notorious that both the Biloxi police and Keesler base officials
vowed to shut them down. One night during a beach gathering,
Trash and Trench were sitting in the bed of a pickup when a car-
load of teenagers drove by and one of them heaved a bottle that
smashed against the side of the truck. The two took off after
them on their motorcycle. They pulled up close enough for Trash
to empty his .22 into the truck's rear wheels, blowing them out.
The police arrived and the brothers were quickly arrested.

To the local judiciary, Trash and Trench looked like errant California hippie scum who never bothered to get a job. They were
also the ones responsible for the wild beach parties that were
corrupting their local Air Force personnel. The gun charges were

dropped but both were charged with vagrancy. During his trial, Trash told the judge he could not possibly be a vagrant. "I'm collecting more in unemployment," he said, "than you make wearing that fucking judge's robe."

Both Trash and Trench were found guilty of vagrancy and sentenced to fifteen and thirty days, respectively, in the county jail (Trash was given less time due to his Vietnam service). After two weeks, Trash was released and then informed that his brother could get out early, too, on one condition. "You guys get the fuck outta the state," they told him. "Go back to California. You're raising too much hell here."

TRASH, TRENCH, AND CRICKET SETTLED IN VAN NUYS, A CITY ON THE western end of the San Fernando Valley. Their house was on Nordhoff Street, just off of Van Nuys Boulevard, the Sunset Strip of the Valley in 1970, where handfuls of speed were available at every intersection.

"Everyone fucking had them," says Trash. "Reds, bennies, white crosses; Van Nuys Boulevard was a cruising boulevard. They had Wednesday Cruise Night. You'd go all the way north to the Arby's, then you'd turn around and go down towards the Ventura Freeway."

Trash bought himself a '66 Harley FL model with no heads on the engine and a '56 Ford pickup truck. He made his living dealing in secondhand bike parts. When he got down to his last five hundred dollars, he would drive out east to buy used Harley parts, which went for a song in places like Oklahoma, Ohio, and parts of the mid-Atlantic and Deep South. "I figured there'd be two hundred dollars in travel expenses and three hundred to buy parts with," he says. "We did that a half dozen times." Motor cases were the most valuable, since an entirely different bike could be created. "If you had a set of motor cases, that was all you needed," says Trash. "Go steal a bike, put those cases into it, and it was your bike." Trash sold used cases to two outlaw bikers named Crazy and Slave. For every set of cases they bought from him, a bike was stolen somewhere in the Valley that night.

Trash had no idea how many of the parts he was buying were legit, so he struck up a friendship with a CHP officer named Don, who was in charge of motorcycle thefts. Whenever Trash came back with a load of parts, he would call Don up and give him the numbers. If the parts were reported stolen, Trash turned them over and Don got a feather in his cap for recovering stolen parts. In exchange, Trash knew which of his parts weren't hot, so he could get a better price for them.

Trash's spare parts business put him in touch with many outlaw bikers, one of them a jaded ex-Navy man named Brother Hank. He and Trash were introduced by a mutual friend at a party and the two spent the next week sizing each other up. The pressure built until finally Trash couldn't stand it anymore. He called Brother Hank out, challenging him to arm wrestling. Brother Hank accepted and they grappled for an hour straight to a dead heat. The two stayed friends ever since. (Years later, Trash asked Brother Hank what he would have done if he had been challenged to a fight. "Aw hell, I woulda shot you," Brother Hank told him. "I wasn't gonna fuck with you.")

Any money that was earned went right back out again. Life was all about pushing the envelope. Trash and his brother usually started drinking as soon as the sun came up, beginning with a pint of Jim Beam and a case of sixteen-ounce Olympia beer at nine in the morning. On other days, they went down to the Oasis bar on Victory Boulevard and spent the entire day hustling pool games for beer; they rarely lost. "By the time night came, we had twenty, thirty beers stashed behind the bar that we'd won playing pool. And we'd drink those the rest of the night."

THE 1974 GAS CRISIS PUT AN END TO TRASH'S EXCURSIONS OUT EAST to scrounge Harley parts. Needing to make money, Trash set about becoming a motorcycle mechanic. It was a trade he knew surprisingly little about but he was confident that he had the aptitude to learn mechanical work, as he once almost became a member of MENSA. Trash had sent off for the official MENSA application exam and once it arrived, he loaded up on speed and whipped through the hour-long test in fifteen minutes while cranked out of his mind. He tested a 138 I.Q., two points shy of the minimum allowed for acceptance. MENSA invited him to take a third test under monitored supervision, but he declined.

Trash had just finished teaching himself Harley mechanics when a motorcycle repair place called the Hog Shop in Ventura went out of business. It had been owned by a biker named Big Jim, who was something of a legend for his custom work on motorcycles. During the late 1960s, he once designed a custom Harley chopper that featured a raised engine frame and a "fat bob" rear fender. The chopper was featured in several biker magazines and became so famous that the prior owner of the Hog Shop traded the entire business to Big Jim in exchange for the bike itself. The owner subsequently got the patent rights to the bike, and made a fortune selling clones of it overseas in Japan. Big Jim, however, was unable to make a go of the Hog Shop and made Trash an offer: Trash could have everything that was inside the shop if he gave him his pickup. Trash accepted and ended up with six tons of Harley parts.

Cricket was gone by this time. Trash had made a pledge to her that if she ever got pregnant, he would take care of her until the child was done nursing, then leave. "I'm too much like my old man," he told her. "Mean, tough, fucking up people in a bar." As fate would have it, Cricket did conceive a child and firmly stated that she would not terminate the pregnancy; the choice of whether he would stay or not was up to him. Trash went off behind the house where a creek ran through the property. "I sat out in that creek for two or three days, trying to decide if I was gonna go back." He left and Cricket had the baby, a boy named Cole, after the Old West outlaw Cole Younger. Trash floated her money and after a few months, she moved to Oklahoma.

After Cricket left, Trash and his brother went to a party where they met a slim girl in her twenties named Cheri. Trash finished the evening by beating up two bikers before he and Trench took her back to their house, where she promptly moved in. When her boyfriend tracked her down a week later and came by to drag her home, Trash pummeled him and chased him off, too. She began dating Trench first, but because he liked to rise earlier in the morning than she did, Cheri soon turned her attention toward Trash.

Trench eventually left the Valley to return to Ukiah and the couple moved to a rented house on Runnymeade Street. It had a small empty cottage in the backyard where Trash set up his repair shop. He continued living the outlaw life, partying, working on bikes, and taking speed, having first been exposed to the drug during his tour of duty in Vietnam. "If you were on ambush patrols, you were issued cross tops. I didn't relate it to something you could buy on the street. I thought it was a military secret." Since his discharge, Trash's intake of speed had never gone much beyond the occasional score on Van Nuys Boulevard during Wednesday Cruise Night, but that all changed in 1976.

A German speed suddenly showed up on the street. It was a pure snowy white powder, with no lumps, that sent its users into the stratosphere without the usual side effects. Nobody knew where this Teutonic dust came from, but it suddenly became highly coveted and everyone was scrambling to score some. "It was around for a couple years," Trash recalls. "Then just dropped out all of a sudden one day."

Having gotten spoiled by the now-vanished German speed, he decided to put his scholastic knowledge of chemistry to practical use and, in 1978, he began manufacturing his own methamphetamine.

CHAPTER 13

Top Speed

"THE ONE THING ABOUT ANY BIKERS YOU SEE, UNLESS IT'S SOME crashed fucker," Trash says, "is they like to have fun. More than anything else, if they have the chance of building an empire here, or having a good day's fun over here, they're gonna go have fun. The only drug I've ever done is speed."

Trash set up a lab inside the cottage in his backyard where he repaired motorcycles, and went to work. Setting the purity bar high, he started mixing metallic sodium and ethyl alcohol absolute-anhydrous to make his own phenyl-2-propanon (P-2-P), a hard to find chemical that, when combined with methylamine and other chemicals, produces wicked speed.* "I'd have the doors locked and a sign out front that said 'Gone Fishing.' All my friends knew if they saw the sign not to knock on the door." Within days of get-

---

* In recent years, more common manufacturing methods involved the reaction of pressurized hydrogen or red phosphorous with ephedrine, a stimulant found in many cold medications. For years, pure ephedrine tablets, or "white crosses," were available at the neighborhood pharmacy where anyone could buy huge jars of them at $150 a pound. This went on as late as 1993, until state governments severely restricted their sales. Now, meth cookers extract ephedrine (or its cousin pseudoephedrine) from over-the-counter medications using heat or chemical reduction. All they do is go to the store and buy up every box of Sudafed they can find on the shelves.

ting started, Trash knocked over a twelve-liter jug of alcohol while cooking a batch of speed and burned the cottage down.

He laid low for several weeks until his landlord, who had no idea what Trash was doing, shrugged it off and let him and Cheri stay. He resumed mixing and cooking in his house and was soon turning out speed by the pound. His place became a regular hangout for biker parties and he got to know most of the outlaw clubs based in the area, particularly the Diablos. A few of them invited Trash to prospect for a membership but he declined. He'd had enough of regimentation from being in the Army, and he didn't trust just anybody who happened to own a stripped-down Harley. A lot of outlaws were flakes and losers with severe drug habits. One was a Diablo named Ratso.

Ratso was an unbalanced kleptomaniac who had a morbid fascination with explosives. One evening during a New Year's Eve party at his house, Trash went outside to his backyard and found Ratso kneeling on the ground about to set a match to a bomb he'd made from a tape-wrapped toilet paper roll stuffed with gunpowder. The bomb had no fuse, though, only a short trail of powder leading up to it. Trash quickly knocked the lighter out of his hand, yelling that the bomb would go off in his face. Ratso demanded that Trash show him how to construct a fuse, or else he was going to light it off, anyway. Trash relented and demonstrated a Rube Goldberg method using a lit cigarette. The crude bomb went off and nearly blew out the windows in Trash's house.

Excited about his newfound expertise, Ratso spent the next several weeks detonating bombs all over the Valley. Even worse, he was openly giving Trash due credit for apprenticing him. Eventually, a sergeant-at-arms for the Diablos showed up on Trash's doorstep, berating him for teaching Ratso how to make explosives. "That crazy fucker is gonna get us all in trouble!" he bellowed. "You gotta do something."

A little while later, Trash was throwing another party at his house when he called Ratso over and told him to guard the bathroom door; he was going inside to make a bomb so he could scare everyone. It's a secret, he told Ratso, so don't come in. Trash went into the bathroom and laid out hydrogen peroxide, nail polish, polish remover, and other cosmetics on the counter, as well as some toilet paper torn into little squares. He waited a few minutes and Ratso suddenly barged in. His eyes lit up when he saw the materials on display. Trash feigned panic, warning him not to fool with this kind of stuff, that it could be deadly. He ordered Ratso out of the bathroom, put everything away, and lit off an M-80 firecracker. The explosion shook the house and impressed Ratso no end.

In the following weeks, women began noticing that their cosmetics were disappearing from their bathrooms. Bottles of hydrogen peroxide vanished from medicine cabinets like planes in the Bermuda Triangle. In some homes, entire medicine cabinets even turned up missing. It was now apparent that Ratso was trying to build the largest Charmin-and-Maybelline bomb ever assembled. It never worked. Frustrated and reeking of acetone, Ratso would ride over to Trash's house and ask for help. Trash drew up diagrams showing the plutonium core to an A-bomb while explaining the principles of nuclear fission. Ratso kept on trying to blow up his cosmetics bomb, until he finally grew bored and gave up. Trash was off the hook with the Diablos. Ratso ended up going to prison for trying to steal a cop's bike while the cop was still on it.

Trash had bought himself a 1969 cone shovelhead Harley which he regularly took on long road trips, usually with Brother Hank. Pulling up in front of his house one day, a fully-outfitted Trash saw Brother Hank come out wearing only his jacket; no sleeping bag, no backpack, nothing.

"Where's your sleeping bag?" Trash demanded.

"Well, we're only gonna be gone four or five days," Brother Hanks said. "And we got an ounce of speed; we don't need to sleep."

"Yeah, but if you *do* need to sleep? You got no sleeping bag. Whatta you gonna do?"

Brother Hank took out a pistol and pointed it at Trash: "Take yours."

Trash shrugged, took out his bayonet, and cut the straps on his backpack. They took off and partied for a week with nothing but speed, money, and weapons.

With the money from his Harley repair work and speed sales, Trash felt immortal. There was always more cash to spend, more parties to throw, more riding to do. It was a wild and errant life, an outlaw life that went on for years. There was never any thought about the future or even the next day. He never held a credit card, drew a salary, or opened a bank account. He simply made money and then spent it. Trash made attempts at getting full-time work, even training to become an ambulance driver, but his brittle resistance to supervision would end up scotching it. More than once, he punched out a manager who tried to tell him what to do.

The seventies became the eighties and Trash hardly noticed. He rarely talked about Vietnam with anyone, continuing to drink and take crank. He taught other people how to cook for him, and gave a lot of his product away. Trash looked at speed as a means to make money and stay wired throughout the day. It wasn't until 1985 that it all caved in on him.

There were two teenaged girls who hung around with the Diablos, a pair of biker Lolitas whom Trash dubbed Crazy Gal and Dumb Gal. Both were fifteen years old. One day, Crazy Gal told Dumb Gal of a great idea she had to get extra money: they would go to Dumb Gal's parents and claim that the Diablos were threatening to kidnap and rape them unless they gave them five hundred dollars. Dumb Gal agreed to the scheme.

"Two Diablos were staying at the house," says Trash. "These girls knew one of 'em. They called us up one day and asked us to take 'em for a ride." Trash and the Diablo rode over on their bikes and picked them up. While out riding, Dumb Gal asked them to drop her off at her house for a second. After pulling up in front of the house, the two girls hopped off the bikes, ran inside and confronted Dumb Gal's parents. There are two Diablos outside, they told them, and they want five hundred dollars or else they're going to make us pull a train. As the two girls waited to be handed the money, the parents called the police.

"The cops went and kicked down every Diablo door in town," Trash says. His house had long been identified by Van Nuys police as a known Diablo hangout and it was quickly raided. Trash managed to track down Cheri, who was not at home at the time, and the two fled the Valley.

A search of Trash's house revealed cans of black powder, thirteen grams of speed, several black powder rifles and other guns, plus containers full of ethyl alcohol, sulfuric acid, and metallic sodium. Police also found some road flares attached to a wall clock to resemble a time bomb and impounded it as evidence. Trash eventually learned everyone had been charged with rape, robbery, kidnapping, and extortion, and that there was a warrant out for his arrest. He came back and turned himself in.

The girls' bizarre scheme had been quickly uncovered but by then it was a moot point. The raids on the Diablos' residences uncovered a major haul of guns and narcotics, and Trash was branded a known associate of the outlaw club. He was in between cooks at the time, though, and there was no speed being processed when the raid took place. Authorities had to settle for charges of possession rather than the more serious one of manufacturing. They also accused him of possessing explosives. Still, Trash was hit with sixty-five thousand dollars bail, later reduced to twenty-five thousand.

During his trial, the prosecutor showed his wall clock to the jury, pointing out how the road flares attached to it resembled sticks of dynamite. The obsolete black powder was also admitted into evidence (though prosecutors knew no mad bomber with any sense would ever use it to make explosives) as well as the chemicals. Trash was found guilty of all charges. He was sentenced to eighteen months in state prison, and shipped off to Chino.

THOUGH IT WAS HIS FIRST TIME IN THE BIG HOUSE, PRISON WAS NO big deal for Trash. Everyone left him alone, particularly after a group of prisoners saw him doing multiple leg presses of 950 pounds on the weight machine. He did his time uneventfully and even got around to proposing to Cheri. The two exchanged vows on the prison grounds.

After his release in 1989, Trash and Cheri moved to a rental house in Kagel Canyon, a remote area hidden away in the arid hills east of Pasadena. The house's cramped interior was all thrift store: worn furniture, a disintegrating throw rug the color of anemic puce, a scarred coffee table. The bedroom was so small that the bed frame and mattress took up almost the entire space. Trash went back to repairing Harley transmissions and cooking meth, while maintaining a low profile. He kept visitors to a minimum, and stopped getting into fights but still took the shovelhead out as often as he could, riding like a madman.

Two years later, on April 15, 1991, Trash was in the middle of a meth batch when he made a run into town on his bike. He was coming around a curve on an access road that led down to the freeway. The bend was marked for 45 mph; Trash was going 90.

At a merging road ahead of him, a pickup truck with its lights off ran a stop sign and pulled in front of him.

"If he'd had his headlights on, I coulda seen him," he remembers. "And if he had stopped at the stop sign, we woulda seen each other. Instead he did neither and I was going way too fast."

Trash broadsided the pickup at 90 mph, and the impact knocked it over on its side. The shovelhead went flying in pieces in every direction. Trash awoke to find himself pinned under the truck with gas pouring all over him. He screamed for help but the shaken driver panicked and ran off. He passed out and awoke to find some people trying to shove the truck off him. An ambulance came and took him to the hospital. The last thing he remembered before passing out was a man in a white lab coat asking him what he wanted to look like.

Trash spent weeks at L.A. County Hospital in full traction while loaded on Demerol. He would awake from a stupor to notice someone drilling holes in his shin with a Black & Decker power tool. Doctors put over a dozen temporary pins into Trash's legs. He continued to recover at home but after several months, his legs began to worsen, and Cheri rushed him back to the hospital. They learned that there'd been an oversight, the pins in his bones should've been taken out weeks earlier. The pins were removed and it was another nine months before he could walk normally.

The bike wreck had left his body a fragile shell of what it once had been. He was forced to give up Harley repair work, as it was agony for him to hunch over a bike frame for hours on end. Trash also stopped making speed, as it was too taxing on him, and instead launched a malpractice suit against the hospital.

In January of 1995, the Northridge earthquake hit the L.A. basin and the extensive damage left by the temblor had caused some areas to enforce a nighttime curfew. A few days after the quake, Trash was at a friend's house across the basin, who told him he had some "packages" that needed to be delivered. He'd be unable to make it back before the curfew went into effect, though, and since the house was near where Trash lived, could he deliver the packages? Though he suspected what was inside them, he foolishly agreed to run the errand. As he was driving back home, curfew went into effect and he was pulled over by the police. "They found it right away," he says. "A pound of speed. Stupid." He was arraigned the next morning and later convicted and sent back to Chino. His lawsuit against the hospital was dismissed.

DURING HIS SECOND PRISON TERM, TRASH WAS PUT IN CHARGE OF producing the prison's In-Service Training manuals (ISTs), which was a kind of newsletter for Chino employees. "I did the layout, typed up all the articles, created the monthly calendar, put in little poems, all that shit," he said. Trash occasionally dropped in cryptic aphorisms of his own among the pages:

A rut is little more than a grave with the ends kicked out.

Upon his release in 1997, Trash set out to become a writer. He sold some short articles to *Thunder Press,* a biker newspaper that paid four cents a word, and began a correspondence with an ex-Hell's Angel named Keith Ball. Ball was an editor at the biker magazine *Easyriders* and Trash wrote him a series of letters asking for a job. His offbeat prose caught Ball's eye, and having two prison jolts didn't hurt either. He was asked to do short features for the magazine's "Readers' Rides" column, which consisted of profiles of customized motorcycles selected from photographs submitted to the magazine by the bikes' owners. Trash would call the owners back, do an interview about the bikes' specifications, and write it up. On occasion, the accompanying phone number was disconnected and the owner had moved, leaving no forwarding address. Rather than choosing another motorcycle, Trash simply studied the photograph, took notes of how the bike had been built, and made up everything else:

> T.J. and ten friends formed a society called the RPM Culture Club in Stockholm. All members are at least seven feet tall, and they specialize in building bikes and painting pretty pictures on the underside of manhole covers, which are used in Tiddly Winks competitions, a fast-growing Scandinavian sport. They even fly the colors of the Stockholm police.

An editorial shakeup at *Easyriders* phased out Trash's "Reader's Ride" assignments but he was still determined to make it as a writer. When he wasn't bombing around on his shovelhead, Trash spent his days writing lengthy e-mails, essays ("The low gravity found in Earth's orbit does some unique things to developing cells, crystallization, and tissue growth," one began), and a few autobiographical stories, all written under the guise of "The Geezer from Hell," or GFH. He sold two GFH stories to *Easyriders,* but his telling of the time he showed the Diablo Ratso how not to make a bomb was turned down. "They told me they don't want any more outlaw stories," Trash says. "No more drug and weapons stuff. No revenge stories."

For Trash, his life after Vietnam had been one long outlaw ride. He never made a connection between the two, figuring his years of brawling, drugging, and free range riding were all part of some primal genetic flux in his emotional makeup rather than a reaction to his having survived a massacre. He got heavily involved in the helmet law issue and even contacted his assemblyman's office in Sacramento, requesting that a motorcycle license plate for veterans be created.

When Trash learned later that his veteran's license plate bill
had been stalled in the California State Transportation Committee, he became infuriated and immediately dashed off a vitriolic
letter. Though he never mailed it to the committee, he did sub-
mit it to *Hustler* magazine in hopes of getting it published:

> My Dear _____,
>
> I wouldn't piss in your mouths if your teeth were on fire,
> you dirty dog dick-lickin' cock-gobbling mother-suckin' fish-
> fuckin' cum-burpin' syphilitic gutter sluts! I'm gonna kick my
> tennis shoes off in your ass, stuff my socks in your mouth,
> reach in your foot-wide adult diapered ass, shove my arm
> up your man-swilling cum tunnel, grab you by that Sheik-
> choked esophagus that runs from your shit bucket to your
> cataracts . . .

It continued for several more lines before closing with:

> Pass AB-1515 . . . or no pollywog soup for you!
>   Thank you for your consideration.
> Respectfully yours,
> Trash, published author, biker,
> veteran (C 2/16 "Rangers" 65-66)
> Initiator of AB-1515.

Hustler did not respond to Trash's submission. Meanwhile he
was thinking more and more about Vietnam.

On July 4, 1999, Trash heard that a traveling replica of the
Vietnam War Memorial was coming to Ventura, California, an
hour's drive north of L.A. He decided to ride up to check it out
and see if he could find the names of some of his buddies from
Charlie Company who were killed at Courtenay Plantation. It

had been thirty-three years since the battle and he never discussed his experiences with anyone.

Trash rolled up the 101 and went into a park where the monument replica was set up. There were thousands of people amassed around the Wall, including hundreds of bikers just like Trash, Vietnam veterans whose own personal phantoms still haunted them at every step.

Trash approached the Wall and scanned the panels, searching for a familiar name. He found one. Then another.

"I was totally unprepared for it," he says. "I had no way of directing it, no way of understanding it..." A flurry of memories, long buried and suppressed, came surging over him rapidly like a jungle rain. Two bikers standing nearby saw what was happening. They gently guided him across the park road and set him down on a sloping stretch of grass. They turned around and stood over him, shielding him from view. "Just let it out, man," one of them said. "Let it go."

Trash huddled on the ground and sobbed for thirty minutes straight.

Part IV:

Blowing It

CHAPTER 14

Getting Organized

IN THE FALL OF 1981, THE BUREAU OF ALCOHOL, TOBACCO, AND Firearms' Cleveland field office received a startling phone call. The caller, who identified himself only as Butch, confessed to having murdered a teenage motorcyclist seven years ago during a drive-by shooting. He also claimed that he was a thirteen-year veteran of the Cleveland Hell's Angels and had loads of information to tell them including information on at least twenty-five other murders committed over the past ten years. He was coming in and needed protection.

The Polish Women's Hall fracas of 1971 caused several Cleveland Angels to cool their heels in jail for months. One of them was a bilious Angel purist with the rustic name of Clarence Addie "Butch" Crouch. Of Louisiana Cajun stock, Butch was a veteran biker who had migrated up to Northern California during the late 1960s to woodshed with the Hell's Angels' Nomad Chapter in San Rafael. After earning his patch, Butch was sent back east to Ohio in 1968 with a few other Angels where they were ordered to rebuild the club's Cleveland chapter, as most of its members were in prison following a shooting in a local bar called Barto's that left two people dead. Using a common and effective approach, Butch and his colleagues absorbed a local outlaw club into their fold, kicked out the dead wood, and resurrected the Cleveland Hell's Angels.

Butch had done his share of carving during the Polish Women's Hall mess, killing one of the Breeds. Though he was exonerated on self-defense grounds, Butch served time along with several other Angels in the Cleveland House of Corrections for various other charges relating to the fight. While there, he claimed that several of his Angel brethren did something that would change the entire focus of the outlaw clan forever: they read *The Godfather.*

Though the movie had yet to be released, Mario Puzo's melodramatic Mafia novel was a bestseller and paperback copies of it were floating around the prison's corridors. It was in Puzo's tome, Butch told authorities, that the Cleveland Hell's Angels found a how-to manual for converting their sloppy chapter into a lean money-making drug operation patterned after the Corleone family, a sort of *Organized Crime for Dummies.*

What impressed the Angels about *The Godfather* was its romantic portrayal of clandestine mob life: their rituals, ruthlessness, and influence over cops and city hall. The Mafia took their graft very seriously; it was their industry, not just a way to flip off the mainstream public. They trafficked in narcotics nationwide and dealt with competition with brutal efficiency. They "took care of business."

Upon their release from prison, the Cleveland Angels regrouped inside their clubhouse, a converted funeral home at the corner of East 67th and Edna Avenue, and went to work. According to Butch, a series of premeditated murders were launched against the remaining Breeds, and also the Outlaws, a fierce club based out of Chicago that had set up a chapter in nearby Akron. Newly-initiated Angels were allegedly ordered to "roll their bones": go and kill rival club members to test their loyalty, a gruesome ritual they lifted from Puzo's novel. The chapter even set up a TCB (taking care of business) fund to underwrite the purchase of weapons to be used in the assassinations.

As the Cleveland Angels restructured themselves into a criminal outfit, Butch started feeling out of touch. He was the atavistic one in the chapter, an outlaw straight out of a Corman biker flick. He longed for the days of endless rides, tavern melees, and beer parties. Mean and stupid, Butch admitted to torturing a dog, gorging on PCP, and fathering a dozen illegitimate children. He ran a multitude of prostitutes and once knifed a woman in the foot because she woke him up. He thought the Polish Women's Hall battle was the greatest thing he ever took part in. But the chapter was becoming more about business and capitalism. Members were selling more drugs than they were ingesting, and getting rich from it. Some had used their proceeds to buy expensive cars and ranch houses in Strongsville. Butch could tell by the rumpled creases in members' colors that they were spending more time driving cars than riding. Most of them didn't even work on their bikes like he did.* To Butch, the Cleveland Angels weren't outlaws anymore, just criminals who were better at vice than he was.

For the time being, though, Butch was a loyal Angel and in 1974, agreed to kill for the club. His target was Akron Outlaws member Steven "Groundhog" Wargo, who had recently moved to South Akron after his Cleveland apartment was firebombed. The Outlaws and the Hell's Angels had been waging war ever since two Angels, along with a third man, were abducted in a Florida bar by several Outlaws, who executed them and dumped their bodies in a quarry. The two clubs were now archenemies and retribution was imminent.

On July 9, 1974, Butch, armed with a 12-gauge shotgun, rode inside a '68 Ford along with two other Angels, one toting a sub-

---

* Cleveland president Eugene Padavick readily confirmed the fact that Butch always worked on his own bike: "He used to say 'I made my bike, Harley-Davidson made yours.' But his wouldn't start."

machine gun, to Wargo's residence at 900 Lover's Lane in South Akron. They'd heard an Outlaws meeting was taking place there. The sun had just gone down and the air was heavy with humidity. As they approached, Butch saw a group of men standing around a motorcycle. The driver pulled the car up and Butch and the Angel in the backseat opened fire. The men all hit the ground. As they sped away, Butch saw one of them crumple, and he was sure he'd hit Wargo.

The next day, it was in the news: an eighteen-year-old motorcyclist named Donald Della Serra had died after being shot during a drive-by shooting; two other men were wounded. None of the victims, including Della Serra, were members of the Outlaws or any other motorcycle gang. There was no meeting at Wargo's house. Butch and the others had killed the wrong men. The murder remained unsolved for seven years.

When Butch surrendered to the ATF's Cleveland field office, he began detailing the murders of fellow Angels, club rivals, drug operatives, and innocent bystanders, including women and children. He claimed the last straw for him was the club's 1981 USA run out east. At the tour's end in North Carolina, Butch learned that several Angels were plotting to kill Michael "Thunder" Finazzo, the president of the Charlotte chapter, in order to take over his drug operations. When a few weeks later Finazzo and another Angel wound up dead, Butch turned himself in to the ATF.

Butch pleaded guilty to the Della Serra killing and was sentenced to ten to forty years for manslaughter, a far lesser sentence than a first degree murder charge would have carried. In exchange for leniency, Butch gave authorities the names of high-ranking Angels whom he said were involved in multiple murders, including one where a house was bombed, killing three people. One member admitted to Butch that he assassinated Outlaws' vice president Bruce R. "Buddy" Sunday as a way to roll his bones for the Angels. Yet another murdered his own wife and stuffed her body inside a barrel. Most of the cases were from years earlier, remaining unsolved. Others, like the killing of the spouse, were not known. Arrests were made and Butch's various testimonies were used to hand down indictments.

Butch was given a $1,245 monthly stipend to testify against the Hell's Angels in no less than five murder trials. Not only was he the star witness for the prosecution, he was also their only source of evidence. His testimony was nothing short of disastrous. He contradicted himself on the stand, gave vague recollections of past conversations and events, and uttered "I don't know" to numerous questions during cross examination. Moreover, Angel defense lawyers used Butch's sordid past against him, accusing the outlaw of being a known pimp, drug user, and convicted killer who was being paid to lie in order to save his own skin. His word was as useless as everything else he'd done with his life.*

It was the first in over a year of trials and endless reams of transcripts that led to nothing. All five of the Hell's Angels under indictment were either found not guilty or had their cases dismissed.

The case that infuriated prosecutors the most was the dismissal of charges against Angels Richard Amato and Harold Chakirelis. Both had been charged with bombing the house of William Sigley, killing Sigley's wife Mary Anne, twenty-one, son Christopher, two, and a family friend Burdell M. (Mike) Offutt, twenty-two. Sigley was neither a member of the Angels nor a

---

* Butch once made an appearance in Washington, D.C. in front of the Senate Judiciary Committee where he made national news by claiming the Hell's Angels had put out a contract on Mick Jagger's life for abandoning the club following the Altamont concert debacle. He recounted two failed assassination attempts, including one involving an exploding boat. Sonny Barger countered the story with a rhetorical question: Why would we try to kill the most famous rock singer in the world?

rival. In fact, they didn't even know him. Butch testified that the Angels mistakenly thought a member of the Outlaws lived at the Sigley residence and left a suitcase bomb on the front step. Offutt found the suitcase and brought it inside the house, setting it on the kitchen table where everyone gathered around it. When the case detonated, Mary Anne's face was rendered unrecognizable and her son Christopher had the top half of his skull blown away. Sigley was at the store when the explosion happened. He returned home fifteen minutes later only to find his family dead.

Five months after the dismissal of the Sigley murder case, the presiding judge, James J. McGettrick, was sitting drunk at Heck's Café in the Rocky River section of Cleveland. The sixty-seven-year-old was an alcoholic widower, known for his combustible temper and steady rotation of young blondes who worked as his personal secretary. As McGettrick drank, a special agent from the ATF who had worked on the bombing case came into Heck's and recognized him. He sidled up next to McGettrick and bitterly thanked the judge for dismissing the charges against Amato and Chakirelis. McGettrick, on his fifth vodka and soda, did not catch the agent's sarcasm (nor, apparently, knew who he was). "Yeah, well, I never got all the money I was supposed to get out of that," he replied.[147]

A sting was set up and in April 1984, McGettrick was caught on videotape accepting a five-thousand-dollar bribe from the agent. He was convicted of judicial misconduct and three counts of bribery, and sentenced to four years in prison. Enfeebled by poor health, McGettrick died behind bars from pancreatic cancer a year later.

The two Angels that McGettrick released could not be retried for the Sigley murders because of double jeopardy, so prosecutors went after the club for bribery and conspiracy. The money McGettrick had received in the bombing case was tenuously traced back to a tavern in South Euclid owned by an enterprising Hell's Angel named Andrew Shission, who had been previously indicted for aggravated murder based on Butch's fuzzy accusations, but was exonerated both times. Shission resembled a Kiwanis member more than an outlaw biker, usually wearing a suit and tie. He owned several businesses and his articulate demeanor on the witness stand in the earlier murder trials impressed both the court and the jury.

Shission and two others were charged with implementing a sixty-nine-hundred-dollar payoff to the judge, but the money trail that the prosecution claimed led to them was so convoluted that the jury could not make heads or tails out of it and voted for acquittals. Butch went into the Witness Protection Program where he said he was writing a book about his experiences as a Hell's Angel. Nobody he testified against was ever convicted.

Still, turncoats like Butch made law enforcement start taking outlaw motorcycle clubs much more seriously. They'd long since discounted the Hell's Angels as an invading threat to small towns and concentrated on their narcotics trade. During the seventies, the federal government began pursuing the Angels with the biggest weapon they had at their disposal: RICO, the Racketeer Influenced Corrupt Organizations Act.

First passed in 1976, the RICO Act was conceived as a way for the government to prosecute organized crime. It is a forbidding federal statute that civil rights attorneys and defense lawyers have screamed bloody murder over for years, accusing it of being overreaching and draconian.

How RICO works is somewhat complex: if a defendant is suspected of committing at least two of thirty-two specific crimes (ranging from wire and mail fraud to homicide) within a ten year period, and these crimes are connected to an illegal enterprise that crosses state lines, a case can be made for racketeering. It becomes a federal beef that can add an additional twenty years to a prisoner's sentence. The genius behind RICO is that it is able to take a series of seemingly unrelated criminal acts committed by seemingly unrelated individuals and toss them all into the conspiracy hopper.

The RICO Act did not exist when *The Godfather* was first published, so outlaws who were jotting notes in the book's margins would not learn of the statute until it started coming down on their heads years later. The first RICO prosecutions against the Angels were made following a series of raids in June of 1979 on club hangouts in California. A twenty-five-count indictment was handed down against thirty-three various Angel members, mostly for narcotics trafficking (Sonny Barger and his wife Sharon were among those charged). The only thing law enforcement had were their suspicions and rashly assumed the necessary evidence would fall in their lap.

The case ended up being a failure. Almost all the charges against the club were dropped later and only five Hell's Angels went on to being convicted, though prosecutors were satisfied that two of the five were Barger and his wife. In 1983, however, all the convictions were overturned by the Ninth Circuit Court of Appeals, who ruled that they could find no connection between the actions of some Hell's Angels and the motorcycle club itself.

The appellate court's decision led to a flurry of mud-slinging between the Hell's Angels and the federal government. Since RICO cases are rarely overturned,* the FBI ominously claimed that it was further proof of the club's immense wealth and power. The Angels countered that the reason their convictions were thrown out was because they're not part of any conspiracy; some of their members just sell drugs, that's all.

---

* Despite the setback, the threat of RICO continues to make American outlaw clubs nervous and this may be why the criminal actions of outlaw clubs are much worse in Canada, a country that has no such statute.

In 1985, the government struck back with Operation Rough-rider, a massive raid on Hell's Angel clubhouses and related haunts nationwide by FBI and DEA agents. The sweep was made in eleven states and over 125 Angel members and associates were arrested on drug and racketeering charges. Operation Roughrider, though not a RICO case, was far more successful for the government. Undercover agents posing as dealers had spent years making drug buys from various Angels, purchasing over $2 million in methamphetamine, cocaine, and heroin. The mass arrests led to a slew of snitching from various members, who were either afraid the club was going to blame them for the raid, or else had the most to gain by informing. Scores of Hell's Angels went to prison.

As with the Mafia, it has always been difficult for law enforcement to infiltrate outlaw motorcycle clubs.* It can take years before a prospect is considered for membership and those who are must supply the club with their social security numbers (federal law forbids undercover agents to use false social security numbers to establish indentities). Probably the most notorious incident of direct infiltration into the Hell's Angels occurred in 1982 when a man named Anthony Tait went undercover in the club's Alaska chapter and stayed there for more than three years. What made the case unusual was that Tait was not a cop but rather a malcontent Army dropout who infiltrated the Angels simply because he bragged that he could.

Tait, having received an undesirable discharge from Fort

---

* One exception was in 1976 when an undercover policewoman, posing as a member's old lady, rode with the California Hell's Angels' Orange County chapter. Members' girlfriends are not made privy to club business but the Orange County Angels had several sloppy members who allowed her open access to their drug deals. Her testimony led to the conviction of over seventy members and temporarily shut down the chapter.

Meade for having an "explosive personality," returned to Alaska in the mid-seventies to find something to do with himself. He settled in Anchorage, a hard-drinking city with a seven to one ratio of men to women, where he found work as a bouncer at a biker bar and several dance clubs. He developed a reputation around town for his cool demeanor and skills as a punch-out artist. Tait mopped the floors with unruly patrons and did not take guff from anybody. After a while, a local outlaw club called the Brothers took notice of him.

Tait did not ride a motorcycle, nor did he hold any opinions either way about outlaw bikers except that they seemed to command respect. One day, some Brothers members approached him and asked if he wanted to buy a gleaming twenty-three-hundred-dollar Harley chopper from them. He could make payments on it for as little as ten dollars a week if he wanted. There was just one stipulation: Tait had to start "hanging around" them. Flattered, he accepted and learned how to handle the rigid-frame monstrosity and service the engine.

Tait liked to play both sides of the fence and was friends with several members of the Anchorage police department, including a vice detective named Larry Robinette. Not long after ingratiating himself with the Brothers, Tait was sitting in a bar with Robinette and a few other cops and started badgering them about why nobody ever busted the outlaw club. "They run all over your town roughshod," he said. "They fuck everybody, they deal dope. They piss on cop cars."[148] Robinette and the others replied that Anchorage was a small town and everybody knew who was on the police force. They didn't have the resources to investigate the Brothers. Tait waved aside their reasons, boasting that he was now riding with the club and he could give the cops everything they would need to know in just three weeks. He made it a bet, with the winner getting a steak dinner and an

---

expensive bottle of Scotch. The detectives took him up on it, though they didn't take him seriously at first.

What was supposed to last three weeks stretched into years. Tait was finally made a Brothers prospect and rode with the club for several months. Prospects, however, were not allowed access to club business and he had nothing to give to Robinette. But the detective was pleased with Tait's association with the Brothers and urged him to stay on. Not surprisingly, Tait demanded money and Robinette scrounged up what he could.

In 1981, the Hell's Angels moved into Anchorage and absorbed the Brothers, converting the club into a prospect chapter (the Brothers had had a long relationship with the Angels and eagerly agreed to be annexed). Eighteen months later, the Brothers were all officially issued Hell's Angel patches, save Tait who became an Angels prospect. Since he was right back where he started, Tait still had nothing of value to offer. He wanted to quit, but Robinette kept persuading him to stay. When Tait was finally issued his Angels colors, club business opened up for him and Robinette brought in the FBI.

The FBI was in the midst of Operation CACUS, which targeted interstate drug trafficking, and met with Tait. As he thrived on flattery, having the FBI taking close note of his undercover work salved his ego. Meanwhile, he also impressed his Angels colleagues with his fighting skills, knowledge of explosives, and ability to procure women for them. They dubbed him Gentleman Tony and he became a close associate of Sonny Barger's. Some Angels, though, were jealous of Tait and felt he was an opportunist.

For the next couple of years, Tait rode, fought, and got stoned with the Angels, taking part in drug deals and regularly beating people up. He married a prostitute named Brenda, whom he fought with constantly (unaware of his undercover work, she tried to inform on him to police, saying he was a major drug dealer). All the while, Tait was feeding information back to the FBI and even started wearing a wire to club meetings. In 1987, a full-scale bust went down and thirty-five Hell's Angels were arrested, including Barger. Most were convicted of drug trafficking and received sentences ranging from three years to life in prison. Tait testified in open court, received $250,000 for his undercover work, and then fled to Europe where he lives to this day under an assumed name.

Though Tait's evidence and Operation Roughrider made dents in the club's organization, in the end, very little was accomplished. The Hell's Angels survived and found new prospects to rebuild their chapters. They continued fending off whatever assaults law enforcement made on them, regularly using club money to hire the best lawyers to file civil suits claiming harassment. The life of an outlaw was becoming complicated, as there was much more at stake.

CHAPTER 15

Worse Than Hippies

On June 23, 1981, the Harley-Davidson Motor Company bought itself out from AMF and went back to being an independent company. The buyback plan cost the company $75 million, all of which had to be borrowed. Harley-Davidson cut corners, laid off several hundred employees, converted to private ownership again, and went about the business of making the company solvent.

The AMF years had certainly not been all bad. AMF money helped Harley-Davidson create the FXS Low Rider in 1977, an enormously popular model that is still being produced, and had funded the development of a new engine to replace the archaic shovelhead. Nevertheless, the company took a hard look at what Harley-Davidson was really about and where the future lay. Everyone readily agreed that it *wasn't* in midsize motorcycles. The Japanese were frankly better at making 350cc models, so Harley-Davidson executives voted unanimously to cease manufacturing smaller road models and go back to what it did best: making big bikes. From 1981 on, Harley-Davidson scaled back production of their motorcycles to strictly models that had an 880cc engine or larger.

A big break for the company occurred in 1983 when the federal government slapped a hefty tariff of 43 percent on any imported Asian motorcycle that was 700cc or bigger in size. Harley-Davidson had spent years accusing the Japanese companies of dumping their bikes into the U.S. market at lower prices than they were selling them for in their own country, and lobbied Congress hard to do something about it. Though Honda cruisers like the luxury Gold Wing remained less expensive than Harley-Davidson's Tour Glide even with the applied tariffs, the price difference was minimal enough for the American company to stay competitive. Harley-Davidson also noticed that their famous name was being exploited by small-time entrepreneurs who fraudulently sold promotional merchandise. Unauthorized Harley-Davidson T-shirts, pins, key chains, cup holders, etc. had been floating around bike shows for years and the company went to great lengths to enforce trademark laws and take control of their name.

Then, in 1984, the company's research and development department came out with a new engine to replace the nearly twenty-year-old shovelhead design. They dubbed it the Evolution V-2, a 1340cc engine that Harley-Davidson engineers had spent seven years developing, and it would have a significant impact on the future success of the company. Unlike the iron shovelhead, the Evo was constructed of lighter alloys and offered higher compression, an improved choke system, belt drive, and a smoother clutch and transmission. It was leaps and bounds superior to any engine they'd designed before, in that the Evo combined Japanese reliability with American heft: it was a powerful sucker that never broke down.

It was around this time that Harley-Davidson realized that its outlaw mystique, something the company had previously treated like the mad wife locked in the attic in *Jane Eyre,* might be a valuable commodity after all. Having learned a thing or two about marketing from AMF, Harley-Davidson launched a major magazine ad campaign that declared their bikes as the ultimate freedom machine, a soaring and powerful vehicle for the human spirit. "The philosophy was about getting back to a reality with the customer," says Marty Rosenblum. "The truth is, yes, there's something edgy about riding a Harley-Davidson motorcycle. One of the banner phrases was, 'The Eagle Soars Alone,' which was Harley-Davidson being on its own and as independent and maverick as our riders. We didn't say it that way but that was the idea."[149]

Still, times remained hard and by 1986, Harley-Davidson was so financially strapped that it came within weeks of going bankrupt. When one of its four lenders, Citicorp, decided that there was no future for the Milwaukee company, it called in the entire balance of its share of the buyout loan. Harley-Davidson quickly went public again, issued stock, and rounded up $70 million to pay back Citicorp and float them along while they tried to sell their motorcycles. And though they'd vastly improved both their marketing and their engines, there was a new and anomalous factor that would eventually play the biggest part in the triumphant turnaround of the company: the *prestige* of being a biker.

Though Harley-Davidson was aggressively promoting their motorcycles to the general public at large, only those with a decent income could really afford them. The new post-AMF Harley-Davidsons had particularly hefty price tags, so there was only a limited class of customer capable of forking over fifteen thousand dollars to buy one. These potential customers were successful and upper-class, with private practices, investment portfolios, and fixed interest mortgages. When Harley-Davidson went public in 1986, the American economy was strong and the stock market bullish, leading a whole new generation of customers, financial types with lots of disposable income, to start absorbing the Harley lifestyle. What better way for a stockbroker to have fun after a hard day in the pit than to go out and be a biker? And as everyone knew, bikers only rode Harleys, the baddest bike on the road.

Probably the epitome of this marketing phenomena was the iconic publisher Malcolm Forbes. A billionaire and hot air balloon hobbyist, Forbes burst on the public scene during the go-getter eighties, where he regularly showed up at events on his Ultra Glide. Though he was seen as an example of the new affluent breed of Harley-Davidson rider, in reality, Forbes had been a dedicated motorcyclist for years. He had come into the sport rather late in life, having bought his first bike when he was already forty-eight years old after his chauffeur gave him a ride on one. Forbes, who previously distrusted motorcycles, enjoyed the ride so much that he bought a fleet of Harleys and other models. He later formed a motorcycle club that he facetiously named the Capitalist Tools, and led them across Europe, Asia, and even the Soviet Union. He wrote several travel books detailing his experiences.

Forbes could be a little campy. His hot air balloons, inflated into the shapes of French chateaus and Harley bikes, were baroque testaments to intentionally gauche tastes, and he once gave his good friend Elizabeth Taylor a gaudy purple Sportster that she dubbed Passion. Still, he never took himself too seriously and remained an impassioned rider right up to his death in 1988. Today, no one has ever promoted a positive image of motorcycling more widely than Forbes did.

With a new upbeat spin to the biker image leading the way, Harley-Davidson sales fairly exploded from the influx of new customers and made the company's comeback a roaring success, though again, not everyone was happy about it. Biker purists started noticing how more and more stretches of the open road were being invaded by corporate types who decided that they, too, wanted to be "bad" and had bought a Harley-Davidson. They saw these new affluent riders as just lemmings being lured into their private pool; these neophytes were hijacking their culture and turning it into a weekend fad.

"These are people that have a family and a job and a mortgage," says *Easyriders'* Dave Nichols. "And they just want to forget about all of their troubles for a few hours on the weekend. They put on the leathers and they look kind of tough and they go out there. It could be your dentist or your lawyer that pulls up next to you and sneers and horrifies your three-year-old. But they're just pretending."[150]

The derisive terms for this new breed of Harley riders came fast and venomous: Rolex riders, RUBS (Rich Urban Bikers), Weekend Warriors, and a slew of other more obscene terms. Though it was considered as a kind of sellout on Harley-Davidson's part, it was yet another variation of the Miscreant's Paradox: The same bikers who criticized the public for judging their culture so harshly were also unhappy more people were embracing it. The Rolex Rider tag was tossed around so much that it became as much of a mythical figure as the Outlaw Biker. The only difference is that nobody would ever declare themselves to be a Rolex Rider; it would be like saying they're "politically correct" or "commercial."

The furor over Rolex Riders hasn't quite died down yet, but one can look back on the eighties and see the sales successes that were achieved as proof of the smartest marketing move Harley-Davidson had ever done. By making the world's most notorious motorcycle available to anyone, the company was in effect telling budding riders that they could experience the rough mystical quality that comes with owning a Harley-Davidson without having to drop a load of speed or smash up a bar. (There was only so much the company was going to condone.)

With the outlaw mythos becoming more sinister, there had to be other reasons why someone should want to buy a Harley besides just being a little daring. Every motorcycle offers the thrill of speed and the risk of impending death to its rider so other more spiritual values had to be expressed. This is where Marty Rosenblum comes into the picture. Along with his position as the official historian for Harley-Davidson, Rosenblum also promotes something he calls biker existentialism.

"Sophisticated psychologists like to divide a person up into personality and self," he says, "personality being the trappings that we present ourselves to the world with. The stuff that's influenced by genetics and childhood. What happens in Harley-Davidson culture is that you really become more of your own person, according to the dreams that you have. The self that you really know you are, that's often restrained by the personality. And this is what happens when you ride a Harley-Davidson motorcycle."[151]

It is difficult to explain Rosenblum's Harley theosophy without having him sound like a terminal Zen victim. Like existentialism itself, many of the ideas that he espouses tend to sound very deep and profound while also not making any sense. This is not a criticism by any means. Existentialism is perplexing because it deals with inner experiences that cannot be defined; they are simply felt. Marty has spent much of his life interpreting Harley-Davidson consciousness to other people while also admitting that much of it is unexplainable. In an effort to better articulate his ideas, he founded the Holy Ranger Project, an earnest study of the myths, mystiques, and cultural auras behind classic Americana, like Colt firearms, Gibson guitars, and especially Harley bikes. The Holy Ranger Project combines folklore, poetry, and transcendental thought to express the cerebral connection between the bike and its rider. He has been known to go into his garage in the middle of the night and sit in silence next to his Harley-Davidson for hours, just to experience what he calls the "mythopoetic process" that exists within the machine:

> When it (a Harley-Davidson) is ridden, let the wind roar and the dirt soar. When the machine is at rest, no fingerprint may be applied. When static, for owner customization ritual, nothing should be contaminated or the mysterious poetic process shall be disturbed. It is this highly personalized treatment that permits the ghost in the machine to haunt. It is the shape and the sound of a Harley-Davidson motorcycle that inspires the rider to let the imagination take over for a visionary ride in the privacy of the garage or, if you will, the place of worship . . . .[152]

Where Marty differs from most other bikers is that he believes that anyone can make this kind of connection with their Harley, and that the experience is open to everyone. "Now we've got a lot of new customers, new riders," he says. "There are new people who are coming into the sport of motorcycling, but the same thing is going on, the same thing happens. You become a member of the culture. You become part of the culture. You don't lose your individuality." This is a welcoming invitation and the Harley-Davidson company should be grateful that they have someone like Marty to clarify it but, in truth, he holds a minority opinion. For most veteran bikers, many of the new generation of Harley-Davidson riders just don't get it.

One of the bigger skeptics is Ugly Paul, a successful lawyer in Los Angeles who has been a motorcyclist since 1967, with a BSA Thunderbolt for his first bike. He is currently the international president of the Uglies Motorcycle Club. The Uglies are the Masons of the motorcycle world, a select organization that doesn't recruit members and who are very particular about who they allow to join. They count a number of luminaries as members, including Larry Hagman, Peter Fonda, and Willie G. Davidson, Harley-Davidson's legendary director of styling (Marty Rosenblum is a member of the Milwaukee Uglies). The Uglies were formed over thirty years ago by a group of sand racers who tore around Pismo Beach before deciding to take their act to the asphalt. Though their colors feature a Jolly Roger, the Uglies are not an outlaw club but remain deadly serious about riding. For Ugly Paul, the last fifteen years have been largely a disappointment and he blames much of it on Harley-Davidson's Evolution V-2 engine.

"That engine brought a lot of people into motorcycling that had never ridden before," Ugly Paul says. "There was no maintenance required anymore. Now you have the Rolex Riders, the yuppie crowd. They buy Harleys and paint them fancy colors, and they may ride them on a Sunday to the Rock Store* or something like that. But they're not serious riders."[153]

It is an interesting viewpoint, being that Harley-Davidson compromised its own soul by building an engine that doesn't break down. For Ugly Paul, it has induced a widespread plague of rider apathy that runs counter to the engine's superlative efficiency. It's something he claims to have witnessed outside Laughlin, Nevada, where a biker rally was taking place. He and a few Uglies parked on the side of the road and counted the number of bikes that were being trailered into town as opposed to being ridden. "And there were more bikes in trucks and trailers," he says. "The big boom has been from those people. I mean, they *trailer* their bike from L.A. to Laughlin. It's 280 miles, it's five hours. There's nothing to it."[154]

---

* A small bar and restaurant east of Malibu in the Los Virgenes forest that is a popular hangout for motorcyclists, including Jay Leno.

Ugly Paul also sees the same thing happening at the famous Black Hills Classic Rally in Sturgis, South Dakota. "I can't imagine trailering my bike to Sturgis," he says. "I remember the first time I went to Sturgis in 1982, I didn't see a single trailer, except for a guy riding a Honda towing his Harley on a trailer. Nowadays, it's pickups and trailers, RVs and trailers. Sturgis used to be a ball. Now it's just a trade show."[155] Ugly Paul does admit there has been a positive impact on motorcycling from these so-called yuppie bikers. "They've been very good for motorcycling," he says. "The more people that are around riding, the higher the visibility and the higher the acceptance."[156] Many biker purists have admitted to this and, again, it adds yet another dimension to the Miscreant's Paradox: We're happy to be earning respectability by the increased presence of a class of bikers whom we don't respect.

It is true that today it's much more socially acceptable to be a motorcyclist than it was twenty or thirty years ago, though Ugly Paul insists that the one thing that remains a problem is the attitude of law enforcement. This, he claims, has never changed.

"It's a siege mentality," Ugly Paul says. "If you've been a biker, a real biker, you *know* it exists." One would expect this from a Hell's Angel, certainly, but not from a wealthy professional who rides a custom Electra Glide with full dressers, ferrings, and an AM/FM stereo system. "You get a little piece of what it's like to be a minority," he continues. "You're seen and judged by what they see. 'I see you, you're on this motorcycle, you're wearing this leather jacket. I may not have caught you but I know you're a criminal. You're part of what I have to control. My life is to control you.' And that hasn't changed."[157]

Like rock 'n' roll and gambling, there's little sense of rebellion left to being a biker anymore; there's too much money and corporate influence involved. The only thing that will never change is the sport's overall risk. There's never been anything practical about owning a motorcycle. They are vulnerable in heavy traffic and utter misery in the pouring rain. One rides for the sheer thrill of it; motorcycles are sexy and fun because they're risky as hell, a visceral enticement that continues to be hampered by helmet laws. Though California has one of the largest percentages of motorcyclists of any state in the nation, bikers have been unsuccessful at overturning the AB-7 helmet law since its passage in 1991. This is largely because helmet law proponents (mostly state insurance commissions) have countered bikers' freedom of choice arguments with something far more pragmatic: money. Their studies show that helmet-less bikers involved in accidents often suffer serious head injuries that leave them needing round-the-clock care and whirring machines to keep them alive. The average biker, they insist, lacks the necessary insurance coverage to offset the enormous medical expenses that accrue; they become wards of the state and a drain on the taxpayers' wallet.

Recently, bikers have challenged this economic argument by arguing that it's the helmeted riders who usually suffer long-term disabilities following an accident; riders without a helmet are more likely to die outright, which is cheaper. They offer as proof a 1990 study by the San Diego Trauma Registry that showed the cost of treating motorcycle accident victims who *weren't* wearing helmets was far lower than those who did wear them (because more of the first group died and, therefore, did not require treatment). Also, since a helmet obscures both a rider's vision and hearing, wearing one is more likely to get you into an accident. Therefore, states that require all riders to wear a helmet are more dangerous to ride in.

Much of this statistical volleying has done little except to cloud the primary issue: should a motorcyclist be required to wear a helmet? No one disputes the fact that a helmet's effectiveness is limited in accidents above speeds of 13 mph, and totally irrelevant during a freeway pileup. As most motorcycle accidents occur at speeds of 40 mph and up, whether or not a rider is wearing a helmet is often a moot point, anyway.

CHAPTER 16

Love and Independence: The End of the Outlaw Biker

JULY 4, 1997

In 1996, Hollister, California, was a year away from the golden anniversary of the Gypsy Tour incident that brought it so much notoriety, and the residents had two choices: either ignore the tour's fifty-year legacy or celebrate it all-out. Many were not thrilled with the notion of an official commemoration; there was something intrinsically weird about organizing a celebration around an alleged riot. Several members of the city council and local law enforcement were firmly against the idea. It didn't help matters that the Oakland Hell's Angels wanted to pay homage to the apocryphal sacking of Hollister by staging their own forty-ninth anniversary event. "The Hell's Angels of Oakland had proposed renting a piece of property outside of town," said a Hollister city councilman. "They wanted to hold a rally on it to have a preview of the fiftieth anniversary. When that happened, it really stirred up the community. The Hell's Angels were not successful in getting the permits to do that. They dropped out."[158]

For years, a few hundred bikers would come into Hollister on July 4* to line up in front of Johnny's Bar and pay

---

* The forty-ninth anniversary in 1996 drew three thousand bikers. Though peaceful, many complained that the police's presence was too strong, and that they were videotaping license plates and writing tickets excessively.

their respects. But now that it was the fiftieth anniversary, everyone in town knew that it would probably draw huge crowds, like swallows flocking to San Juan Capistrano. But while residents spent the ensuing months fretting over what to do, a local man named Mark Maxwell, along with several others, formed the Hollister Independent Rally Committee (HIRC) in order to take advantage of the growing interest in the fiftieth. "We wanted to figure out a way that it wouldn't cost the taxpayers of Hollister a penny to put this thing on," says Maxwell. "We figured if we brought in vendors and charged for spots, it wouldn't cost the city a dime which let them off the hook a little bit by not having to foot the bill for this big monster fiftieth celebration."[159]

The Hollister city council warily agreed to sanction the fiftieth anniversary celebration, their appreciation of a sound dollar outweighing the fear of a potential blitz. The HIRC set about handling the task of how to promote it. Their publicity materials firmly emphasized how the 1947 Hollister incident had always been blown out of proportion and there had been, in fact, no riot. Using a stellar variation of the Miscreant's Paradox, they proclaimed Hollister as being the birthplace of the original Wild Ones, and the Independence Rally was celebrating the legacy of all those insane outlaw bikers that the irresponsible media falsely accused of being insane outlaw bikers.

"We decided on [calling it the] Independence Rally," Maxwell says, "because there were a lot of people who felt it was a coincidence that it [the 1947 Incident] happened on the fourth of July.... Bikers won their independence from other motorcycle enthusiasts when the '47 deal went on here. So that's why we've been adamant about leaving out the word "day" in the name. It's not an Independence Day rally, it's an *Independence* rally. And that's because we won our independence as bikers here."[160]

The Independence rally took place in Hollister on the July Fourth weekend, 1997, and drew an estimated forty thousand attendees. Law enforcement was in full riot mode. "There were some 160 officers, not counting the California Highway Patrol," says Maxwell. "They came in riot gear. They wouldn't let us use the Fourth Street lot corner because that was a staging area for the busloads of law enforcement to land in case something broke out. And to say they were paranoid . . . well, what they did is they hoped for the best but they planned for the worst. It was, um, very intimidating."[161]

Yet the 1997 Independence Rally went off without a hitch, though the cost of footing the bill for the unwanted security left it in the red. An ailing Wino Willie Forkner was even invited to be the Grand Marshall for the opening day parade, an honor which he happily accepted. Sadly, Wino passed away just a few days before the event and a memorial service was held for him on the steps of City Hall. Hundreds of people showed up to pay tribute to the man who didn't start a riot in their town.

The following year, organizers persuaded authorities to cut down on the number of police personnel for the event. Security costs plunged some 70 percent and the fifty-first anniversary celebration yielded a tidy profit. Today, the Independence Rally is Hollister's biggest source of tourism and many locals now see the 1947 fracas as the best thing that ever happened to their town.

"I believe that if it wasn't for what happened in '47," says Maxwell, "if it hadn't been blown out of proportion, if the police hadn't reacted the way they did . . . then it would have just been nothing and it never would have turned into the event it is today."[162]

NOVEMBER, 1999

On the second Sunday of November, Glendale, California, hosts the world's largest charity motorcycle ride, the Love Ride.

It is one of the major attractions of a city known mainly for its large Armenian populace and a huge shopping mall that resembles something Albert Speer would've built if Hitler had won the war. City officials must reroute traffic on several major streets in order to assemble the massive number of motorcyclists who take part in the ride. Confused drivers unaware of the event usually wind up trapped in a massive snarl of motorcycles.

Registration for the ride starts at dawn and by 7 A.M., a column of bikes stretches back more than a mile on Glendale Boulevard with more lining up by the hour. On this November morning, the air is thick with fog, cutting visibility down to a hundred feet and obscuring the Hollywood hills to the west. The sign-up area on Mira Loma Street is packed with riders who didn't register in advance and must stand in long lines to pay their fee and get an entry bracelet. With members of the Soldiers for Jesus directing traffic, thousands of bikers jockey into position: Mongrels, Loners, Uglies, Hell's Angels, Sons of Silence, RUBs, the stray Ducati rider, and members of HOG chapters from most of the western states. The din of rumbling engines is deafening, and local residents trying to sleep in are pretty much screwed. Anyone with motorized transportation can take part in the Love Ride for a pledge of at least fifty dollars. If you donate more, you get extras like bandanas, shirts, and jackets. Pledge a thousand dollars and you are a Top Gun and get to hang with the celebrity riders in the VIP area.

At the festival stage, a band called the Fryed Brothers cranks out a version of "Orange Blossom Special" that sounds like Megadeth doing bluegrass while burly bikers dance a mad two-step on the asphalt. Next to the stage, against the southeast wall of Glendale Harley-Davidson is the VIP area where Top Gun pledges can mingle with the celebrities, mostly cast members from seventies-era TV shows: *The Bionic Woman*'s Lindsay Wagner chats with a TV news crew; Dan Haggerty *(Grizzly Adams)* talks with some Harley reps while two patrolmen scold his manager for not wearing a helmet and trying to cut in line; Larry Hagman ambles around with a skunk pelt on his head; Robert Blake of *Baretta* fame waves to a few fans and puts drops in his eyes. Marty Rosenblum and Willie G. Davidson visit with a few Top Gun pledges. Billy Idol jumps on the bandstand and bellows out "L.A. Woman" with the band thumping behind him. Several in the crowd are wondering why Jay Leno isn't riding this year.

The Love Ride is the creation of Oliver Shokouh, the owner of Glendale Harley-Davidson and a long-standing member of the Uglies. Participants pledge to take a fifty-five-mile-long trek from his dealership up to Castaic Lake (though many simply make their pledges in advance and skip the opening ceremony, heading straight to the lake, instead). Shokouh organized the first Ride in 1984, three years after Harley-Davidson became an official corporate sponsor of the Muscular Dystrophy Association. Peter Fonda served as the grand marshal for the 1984 event, which drew around five hundred bikers with pledges totaling three thousand dollars. Currently, the Love Ride annually attracts close to twenty-five thousand riders and to date has raised more than $16 million for the MDA and other charities.

The Love Ride has long been held up as a shining example of biker altruism and outlaw chic, which the media plays to the hilt. News crews pan their cameras around looking for the biggest tattooed freak they can find while TV reporters utter groan-inducing puns as they file their reports: *These outlaws are out for love.... They may look like the Hell's Angels but today, they're heaven sent....* In recent years, Harley-themed charity rides have become increasingly popular, as the novelty of large numbers of Harley-Davidson bikes rumbling through the streets never fails to draw attention. One 1997 ride, dubbed "Harley

Days," was held on Rodeo Drive in Beverly Hills and featured Cher leading the pack while dressed in leather *haute couture.* Bikers on Road Kings and Ultra Glides slowly rolled past the stores selling Gucci and Harry Winston jewelry while photographers snapped away at Cybill Shepherd lounging seductively on the back of an FXR Lowrider. It's enough to make a dead outlaw spin out in his grave.

The Love Ride's opening ceremony finally gets underway and the celebrities are brought up onstage to address the crowd. The honorary chairman this year is actor Lorenzo Lamas, sporting a four-day shadow on his face, a biker Festus, while the co-chairman is Peter Fonda, who had spent the past several months promoting the thirtieth anniversary release of *Easy Rider.* Fonda gives a rambling speech that he punctuates with a joke about pedophilia, that goes over like a Honda at a Hell's Angels party. Even he knows it bombed; "I never could get that joke right."

When Larry Hagman comes on with his skunk pelt, it is business as usual and the crowd takes in the sight of J.R. Ewing wearing a dead varmint on his head (Hagman, like Fonda, is no newcomer to the Harley scene, having been a rider for over forty years). Eventually, the assembly line of celebrity speakers gets old and riders grow impatient. Everyone wants to climb back on their bikes and head up to the lake where the real party is going to be. By the time Disco the emcee introduces a cast member from *Days Of Our Lives,* much of the crowd is ready to torch the platform. A bearded mastodon grumbles, "Christ, can't we just ride?"

The Ride gets underway around 11 A.M., more than half an hour behind schedule, and many of the riders push it. The long column of bikes roars out of the city and jumps onto the Golden State Freeway. Scores of people standing on the overpasses watch eagerly with many holding up signs saying "Go, Love

Ride" and "Bikers Forever." News helicopters follow for miles as they head up the freeway.

Castaic Lake is a man-made oval lake surrounded by small semi-perfect beaches next to a campground. A large stage is set up in front of the lake at the base of a natural grass bowl that rises up to a parking lot. Beer and barbecue stands, vendors, and other exhibits rim the top of the bowl, as the crowd moves to take their place on the grass incline. Sammy Hagar is the main attraction today, delivering the kind of testosterone-fueled frat rock that he's known for. The crowd is close to forty thousand, rowdy during the concert but well-behaved otherwise. However, one skinny tattooed biker with no shirt draws a small crowd with his repeated attempts at feigning copulation with his girlfriend. As she giggles madly, the biker grabs her around the waist from behind and thrusts her up and down against his loins, his pants down to his knees. He tries to pull down her jeans as she struggles to keep them on. A news camera crew comes running in and films the whole thing, delighted at the spectacle unfolding before them. Afterward, the pair are gleefully interviewed.

Epilogue

TWO WEEKS AFTER THE ABATE RALLY IN SACRAMENTO, TRASH phoned me to say he had something really big in the works. "I'm going to kick my helmet out the front door of my house," he said, "and keep kicking it all the way to Sacramento."

"Why?"

"I'm sending you an e-mail that explains everything," he answered.

Six hours later, his e-mail finally arrived:

> Hi Ya Kid!
>
> What a punk [Assemblyman] Dick Floyd is. And why would the *Daily News* and the *Pasadena Star-News* even print such an obviously stupid and poorly written story? Have they no journalistic integrity, or is it just a willingness to kick an underdog by printing an outdated, stereotyped and sensationalistic story just to boost sales?

I had no what idea Trash was talking about until I saw a copy of an article from the *Los Angeles Daily News* attached:

Motorcycle Riders Take Helmet-Law Protest to Capitol

by Dorothy Korber and Terri Hardy

With the throbbing strains of "Born to be Wild" blaring from loudspeakers, California's bikers roared in the capital last week wearing lots of black leather, with leering skulls on their jackets and chains on their boots, scars seamed their faces; menacing tattoos writhed on their biceps. Their hair was pulled back in short pigtails. Thinning, gray pigtails.

Their rally on the Capitol steps, though spirited, exuded a kind of creaky poignancy. For, like everyone else, the fierce outlaw bikers of the 1960s are growing old. They spoke of freedom—the freedom from helmets. "We're never going to forget—and we'll never get used to it," bellowed one speaker.

After the rally, a few of the bravest bikers headed over to confront Assemblyman Dick Floyd, the Carson Democrat who authored the 1991 law requiring all motorcyclists to wear helmets. Profane and feisty, Floyd is the Legislature's own hell's angel. Floyd was unimpressed by his visitors.

"I told them: 'Get a life. You ain't going to change this thing. The Highway Patrol statistics show the helmet law is working and saving lives.' They started to protest, so I said: 'You are a weak-kneed bunch of losers. You keep coming in here and talking about your freedom. If you really believe in this, do something dynamic, for God's sake. Set fire to your helmets! If you had any guts, you'd defy the law and ride without a helmet.'

"Know what they said to that?" Floyd's voice rose to a sarcastic whine. "They said, 'Yeah, but we'd get a ticket!' They're born to be wimps."[163]

The comments from Dick Floyd were true to form. The assemblyman has long held contempt for bikers and the "get a life" dismissal summed up his entire view of their crusade to repeal helmet laws. I read on:

> Me again,
>   When I read that article, my mind went numb...for a moment....I know I've got a few problems, but I've worked hard over the last two years trying to get better...Dick Floyd called us a bunch of wimps, so "WIMPs" it shall be. It's catchy, and lends itself well to the roll of acronym for: Why I Must Protest.
>   Thanks, Dick.

In his e-mail, Trash announced he was staging a WIMP walk. He was going to kick his motorcycle helmet out the front door of his house and keep on kicking it for 458 miles until he reached the steps of the California state capitol in Sacramento. He would travel in five mile increments, then have Cheri come to pick him up.

The next day, Trash phoned to say he had kicked his helmet out his front door the previous evening at exactly five minutes to midnight. He continued kicking it for three blocks, then turned around and walked back home. It had been drizzling and his legs got sore. But in a little while, he was going to pick up where he left off and kick his helmet around the San Fernando Valley, stopping at various motorcycle shops to drum up support and draw publicity.

"Oh, by the way," he added. "I'm going to a funeral out in Riverside this Friday. One of the old Boozefighters passed away. You're invited."

The funeral was for Edward "Red Dog" Dahlgren, who made his contribution to outlaw myth by getting tossed in jail for riding his motorcycle down the sidewalk on San Benito street during the 1947 Hollister rally. He was seventy-eight years old. A memorial service was being held at the Riverside National Cemetery complete with a color guard.

The morning of the memorial, I drove down to meet Trash in Gardena, a slightly seedy industrial township just west of the Harbor freeway in south L.A. County. He wanted us to hook up at the workshop of Big Jim, the man who, in 1972, traded the entire inventory of the Hog Shop to Trash in exchange for his pickup truck. Big Jim was currently a Boozefighters prospect, as the club had been resurrected in 1995 with the blessings of an aging Wino Willie. They had chapters in both California and Texas. I had met the Mother chapter in San Diego once before, after driving down to have beer and grilled salmon with Snowman, Rebel, Buckshot, Ghost, Polack Paul, Cadillac Jack, Red, and several others. They all rode Harleys and many of them were Vietnam veterans. I hadn't seen them since, but they would occasionally e-mail me.

Big Jim's workshop was in back of an aluminum and canvas store on 135th Street off Normandie, an industrial area of machine shops and wholesale lighting dealers. There was a dilapidated eatery down the street, a schizoid walk-up that offered burgers, burritos, and teriyaki bowls. He was inside an open garage space holding a couple of vintage Packards and Hudsons in various states of restoration. A garish pink Studebaker was perched on a lift with its right front brake assembly in disrepair. There were a few old rusted Harley frames, too, outfitted with wheels and not much else.

Big Jim was sitting at a workbench eating a sandwich when I walked in and he rose to greet me. "Hi, nice to meet you," he said with a casual rumble. "Trash isn't here yet." There was nothing facetious about his moniker. He *was* big, at least 6′3″ and around 300 pounds, and wearing a Hollister commemorative sweatshirt with a photo of Wino Willie ("The Original Wild One") silk screened on the front. Big Jim was in his early fifties,

---

with a balding forehead and lanky hair that swept back around his head and fell flaring over his ears. Clean shaven with a large round face and friendly eyes, he resembled a Teamsters version of Jonathan Winters.

As a potential Boozefighter, Big Jim was somewhat of an anomaly in that he rode an early seventies BMW, a black boxy bike with a pair of cam heads that stuck out on either side of the engine block like concertinas. The Boozefighters were all Harley purists and I wondered if this old kraut bike was a problem with them. "Oh, I got two Harleys," Big Jim said. "I'm still rebuilding them."

When Trash arrived, we all took off and headed down the Harbor Freeway for the 91 East, a route that would take us through the heart of staid Orange County straight toward Riverside, fifty miles away. Riverside County is a rolling landscape of orange groves, high arid mountains, and freeway overpasses constantly under construction. Every few miles, a dreary shopping mall could be seen off the highway, cropping up as predictably as billboards.

I arrived at the Riverside National Cemetery a full hour before the memorial was scheduled to start. Trash and Big Jim had disappeared, so I drove in and parked at a staging area where the procession was to begin. There were ducks swimming in a large cement pond across the road, splashing about under the spray of three gushing fountains. The cemetery was so quiet I could hear the rustling of leaves and the wind sighing over the rolling grounds. I went for a walk and studied the linear rows of white headstones and small square plaques set flat into the ground. They seemed to symbolize the regimented aspect of military life; wearing the same uniform, saluting the same superiors, and fighting the same enemy.

A GMC Safari van pulled up and five bikers wearing Boozefighters shirts got out. I didn't recognize any of them and guessed they were from Texas, which was the only other chapter I knew about. One of them saw me taking notes and walked up. He was Big John of the Boozefighters Texas Chapter and he called over the others—Dancer, Running Bear, Irish Ed, and Jim Quattlebaum—who introduced themselves. They had flown out to attend the memorial for Red Dog and pay their respects. Many of them had gotten to know him before he died and were somewhat in awe of him. Red was ground zero, a class original who loved to ride, party, and flirt with girls. His sole brush with the law had been from getting busted for riding on the sidewalk.

We talked for a while until I heard the dull roar of engines rumbling in the distance. I looked over and saw a stretch limousine coming around a curve followed by a processional of at least fifty Harleys. They rolled up and parked on the opposite side of the road. It was the San Diego Boozefighters, with Trash and Big Jim riding along. Most of them weren't wearing helmets and I found out later that they had removed them at the cemetery's front gate and thrown them into a ditch.

As I watched the horde kill their engines and dismount, I recognized Snowman, the one Boozefighter I knew best, as he began mingling with the crowd. Snowman is a direct but friendly man with a long gray beard. He'd fought in Vietnam, serving in a tank command, and worked as a postal employee. Snowman often hosts club parties at his La Jolla house and even erected a ten-by-six foot plywood barricade in his backyard to serve as a "piss wall," which reduces the traffic to his bathroom. Snowman was Big Jim's sponsor.

"The Boozefighters concentrate on family, work, and the club," Big Jim had told me earlier, ticking off his massive fingers. "They're not into any of that one-percenter shit." When I first met the Boozefighters in San Diego the year before, though, they were evasive with me about the size of their membership. "You should never ask a biker club how many members it has," Snowman had told me politely. "We like to keep that confidential."

The Boozefighters don't wear one-percenter patches, but because green dominates their colors, the club occasionally gets mistaken for the Vagos, an outlaw group who shares the same color scheme and with whom some Hell's Angels chapters don't get along. There are stories where a group of Angels would pass some Boozefighters on the highway during a run, catch sight of a flash of green, and make screeching U-turns to give chase, only to discover they had the wrong bikers. As a rule, Angel chapters get along well with the Boozefighters whenever they cross paths, but they're not prone to apologizing or backing down from a fight. Consequently, what would follow was an unsteady attempt at resolving the situation without the Angels losing face, and this usually involved the Boozefighters having to wax diplomatic. Most of the Boozefighters are big guys who could readily handle themselves if the going got tough, but fighting is not their style. Nothing physical has ever occurred.

While greetings were being exchanged, I walked over and said hello to Trash, who was in a good mood that day. I asked him how his helmet-kicking project was going. "Pretty good," he said, stroking his beard. "But my toe hurts like a bitch." I looked down to see that he was wearing a pair of wide boots made out of weathered suede.

"I thought maybe you had a pair of steel-toed boots," I said, thinking most bikers at least wore protective foot gear. "Wouldn't they work better?"

"Yeah, probably," Trash said, shrugging. We wandered over to where Big Jim and some of the others were standing in a circle. Someone produced a flask filled with bourbon and everyone took a nip and began pulling out cameras. Trash produced a disposable Kodak and ordered everyone to pile on top of me.

No one did but Big Jim playfully put me in a bear hug that bordered on the Heimlich maneuver as Trash snapped away, all the while whipping off one-liners with rim shot efficiency. He is a fan of the comedian Steven Wright and often quotes his material. "I have a life-size picture of my entire body tattooed on the front of me," Trash said, passing the flask. "Only it's three inches taller."

"I've always told jokes," Trash said to me a few minutes later, as if explaining his jocularity during such a solemn occasion. "I was just thinking how it was the morning after the battle in '66. We were just sitting around cracking jokes and playing high-stakes poker while waiting for somebody to come and pick up all the guys who got killed. Everyone was dead around us but we didn't feel like collecting them. I mean, all we could do was just tell jokes. Even in jail, I had a good time. I was telling jokes when I was in a lineup once."

When it came time, everyone mounted up and followed the limousine out to a square gazebo that had been set up. I rode on the back of Trash's shovelhead and noticed how he seemed unable to keep from pushing the envelope, even at 5 mph. He hugged the side of the concrete path near the grass's edge and made quiet "whoopee" noises while pushing his feet off the pavement. Everyone parked their bikes and filed into the gazebo, walking between an honor guard of ten elderly VFW members wearing white windbreakers. Inside were chairs and two easels holding poster boards covered with photos of Red's life. We were each given a small program printed on green paper with a picture of a smiling elderly Edward Dahlgren on its front. *In Remembrance of Red Dog,* it read. The inside included a brief history of the Boozefighters and a picture of a patch commemorating Red's 1947 "jail break." On the back was a passage from the Book of Ephesians, followed by a didactic comment in response:

Be imitators of God, therefore, as dearly loved children.
—Ephesians 5:1

The memorial service was all nostalgia and memory. Red's closest friend of fifty years, an elderly Hispanic man named Rudy, spoke of his steady work ethic, dancing skills, and devotion to his wife Virginia. Jim Quattlebaum and Irish Ed of Texas told of a gentle loving man whom they got to know only too briefly. A VFW chaplain uttered a poem in indecipherable English.

As everyone spoke, I looked over at the photo collage of Red's life. I saw a grinning youth with movie star looks relaxing at the beach, and sitting astride a four-stroke Triumph. The youth enlists in the Navy and wears a sailor's uniform. Returning from the war, he digs his bike out of storage, rides it like a dust devil, and spends the night in a Hollister jail. He marries, holds a tiny infant in his arms, and clowns with friends in his living room. The photos turn to color as he and his wife pose in formal wear under an archway at one of their children's weddings. He grows older but keeps riding. He and his wife wave from a Harley. Finally, he passes away from a tired heart and is interred alongside a million other souls.

A twenty-one-gun salute was fired and "Taps" played from a loudspeaker. The honor guard marched in carrying a folded American flag. They were old and moved shakily but held their precision. The flag was presented to the widow. I looked over and saw that Trash had a trembling lower lip and I gave his massive shoulder a squeeze. It was over. Life went on.

TRASH STILL LIVES WITH CHERI IN KAGEL CANYON WHERE THEY TRY to scrape by doing whatever odd jobs they can. He does engine repairs on the occasional Harley-Davidson but is unable to work at it full-time. Money is a constant struggle and he and Cheri worry that their water and power will be shut off again. Trash sold one of his Harley-Davidson commemorative knives for eighteen hundred dollars. It was like winning the lottery. He recently received his first ATM card and used it for the first time in his life.

The helmet-kick to Sacramento ended after just a few weeks. Assemblyman Dick Floyd lost his bid for reelection during the 2000 California primary, so Trash felt vindicated. He also learned that his AB-1515 bill was approved by the Senate Transportation Committee, and passed in the legislature. He can finally get a plate for his bike that shows where he was and what he did.

Trash still gets extremely depressed and dispirited on occasion, though he won't admit it. He continues to receive counseling at the Sepulveda VA hospital where he has been diagnosed as suffering from PTSD. He recently qualified for full veteran's disability benefits and currently receives a monthly stipend. "I've been thinking more about Vietnam," he told his counselor one day. "I have worked so hard not to think about it."

Trash still writes fervid essays on a wide range of topics and e-mails people daily. Old friends stop by the house in the middle of the night to visit since that is when he and Cheri are usually up. They bring over their spare parts and talk engines and transmissions.

Trash rides his shovelhead almost every day, jamming it down the freeway as he weaves in and out of traffic like an adder, always pushing the engine to its absolute limit. It is an outlaw bike, more than thirty years old, and held together with welds, spare parts, and blind faith. Trash remembers how it blew an oil seal during his trip to Sacramento. He is waiting for the next breakdown to happen.

Notes

THE RESEARCH FOR THIS BOOK WAS COMPILED FROM INTERVIEWS with over forty individuals, plus secondary sources, including biographies, newspaper and magazine articles, government documents, archival footage, and materials available on the World Wide Web

AI = Author's Interview

Introduction
From personal reportage of the 2000 ABATE Rally in Sacramento and interviews with Ron AKA Trash Haley.

Part I—Boozefighters and Pissed-Off Bastards
The research for this section was compiled from interviews with several of the surviving Boozefighter members, Dr. Martin Jack Rosenblum, articles from the *San Francisco Chronicle, Life* magazine, biographies on the lives of Stanley Kramer, Gene Vincent, and Marlon Brando, and raw film footage of interviews with member of the Hell's Angels San Bernardino Chapter circa 1965.

1. William Forkner, *Easyriders* video interview, 1987.
2. Dave Nichols, AI, 1999.

----

3. Forkner, *Easyriders* video interview, 1987.

4. *Ibid.*

5. *Ibid.*

6. *Ibid.*

7. *Ibid.*

8. Jim Cameron, AI, 1999.

9. *Ibid.*

10. Gil Armis, AI, 2000.

11. Forkner, *Easyriders,* 1987.

12. *Ibid.*

13. *Ibid.*

14. Cameron, AI, 1999.

15. Forkner, *Easyriders,* 1987.

16. *Ibid.*

17. *Ibid.*

18. *Ibid.*

19. *San Francisco Chronicle,* July 5, 1947.

20. *Ibid.*

21. *San Francisco Chronicle,* July 7, 1947.

22. Quoted by William Smith, AI, 1999.

23. Cameron, AI, 1999.

24. Forkner, *Easyriders,* 1987.

25. Stanley Kramer, *It's A Mad, Mad, Mad, Mad World* (Harcourt Brace & Co., 1997), p. 53.

26. Donald Spoto, *Stanley Kramer: Film Maker* (G.P. Putnam & Sons, 1978), p. 157.

27. Kramer, *Mad World,* p. 53.

28. *Ibid.,* p. 55.

29. Peter Manso, *Brando: The Biography* (Hyperion, 1997), pp. 339–40.

30. *Ibid.,* p. 340.

31. *Ibid.,* p. 341.

----

32. Spoto, *Film Maker,* p. 159.

33. Manso, *Brando,* p. 344.

34. Brando himself readily admits to both its shortcomings and relevance: "It was only seventy-nine minutes long, short by modern standards, and it looks dated and corny now. But it became a kind of cult film, and it certainly helped my career . . ." Marlon Brando, *Songs My Mother Taught Me* (Random House, 1994), p. 258.

35. Dr. Martin Jack Rosenblum, AI, 1999.

36. *Ibid.*

37. *Ibid.*

38. *Ibid.*

39. *Ibid.*

40. *Ibid.*

41. Craig Morrison, *Go Cat Go!: Rockabilly Music and Its Makers* (Univ. of Illinois Press, 1996), p. 48.

42. Morrison, *Go Cat Go!,* pp. 49–50.

43. Brett Hagarty, *The Day The World Turned Blue: A Biography of Gene Vincent* (Blandford Press, 1984), p. 54.

44. Rosenblum, AI, 1999.

45. Al Griffin, *Motorcycles* (Henry Regnery Company, 1972), p. 135.

46. Paul Morin, *Classic Bike* interview, May, 1982.

47. "I was in Sweden in 1965 and saw some mods and rockers go after each other in a market place," says Marty Rosenblum. "The mods would sit on one side, they wore makeup, and on the other side were all the rockers in their leather. On the left were the scooters and on the right were the motorcycles. They would sit there for days and every once in a while, one side would taunt the other. Finally, they just beat the crap out of each other. These were *Swedish* mods and rockers."

48. James Meredith, AI, 2000.

49. *Ibid.*

50. Ruby Miles, AI, 2000.

51. Meredith, AI, 2000.

52. George Wethern with Vincent Colnett, *A Wayward Angel* (R. Marek Publishers, 1978), p. 26.

53. *Ibid.,* p. 29.

54. Meredith, AI, 2000.

55. Wethern, *Wayward Angel,* p. 84.

56. Excerpt from KCBS television interview, 1965. Interviewer unknown.

57. *Ibid.*

58. *Ibid.*

59. *Ibid.*

60. *Ibid.*

Part II—The Counter Counterculture

From interviews with Ken Kesey, Marty Balin, Roger Corman, Peter Fonda, Bill Hayward, Jim Meredith, and William Smith, plus research from biographies of Hunter S. Thompson and Bill Graham. My special thanks to Peter Coyote for his fascinating memoir *Sleeping Where I Fall* and Peter Biskind for his riveting account of the making of *Easy Rider* in his book *Easy Riders, Raging Bulls: How the Sex-Drugs-and-Rock 'n' Roll Generation Saved Hollywood.*

61. Hunter Thompson, "Motorcycle Gangs: Loser and Outsiders," *The Nation,* May 17, 1965.

62. Peter Coyote, "Sleeping Where I Fall," *Counterpoint,* 1998, p. 236.

63. *Ibid.,* p. 241.

64. Ken Kesey, AI, 1999.

65. Paul Perry and Ken Babbs, *On The Bus* (Thunder's Mouth Press, 1990), p. 116.

66. Kesey, AI, 1999.

67. *Ibid.*

68. Wethern, *Wayward Angel,* p. 178.

69. Babbs and Perry, *On The Bus,* p. 119.

70. *Ibid.,* p. 122.

71. Kesey, AI, 1999.

72. Hunter S. Thompson, *Hells Angels: A Strange & Terrible Saga* (Ballantine Books, 1966), p. 316.

73. Roger Corman, AI, 1999.

74. *Ibid.*

75. *Ibid.*

76. Peter Fonda, AI, 1999.

77. *Ibid.*

78. Corman, AI, 1999.

79. *Ibid.*

80. Fonda, AI, 1999.

81. *Ibid.*

82. Roger Corman (with Jim Jerome), *How I Made a Hundred Movies in Hollywood and Never Lost a Dime* (Da Capo Press, 1998), p. 154.

83. *Ibid.,* p. 156.

84. Fonda, AI, 1999.

85. *Ibid.*

86. Corman, AI, 1999.

87. *Ibid.*

88. Rosenblum, AI, 1999.

89. William Smith, AI, 1999.

90. Rosenblum, AI, 1999.

91. Barry Mayson, *Fallen Angel: Hell's Angel to Heaven's Saint* (Doubleday, 1982).

92. Smith, AI, 1999.

93. *Ibid.*

94. Fonda, AI, 1999.

95. Bill Hayward, AI, 1999.

96. *Ibid.*

97. Fonda, AI, 1999.

98. Peter Fonda, *Don't Tell Dad : A Memoir* (Hyperion, 1998), p. 221.

----

99. Hayward, AI, 1999.

100. Corman, AI, 1999.

101. Fonda, *Don't Tell Dad,* p. 229.

102. Biskind, *Easy Riders, Raging Bulls,* p. 69.

103. *Ibid.,* p. 68.

104. Hayward, AI, 1999.

105. *Ibid.*

106. Fonda, AI, 1999.

107. *Ibid.*

108. *"When we finally . . . worked just great,"* Ibid.

109. Hayward, AI, 1999.

110. Fonda, AI, 1999.

111. Hayward, AI, 1999.

112. Peter Rainer, AI, 1999.

113. Fonda, AI, 1999.

114. Dick Carter, AI, 1999.

115. Bill Graham, and Robert Greenfield, *Bill Graham Presents: My Life Inside Rock and Out* (Dell Publishing, 1992), p. 187.

116. *Ibid.,* p. 189.

117. Coyote, *Sleeping . . .* , p. 298.

118. Dick Carter, AI, 1999.

119. *Ibid.*

120. *Ibid.*

121. Albert Maysles, AI, 1999.

122. Carter, AI, 1999.

123. *Ibid.*

124. Maysles, AI, 1999.

125. Carter, AI, 1999.

126. Coyote, *Sleeping . . .* , p. 211.

127. Maysles, AI, 1999.

128. Coyote, *Sleeping . . .* , p. 212.

129. Marty Balin, AI, 1999.

----

130. *Ibid.*

131. Coyote, *Sleeping...*, p. 223.

132. Carter, AI, 1999.

133. *Ibid.*

134. Maysles, AI, 1999.

135. Carter, AI, 1999.

136. Maysles, AI, 1999.

137. Carter, AI, 1999.

138. Wethern, *A Wayward Angel,* p. 155.

139. Nichols, AI, 1999.

140. Rosenblum, AI, 1999.

141. *Ibid.*

142. *Ibid.*

143. Nichols, AI, 1999.

144. Ron Simms, AI, 1999.

145. Arlen Ness, AI, 1999.

146. Forkner, *Easyriders* video interview, 1987.

Part III—Trash: An Outlaw's Tale

From numerous interviews done with Ron AKA Trash Haley from January—June, 2000, plus medical reports from the Veterans Administration supplied by the interviewee.

Part IV—Blowing It

From extensive reportage on the Hell's Angels from the *Beacon Journal, The Plain Dealer, Cleveland Magazine, Time, Newsweek, San Francisco Chronicle, San Franciso Examiner,* and *Rolling Stone.* My special thanks to John Michaels for his collection of archival materials from the above-mentioned publications.

147. Stephen Sawicki, "The Judge, the Blonde and the Sting," *Cleveland,* p. 54.

----

148. Lavignem Yves, *Hells Angels: Into the Abyss* (Harper Paperbacks, 1997), p. 68.

149. Rosenblum, AI, 1999.

150. Nichols, AI, 1999.

151. Rosenblum, AI, 1999.

152. *Ibid.*

153. Ugly Paul, AI, 1999.

154. *Ibid.*

155. *Ibid.*

156. *Ibid.*

157. *Ibid.*

158. Hollister councilman, AI, 1999.

159. Mark Maxwell, AI, 1999.

160. *Ibid.*

161. *Ibid.*

162. *Ibid.*

Epilogue

From interviews and e-mail correspondence with Ron aka Trash Haley and *Los Angeles Daily News.*

163. Korber, Dorothy and Hardy, Terri, "Motorcycle Riders take Helmet Law to Capitol Steps," *Los Angeles Daily News,* Jan. 3, 2000.

Bibliography

Bacon, Roy. *British Motorcycles of the 1940s and 1950s.* Osprey Publishing, 1983.

Biskind, Peter. *Easy Riders, Raging Bulls: How the Sex-Drugs-and-Rock 'n' Roll Generation Saved Hollywood.* Touchstone, 1997.

Brando, Marlon. *Songs My Mother Taught Me,* Random House, 1994.

Carrol, E. Jean. *Hunter.* Dutton, 1993.

Corman, Roger. (with Jim Jerome) *How I Made a Hundred Movies in Hollywood and Never Lost a Dime.* Da Capo Press, 1998.

Coyote, Peter. *Sleeping Where I Fall.* Counterpoint, 1998.

Detroit, Michael. *Chain of Evidence.* Dutton, 1994.

Fonda, Peter. *Don't Tell Dad: A Memoir.* Hyperion, 1998.

Girdler, Allan. *Illustrated Harley-Davidson Buyer's Guide.* Motorbooks International, 1992.

Graham, Bill and Robert Greenfield. *Bill Graham Presents: My Life Inside Rock and Out.* Dell Pub., 1992.

Griffin, Al. *Motorcycles.* Henry Regnery Company, 1972.

Hagarty, Brett. *The Day The World Turned Blue: A Biography of Gene Vincent.* Blandford Press, 1984.

Halberstam, David. *The Fifties.* Villard Books, 1993.

Hayward, Brooke. *Haywire.* Knopf, 1977.

Kramer, Stanley. *It's A Mad, Mad, Mad, Mad World.* Harcourt Brace & Co., 1997.

Lavigne, Yves. *Hells Angel: Into the Abyss.* Harper Paperbacks, 1997.

Manso, Peter. *Brando: The Biography.* Hyperion, 1997.

Marwick, Arthur. *The Sixties.* Oxford University Press, 1998.

Mayson, Barry. (with Tony Marco) *Fallen Angel: Hell's Angel To Heaven's Saint.* Doubleday, 1982.

Morrison, Craig. *Go Cat Go!: Rockabilly Music and Its Makers.* University of Illinois Press, 1996.

Motorcycle Mania: The Biker Book. Matthew Druitt, editor, Solomon Guggenheim Foundation and Universe Publishing, 1998.

Perry, Paul and Ken Babbs. *On The Bus.* Thunder's Mouth Press, 1990.

Perry, Paul. *Fear and Loathing: The Strange and Terrible Saga of Hunter S. Thompson.* Thunder's Mouth Press, 1992.

Renstrom, Richard. *Motorcycle Milestones.* Classics Unlimited Inc., 1980.

Schickel, Richard. *Brando: A Life In Our Times.* Atheneum, 1991.

Schumacher, Michael. *Dharma Lion: A Biography of Allen Ginsberg.* St. Martin's Press, 1992.

Spoto, Donald. *Stanley Kramer: Film Maker.* G.P. Putnam & Sons, 1978.

Thompson, Hunter S. *Hells Angels: A Strange & Terrible Saga.* Ballantine Books, 1966.

Weisner, Wolfgang. *Harley-Davidson Photographic History.* Motorbooks International Publishers & Wholesalers, 1989.

Wethern, George. (with Vincent Colnett) *A Wayward Angel.* R. Marek Publishers, 1978.

Whitmer, Peter O. *When The Weird Turn Pro: The Twisted Life and Times of Hunter S. Thompson.* Hyperion, 1993.

Wright, David K. *Harley-Davidson Motor Company: An Official Ninety-Year History.* Motorbooks International Publishers & Wholesalers, 1993.

Index

About the Author

A native of Wisconsin, TOM REYNOLDS attended college at the University of Wisconsin–La Crosse where he majored in English. He worked as a radio announcer at KTXJ radio in East Texas before going to produce industrial training films and commercials in Beaumont and Houston.

After moving to Los Angeles, he worked as technical director for the Groundlings Comedy Theater for six years before leaving to become a producer at E! Entertainment Television. Tom went on to produce the A&E Special *The Wild Ride of Outlaw Bikers* in 1999 and currently writes for the syndicated reality crime series *Arrest & Trial* for Studios USA and Dick Wolf Productions. He lives in Los Angeles.